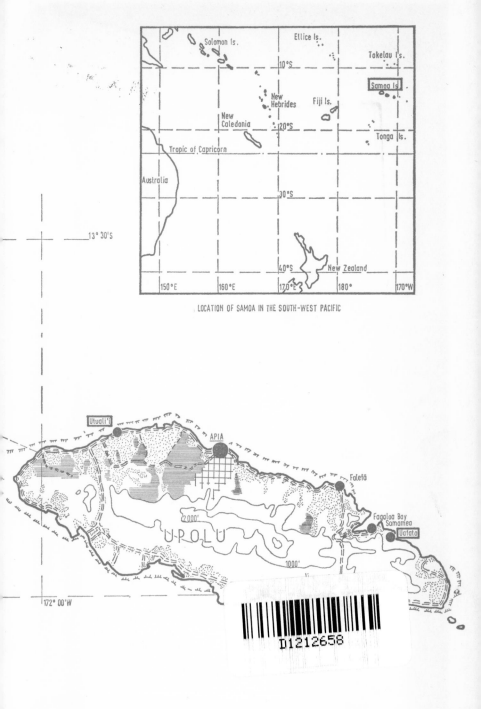

LOCATION OF SAMOA IN THE SOUTH-WEST PACIFIC

Solomon Is.

Ellice Is.

Tokelau I's.

10°S

Samoa Is

New
Hebrides

Fiji Is.

New
Caledonia

120°S

Tonga Is.

Tropic of Capricorn

Australia

30°S

40°S

New Zealand

150°E

160°E

170°E

180°

170°W

13° 30'S

Utuali'i

APIA

Falefā

Fagaloa Bay
Samamea

U P O L U

2 000'

1000'

Uafato

172° 00'W

0  2  4  6  8  10miles

# SAMOAN VILLAGE ECONOMY

# SAMOAN VILLAGE ECONOMY

BRIAN A. LOCKWOOD

MELBOURNE
OXFORD UNIVERSITY PRESS
LONDON   WELLINGTON   NEW YORK

1971

*Oxford University Press, Ely House, London, W.1*

GLASGOW   NEW YORK   TORONTO   MELBOURNE   WELLINGTON
CAPE TOWN   SALISBURY   IBADAN   NAIROBI   DAR ES SALAAM   LUSAKA   ADDIS ABABA
BOMBAY   CALCUTTA   MADRAS   KARACHI   LAHORE   DACCA
KUALA LUMPUR   SINGAPORE   HONK KONG   TOKYO

*Oxford University Press, 7 Bowen Crescent, Melbourne*

© *Oxford University Press 1971*

*First published 1971*

ISBN 0 19 550335 X

*Registered in Australia for transmission by post as a book*
PRINTED IN AUSTRALIA BY HALSTEAD PRESS, SYDNEY

FOR
HEATHER
JENNIFER AND ADRIAN
WHO SHARED IT ALL

# CONTENTS

*page*

List of Tables                                    ix
List of Figures                                   xi
Glossary and Abbreviations                       xiii
Introduction                                      xv

PART I: THE FRAMEWORK
1 From subsistence to market                       3
2 Scope and method                                 9
3 The Samoan economy and society                  22

PART II: FOUR VILLAGES
4 Uafato                                          39
5 Taga                                            85
6 Poutasi                                        124
7 Utuali'i                                       155

PART III: THE PROCESS OF ECONOMIC
          CHANGE
8 From primitive affluence to economic
  development?                                   187

Appendix Tables                                  211
Bibliography                                     225
Index                                            229

# LIST OF TABLES

|  |  | page |
|---|---|---|
| 1 | Sample households and village populations | 17 |
| 2 | Fieldwork timetable | 20 |
| 3 | Sources of employment in Western Samoa in 1961 | 26 |
| 4 | Principal occupations of wage and salary earners in Western Samoa in 1961 | 27 |
| 5 | Disposition of land in Western Samoa in 1955 | 28 |
| 6 | Western Samoa's principal exports: five-year annual averages 1915-64 | 29 |
| 7 | Western Samoa: imports by commodity groups in 1965 | 30 |
| 8 | Uafato: *matai* land holdings and land use in 1966 | 43 |
| 9 | Uafato: producers' capital | 51 |
| 10 | Commodities shipped in Mamea's whaleboat to Fagaloa Bay | 65 |
| 11 | Cash subscriptions for the Uafato school 1961-2 | 71 |
| 12 | The estimated cost of the Uafato school | 73 |
| 13 | Uafato: social and village capital | 75 |
| 14 | Uafato: subsistence and cash incomes | 76 |
| 15 | Uafato: cash outlay | 77 |
| 16 | Uafato: commodity purchases | 79 |
| 17 | Stock and prices—Mamea's store April 1966 | 80 |
| 18 | Uafato: cash donations by the sample *'āiga* to the Congregational Church and pastor | 83 |
| 19 | Taga: land use in 1966 | 93 |
| 20 | Taga: *matai* land holdings in 1966 | 93 |
| 21 | Taga: producers' capital | 99 |
| 22 | The estimated cash and subsistence costs of five open-houses in Taga | 103 |
| 23 | Copra and cacao purchased by the two Taga trading-stations 1948-52 and 1961-5 | 108 |
| 24 | Taga: social and village capital | 115 |
| 25 | Taga: subsistence and cash incomes | 116 |
| 26 | Taga: cash outlay | 117 |
| 27 | Taga: commodity purchases | 118 |
| 28 | Poutasi: *matai* land holdings and land use in 1966 | 131 |
| 29 | Poutasi: producers' capital | 135 |
| 30 | Poutasi: cash income from agriculture 1960-5 | 138 |
| 31 | Copra sold to three Poutasi trade-stores 1960-6 | 140 |
| 32 | Poutasi: social and village capital | 146 |
| 33 | Poutasi: subsistence and cash incomes | 148 |

*page*

34  Poutasi: cash outlay                                                     149
35  Poutasi: commodity purchases                                            150
36  Money owed by the sample *'āiga* to three Poutasi stores, May
       1966                                                                 151
37  Utuali'i: *matai* land holdings and land use in 1966                    161
38  Utuali'i: producers' capital                                           164
39  The proportion of traditional to non-traditional dwellings in
       1966                                                                 168
40  The estimated cash and subsistence costs of three guest-*fale* and
       two non-traditional *fale* in Utuali'i                               169
41  Utuali'i: social and village capital                                    176
42  Utuali'i: subsistence and cash incomes                                  177
43  Utuali'i: cash outlay                                                    178
44  Utuali'i: commodity purchases                                           179
45  The availability of land for bush fallow cultivation in 1966            189
46  The average number of hours spent a week per adult male in
       the main productive activities                                       191
47  Comparisons of labour surveys 1950, 1961 and 1966                       191
48  Travel costs in 1966                                                     197
49  The villages ranked by cash returns to labour in the production
       and sale of copra                                                    198
50  Incomes                                                                  202
51  Income adjusted for hurricane and bunchytop losses, 12 months           203
52  Proposition 2 test results                                              204

APPENDIX TABLES

1  Four villages: population data 1950-65                                   211
2  The estimated average supply of staple foods by months, Decem-
      ber 1965-November 1966                                                212
3  The estimated production from the village coconut lands and the
      disposal of output in 1966                                            214
4  Copra Board of Western Samoa price order, February 1965                  215
5  Quantities and value of banana sales                                     215
6  Questionnaires                                                           216

The detailed village and household data assembled for each village during the survey have not been included in this book, but may be of interest and use to researchers undertaking further work of this kind. This material has been duplicated and is available on request, for a small charge, from the Department of Economics, the Research School of Pacific Studies, Australian National University, Box 4, P.O., Canberra, A.C.T. 2600, Australia.

Briefly, this publication includes the following material for each of the four villages studied: population details, foodcrop planting, banana exports, hours of productive work, cash income and expenditure, and ownership of work-tools and equipment, domestic durables and semi-durables, and housing. The more detailed material is given for individual sample households.

# LIST OF FIGURES

|  |  | *page* |
|---|---|---|
| Endpaper map: Western Samoa |  |  |
| 1 | Uafato village in 1966 | 40 |
| 2 | Uafato: land use in 1966 | 44 |
| 3 | Uafato: *matai* land holdings in 1966 | 45 |
| 4 | Taga village in 1966 | 86 |
| 5 | Taga: land use in 1966 | 92 |
| 6 | Taga: *matai* land holdings in 1966 | 94 |
| 7 | Poutasi village in 1966 | 125 |
| 8 | Poutasi: land use in 1966 | 128 |
| 9 | Poutasi: *matai* land holdings in 1966 | 130 |
| 10 | Utuali'i village in 1966 | 156 |
| 11 | Utuali'i: land use in 1966 | 160 |
| 12 | Utuali'i: *matai* land holdings in 1966 | 162 |

# GLOSSARY AND ABBREVIATIONS

SAMOAN WORDS USED IN THE TEXT FOR WHICH THERE IS NO EXACT EQUIVALENT IN ENGLISH

| | |
|---|---|
| *afiafi* | Sleeping-mat |
| *'āiga* | A relative, a nuclear family, or an extended family. I use the term to designate a local village lineage under the authority of one elected chief (*matai*). It might embrace several nuclear families, relatives and adopted members. |
| *amo* | Yoke; stick resting on a man's shoulder and used for carrying two heavy loads, one at each end. |
| *'aumāga* | The association of untitled men (non-*matai*) in a village—the male village work force. |
| *falalau'ie* | Sleeping-mat made from a soft pandanus material taken from the same plant as the material used for the *'ietōga*. |
| *fale* | A traditional Samoan house |
| *faleo'o* | Small traditional house |
| *faletua ma tausi* | Wives of the *matai* |
| *fono* | The village council or meeting of *matai* |
| *'ietōga* | Fine mat—the most valued and significant object in Samoan custom |
| *laulau* | Coconut-leaf food mat or tray |
| *malae* | Ceremonial centre of a village |
| *mamalu* | Dignity, respect, honour |
| *matai* | Elected leader and titleholder of an *'āiga* |
| *moso'oi* | Tree, *cananga* sp., flowers used for scenting coconut oil |
| *oso* | Digging stick |
| *paopao* | Small dugout canoe |
| *papa* | Coarse floor mat |
| *pule* | Authority, control |
| *pulenu'u* | An appointee, by the government, from among the *matai* of a village, to perform local administrative duties |
| *siapo* | Tapa; bark-cloth made from the bast of paper mulberry—a traditional valuable |

| | |
|---|---|
| *ta'amū* | Giant taro, *alocasia* sp. |
| *tāuga* | Pledge payment for the services of a carpenter, canoe-builder etc. |
| *taule'ale'a* | A young or untitled man; plural—*taulele'a.* |
| *tautua* | The service given by an untitled dependant to the *matai* |
| *tu'ulaufala* | Large pandanus sleeping-mat |
| *uli* | Small corm which grows under the sucker of a taro plant |
| *'umete* | Wooden bowl |
| *umu* | Earth oven |
| *va'aniue* | Small dugout canoe |

### ABBREVIATIONS USED IN THE TEXT AND APPENDIX TABLES

| | |
|---|---|
| C.C.C.S. | Congregational Christian Church in Samoa; direct descendant of the London Missionary Society. |
| W.S.E.D.P. 1966-70 | *Western Samoa's Economic Development Programme* 1966-70 |

# INTRODUCTION

THE JOURNALS of early explorers of the Pacific will always hold a special fascination: the trials and tribulations of men and ships, fear and heroism, exotic places and people, island gods and seamen gods, gifts of trinkets, mirrors, cloth and iron, canoes laden with coconuts, breadfruit, pigs and fish. Sometimes there would be a long gap between the visit of an explorer and the beginning of regular visits by whalers, traders and blackbirders, and the coming of castaways, beachcombers, resident traders and missionaries, and sometimes the gap would be short. But for most islands of any size this second phase of contact with a world beyond the reef and horizon was inevitable and quickly dispelled any notions the islanders may have had about the godliness of the white man: new diseases, alcohol, firearms, kidnapping, increasingly bloody and destructive fighting. Protestant and Catholic, new and old testament gods, broken idols and beliefs, missionaries and traders competing for coconut oil and followers, unhealthy clothing and ideas; this was the end of the dance.

Such disruption was of no real advantage to the larger companies operating the copra and other Pacific island trade, nor could it be tolerated by the missionaries. The influence on home governments of these two groups led to the third stage of Pacific island domination, to annexation and colonial status. This at least brought internal peace and an end to the worst abuses of the second or fair-game phase. It allowed the consolidation and expansion of foreign institutions of government, commerce and church in most Pacific island communities.

This book is concerned with one such Pacific community, the Polynesian people of Western Samoa. Their history follows quite closely the general tale just told; but in 1962 it entered a fourth phase with the achievement of independence. Western Samoa's political and social history has been well documented, but there has been little attempt to examine the effects of foreign institutions on the lives of the majority of Samoans who continue to live and work in villages. They have long since become part of the world economy:

they produce copra and other commodities for export; they buy imported goods in their stores; they go to school and to church; they ride buses to visit their neighbours and the stores and government offices in Apia, the capital; they take their land disputes to court; they listen to Samoan and foreign news and music on the radio; and they have come to know the value of money. At the same time they observe the moral code of their forefathers, and maintain most of the inherited Samoan institutions of family, and village government. In many respects these inherited socio-economic characteristics remain dominant in the lives of the village Samoans, absorbing their interest and much of their time and energy and, often, providing the incentive for much of their participation in the newer market sector. They want many of the goods and services money will buy, but they want more the honour and prestige of a chiefly title which money alone normally cannot buy.

Long contact with the market system and other foreign institutions, however, have brought about changes in the economic organization of Samoan villages and the lives of all Samoans, and the type and extent of these changes in four villages are the subjects of this study. The study is presented in three parts. The precise problem and the theoretical background in which it is set are described in Chapter 1. Chapter 2 outlines the scope and method of the study, and Chapter 3 completes Part I with a brief introduction to the Samoan economy and social system. The four chapters of Part II describe the resource endowment, the production of goods and services, the levels of monetary and commodity incomes and consumption of each of the four villages in turn. The level of market participation and the extent to which this has been influenced by inherited and foreign institutions is discussed in detail. The villages varied a great deal in their exposure to the market and in their interest and participation in it. These differences are analysed in Part III in terms of the theory of transition from subsistence to market economy described in Chapter 1. This analysis tells us a good deal about Samoans' attitudes to their economic future which will soon be affected by a rapidly increasing population and a reluctance at the present time to invest in productive assets.

IN UNDERTAKING a study of this kind one accepts a great deal of help from a great many people. To acknowledge each person individually, particularly those who gave their friendship and assistance to my family and myself in Western Samoa would take many pages, and this I will not attempt. Through their generosity and warmheartedness the Samoans made us feel welcome and part of their great family. I would like to mention with special thanks our hosts in Apia and the villages: Dr and Mrs Leausa Kitiona, Reverend and Mrs Enari, Reverend and Mrs Fuafiva, Reverend and Mrs Maene and Reverend and Mrs Vasa; the *matai* and '*āiga* of Poutasi, Taga, Uafato and Utuali'i, and Mr Viliamu Brown who was my very able assistant and delightful companion during the twelve months we spent in Western Samoa. *Malo tele lava le fa'aaloalo ma le felagalagoma'i.*

My interest in the general problem of transition from a primitive economic system to a market economy was stimulated initially and encouraged continuously by Mr E. K. Fisk of the Department of Economics in the Research School of Pacific Studies, the Australian National University. His appreciation and clear exposition of the economics of this transition provided a useful model for my work in Samoa in which he took an active and very much appreciated interest. Dr D. H. Penny, of the same department, helped me to understand my data better and to use it more effectively, and did a great deal to keep my spirits from flagging while writing the book. I offer my grateful thanks to both. I am grateful also for the help given me at different stages of the study by all members of the department, and I would like to extend special thanks to two colleagues whose comments have made the book much better than it would have been otherwise—Dr T. Scarlett Epstein and Dr Paul Luey. For the same reason I would like to thank Mr Laurie Virr, a Canberra architect and friend who put a lot of time, patience and skill into the maps.

I wish to acknowledge my debt to the Australian National University which generously supported my efforts through its research funds and facilities. My thanks also to Mrs Heather Harding, Mrs Florence Johnson and Mrs Helena Michel whose help in preparing tables and typing the manuscript is much appreciated; and to Mrs Kate Miller for help with the index.

My final words of thanks are reserved for my wife, Heather, and Jennifer and Adrian, our children. While they enjoyed our work in Samoa as much as I did they have had to endure the consequences ever since.

Canberra                                                    B. A. LOCKWOOD
June 1970

# PART I:
# THE FRAMEWORK

# Chapter 1

# FROM SUBSISTENCE
# TO MARKET

OVER the past twenty or thirty years, a great deal of practical experience in formulating and implementing policies of economic development has been obtained in societies with vastly different economic, social and religious backgrounds and resource endowments. With this experience has come greater knowledge and understanding of the economies of underdeveloped areas. But most attention has been given to societies with relatively sophisticated economic organizations; where some basic specialization and division of labour is a feature of the economy, where money has been in wide use for a long time, where internal and external trade are important aspects of the economy, and where there are market towns and large cities. Less attention has been given to societies with primitive economic organizations; where non-monetized production is a major, or even the main, component of income, where there has been no growth of towns, where specialization and trade are but weakly developed, and where there is no all-purpose medium of exchange. Such societies have long been the province of anthropologists and geographers who have described the mechanisms of production and distribution in great detail; but economists, perhaps because they are schooled to concentrate on the exchange economy, have generally less understanding of development in primitive economies.

Because primitive economies develop in isolation, and are found in most parts of the world, the details of their economic and social systems vary a great deal. It is not necessary for the purposes of this study to define rigorously the term 'primitive economy', but it will be useful to list a number of characteristics which appear to be common to many economies described in this way. These characteristics are:

(1) The primitive economy consists of a number of relatively small independent subsistence[1] units each of which controls its own

---

[1] In this study the term 'subsistence' refers to goods and services which are not obtained or exchanged in the market sector; it is synonymous with such terms as 'non-market' and 'non-monetary'.

means of production such as labour, land, useful trees and livestock, and tools and equipment.

(2) Technology is simple, although the producer may exploit the natural resources available to him with great skill.

(3) The subsistence community is small so that there is little opportunity for specialization and division of labour.

(4) Within each subsistence community most production is planned for the use of the producers and to discharge kinship and other social obligations.

(5) The exchange of goods and services is regulated through the social system and has an underlying basis in reciprocity.

(6) There is no all-purpose medium of exchange such as relates all goods and services to each other in a market exchange system, although there may be commodities which have special social value and act as a medium of exchange in some circumstances.

The economist is unlikely to meet primitive economies in their pure state since they are essentially isolated and are therefore not subjects for development. They become eligible only when this isolation is ended through regular contact and trade with an outside market economy. The economist in effect sees a market sector operating in a community whose basic economic organization has been, and usually remains to an important extent, of the primitive type. Such mixed economies are common and present special problems for the development economist who, although he is equipped to deal with the market sector, generally understands little of the primitive sector or how the two sectors interact.

In two recent papers Fisk (1962, 1964) has tackled this problem of the interaction between a primitive subsistence-based economy and an advanced market sector in the context of Papua-New Guinea. He has presented a theoretical analysis which demonstrates the mechanism through which this interaction can lead to an increase in the output of the subsistence unit. The analysis is based on a number of general propositions about human economic behaviour in a particular economic environment, and as it is with these propositions that the following study is concerned, it is necessary to outline the main points of the Fisk argument.

In his first paper Fisk (1962) concentrates on the factors which determine economic activity in a primitive economy before contact is made with an advanced market sector. He assumes that the primitive economy is fragmented into a number of small self-sufficient units, and he takes one of these as his basic unit of analysis. He defines an ideal pure subsistence unit in the following paragraph:

The pure subsistence unit is one that is entirely independent of the outside world for the necessities of life and all items of normal consumption. The community comprising the unit produce their food, clothing, shelter, tools and recreational requirements from their own lands, fishing and hunting grounds. What they produce is either consumed by themselves or goes to waste. Saving is limited to the storage of such necessities as can be stored as a reserve against a rainy day, a poor harvest or sickness, and to occasional preparation for increased consumption in feasts and ceremonial. Beyond that there is no incentive to save, or to produce at a level beyond their normal immediate consumption. The level of production is therefore subject to a very definite ceiling, which may be well below their potential capacity to produce, in that when they have produced sufficient of what they know how to produce to meet their immediate needs, there is no point in producing more. The production of a surplus beyond that requirement adds nothing to their satisfactions, present or future. (p. 463)

By showing that output is limited by a demand ceiling Fisk is able to show also that, in a subsistence unit with a productive natural environment, there will be a fund of unused resources which, if the need arose, could be used to raise the level of output. This would not involve changes in the techniques of production or important changes in the social system. Included in these idle resources will be that proportion of the potential supply of labour not required for production to the level of the demand ceiling. The level of planned output per head will rise only in response to a rise in the level of the demand ceiling such as can be expected to take place if trade links are established with an outside economy which can offer new goods and services in exchange for the goods and services produced in the subsistence unit. Substantial and continual rises in the demand ceiling can come only after trade links have been established with an advanced market sector which can offer a very great range of new goods and services.

Fisk also examines the effect of simple technological changes such as the introduction of steel knives and axes, which usually follow contact and usually reduce the quantity of labour necessary for a given productive task. He suggests that changes of this type are unlikely to lead to a large increase in the variety of goods and services produced in the subsistence unit and thus to a substantial rise in the level of the demand ceiling. They will rather be used to reduce the labour effort required to satisfy the given needs of the unit, and will increase the size of the potential surplus of labour which could find employment in the market sector if the incentive to do so were provided.

In his second paper Fisk (1964) takes the analysis a step further and examines the conditions under which the subsistence producer will be persuaded to apply some, or all, of his surplus labour in supplementary market production. The incentive to do this will come from his desire to possess and consume the new goods and services which become available in the market sector. But a complex array of other considerations could influence his final decision and his ability to carry this decision through. Fisk has classified these many considerations as follows:

> In its simplest form, the basic proposition is that supplementary cash production is the response of the subsistence group to the force of incentive. The growth of cash production is therefore dependent on the relative strength of two factors. On the one hand there is the strength of the incentive transmitted to the subsistence group by the market forces, which may be termed the *incentive factor*. On the other, there is the strength of the resistance or inertia of the subsistence group to changes of the types required for supplementary cash production, which may be termed the *response factor*.
>
> However, both these factors are resultants of a complex manifold of components, which may broadly be classified as internal and external. . . . In the case of the incentive factor, the internal components are the market forces which operate in a deterministic fashion in accordance with known laws. The external components are the non-market forces through which the framework in which the market forces operate can be modified, and by which intervention is possible. In the case of the response factor, the internal components are the cultural, political, physical and economic characteristics of the subsistence group itself, and in the absence of external influence, these also can be taken as largely deterministic and given. The external components are the non-market forces that influence and modify the internal characteristics of the group, and through which intervention in the response factor is possible. (p. 157)

The role of the response factor is passive or inert in that it determines how the subsistence producer will react to the forces of incentive but it does not initiate change itself. For the rest of the paper Fisk concentrates on the active incentive factor, not because it is more important than the response factor, but because it is generally less well understood. The strength of the incentive factor results from a comparison by the subsistence producer of the disutility of the additional labour (or negative leisure) necessary to produce for the market, with the utility of the goods and services his money earnings will command. Since the market sector is highly monetized and participation in it involves the use of money, Fisk examines the incentive factor from two sides of the necessary coin. One side gives the labour cost of earning money while the other shows the level of satisfaction gained from the use of this money. The effort cost of earning a certain sum will largely depend on factors such as 'the range, accessibility, cost and efficiency of processing, marketing, transport and distribution services' (p. 160) which reflect the effectiveness of the physical linkage between the subsistence producer and the market sector. Other factors, such as 'the range and appropriateness of the goods and services offered for money, their availability at the time and place they are required, and the cost of retailing' (p. 161) affect the level of satisfaction that can be derived from the money earned. In the early stages of contact with the market sector the incentive factor can be particularly weak and initiate little response from the subsistence producer. Once the subsistence producer has earned sufficient money to acquire a few basic items like knives and axes and a few simple luxuries like beads and a mirror, he may retire from the market sector. As the market sector expands, economies of scale can raise the level of incentive to a point where the subsistence producer is again willing to exchange his labour for market sector goods, or to exchange more labour than he had felt the need to earlier. The important point here is that the strength of the incentive factor is a variable and, other things being equal, the greater the strength of the incentive factor, the more labour the subsistence producer will be willing to put into supplementary market production. This does not preclude him from reducing his effort if the level of incentive falls; if, for example, his cash earnings per hour of labour rise faster than his demand for market sector goods and services. Fisk goes on to show that it could take substantial upward shifts in the level of incentive to call forth any significant response in the subsistence unit, and that the supplementary market output from the subsistence sector is likely to alternate between periods of stagnation and growth rather than to respond smoothly to a gradual strengthening of the incentive factor.

As a result of this analysis, of which the above is only a part, Fisk has shown that in certain circumstances there will be a potential for substantial increases in output from the subsistence sector and he has also shown the mechanism through which this increased output can be achieved. The analysis was intended to apply to the special problems of development planning in Papua-New Guinea. It was based on experience in Papua-New Guinea, and there is a good deal of empirical evidence from there to support it. But the validity of the analysis does not depend on what has happened in Papua-New Guinea, but on the validity of a number of general propositions about human economic behaviour in a particular economic environment which is found in many parts of the world. This particular economic environment has been described earlier but its essential conditions are satisfied where a primitive economy exists in surroundings of abundant and productive natural resources.

Three basic propositions underlie the Fisk analysis. The first concerns the primitive economy in conditions which may be termed 'primitive affluence', before contact is made with an advanced market sector, and is as follows:

(1) That subsistence production in a situation of 'primitive affluence' is limited by demand for the goods and services that the subsistence unit can produce rather than by any shortage of factors of production, and therefore *per capita* output tends to be maintained at a constant level.

The second proposition deals with the same subsistence unit after its isolation has ended and regular contact is, or could be, maintained with an advanced market sector. In this new situation:

(2) The degree of participation in the market sector by the subsistence unit will vary with the strength of the incentive factor which in turn will depend largely on the development of effective linkage with the market sector.

The third proposition is central to the argument that increased involvement in the market sector and, as a corollary, increased monetization in the subsistence unit, will lead to increased output per head in the subsistence unit and thereby meet the requirements of economic development. It is that:

(3) Participation in the market sector may be expected, initially, to be supplementary to subsistence production, and therefore to represent additional income and consumption rather than mere substitution.

While Fisk has described, in the abstract, the relationship between monetization and output, there has been little empirical work, particularly outside Papua-New Guinea, to show how the relationship works or if it exists. It was felt that a rigorous empirical test of the three main propositions in the Fisk analysis would test the validity of the general hypothesis; that such a test would be practicable; that it should be attempted away from Papua-New Guinea; and that, as more and more primitive subsistence-based communities are being drawn into the development web in various parts of the world, such a test would have some practical value.

Chapter 2

# SCOPE AND METHOD

A DISCUSSION of fieldwork methods and problems is necessary for two reasons. First, it helps the reader assess the reliability of the primary data presented in the study, and second, a description and appraisal of a somewhat novel survey design used to collect most of the household data may be of interest to fellow fieldworkers. A brief description of the general research design will be followed by discussion of the selection of Western Samoa as the location for the study, the selection of four villages as case studies, and the collection of data.

## The general research design

In his theoretical analysis Fisk followed a model of a single subsistence-based community through time to examine its responses to a changing economic environment. Obviously an empirical study along these lines could take decades to complete, and it would hardly be a feasible research project. But if the element of continuity through time is removed from the Fisk analysis one is left with a series of static situations, each with its own peculiar level of market incentive, and the resultant level of output and market participation. If, further, the continuity of community is removed, one could have a series of static situations, with different levels of incentive and response, represented by several different communities. This study is based on a comparison of four separate communities which were selected because they were faced with markedly different levels of market incentive. Each provides an independent case study of economic behaviour in a subsistence-based village community partly dependent on an advanced market sector for the maintenance of its living standards. But the subjects of investigation and methods used in each case study were identical so that a firm basis was laid for comparison.

## The selection of a suitable primitive economy

The first task was to select a primitive economy in which could be found, in addition to the necessary conditions of co-existence of a

9

high level of subsistence production and an advanced market sector, a number of small subsistence-based communities with similar social and pre-contact economic backgrounds and markedly dissimilar relationships with the market sector. The requirement that the communities have similar social and pre-contact economic backgrounds is a practical rather than theoretical condition as it was felt that the relationship between output and incentive in each community could be compared best if Fisk's response factor could be assumed to be substantially the same in each community.

A great number of societies with suitable conditions for this study have been described by anthropologists and others, and several were studied through the literature before the final choice was made. In fact, the selection of Western Samoa came only after a first choice of the Redjang of south-west Sumatra had to be abandoned as the political situation worsened in Indonesia during 1965.

The Samoan islands (inset, endpaper map) were effectively isolated from regular external contact until the 1830s when missionaries and traders settled permanently in the islands. Earlier political and perhaps social contact with the Fiji and Tonga Islands was irregular and trade links had not developed. The two largest islands of the group—Upolu (430 square miles) and Savai'i (660 square miles) were covered by lush tropical forest and ringed by coral reefs and lagoons. The population of these islands during the first two decades of regular contact with the west was estimated to have been between 30,000 and 50,000 (*Census* 1961, p. 8). Many writers have described the 'primitive affluence' of the Samoans but two were particularly influential in the selection of these islands for the study. La Perouse (1798), the first European known to have landed in the Samoan Islands, left little doubt as to the primitive affluence of one community he visited:

> . . . a charming village situated in the middle of a wood, or rather of an orchard, all of the trees of which are loaded with fruit. The houses were placed on the circumference of a circle, of about a hundred and fifty *toises* [300 yards] in diameter, the interior forming a vast open space, covered with the most beautiful verdure, and shaded by trees, which kept the air delightfully cool. Women, children, and old men, accompanied me, and invited me into their houses. They spread the finest and freshest mats upon a floor formed of little chosen pebbles, and raised about two feet above the ground, in order to guard against the humidity. . . . The best architect could not have given a more elegant curve to the extremities of the ellipses that terminated the buildings.
>
> . . .
>
> The trees that produce the breadfruit, the cocoa-nut [sic], the banana,

the guava, and the orange, hold out to these fortunate people an abund-
ance of wholesome food; while fowls, hogs, and dogs, which live upon
the surplus of these fruits, afford an agreeable variety of viands.

. . .

They were so rich, and in want of so little, that they disdained our
instruments of iron and stuffs, and would only have beads. . . . These
Islanders, were we incessantly repeating, are undoubtedly the most
happy inhabitants of the earth. (pp. 58-130)

Perhaps the most complete description of the affluence of the
primitive Samoan economy is in a paper by R. F. Watters in which
he reconstructs the main features of Samoan agriculture in the
1840s:

In Samoa the physical and social environments modified slightly a system
of primitive cultivation from its intrinsically Polynesian form. Aims and
practices were a little different and revealed themselves in a subsistence
system that was rather more extensive, more static, and socially less
important. Agricultural methods of the Polynesian heritage appear to
have been gradually sublimated, for the wealth of resources in the
Islands seems to have resulted in a narrowing rather than a broadening
of agricultural practices. The practice of irrigation, common in Fiji
and various Polynesian islands, was absent. Slopes were not terraced.
Methods of cultivation were casual and weeding desultory. In the larger
islands, the pressure of population on the land was only light and prodigal
use of the land could be made.
In spite of the depredations of wild pigs, flying foxes (*Pteropus ruficollis,
pe'a*), birds, rats, the dreaded rhinoceros beetle (after white settlement),
or destruction caused through gales, tropical cyclones, or human agency
in wartime, the loss of the entire taro or yam crop did not produce
much hardship. Storms, droughts and pests were regarded as ministers
of the wrathful god *O le Sa*, to whom propitiatory offerings were made
before vigorous efforts by the gardener were begun, to redeem his losses.
The fact that planting could be done all the year round in most parts
meant that losses would soon be recovered, and in the meantime the
bounteous natural environment provided fish from the sea, wild yams
and roots from the forest, and coconuts along the seashore.
Although supplementary food resources could be found in profuse and
varied quantities, the fact that the Samoan neglected to utilize many
of them, or did so only intermittently, is striking testimony to the produc-
tivity of his natural environment in relation to population pressure.
Thus, wild fruits were rarely eaten, and wild dogs and rats—food relished
in other parts of the Pacific—were generally scorned as food. Insects
were rarely eaten. The deification of various birds and fish as family
gods made them taboo to the villagers, but this was no great loss to the
food supply. The absence of any method of drying fish was a disadvantage
of little moment. So liberal was the Samoan natural environment that
a subsistence system was supported more easily than in most other groups

of the Pacific, and little effort was required to maintain comfortable living standards. The challenge of the natural environment was on the whole only slight, and the response of the Samoan culture was accordingly small. (1958a, pp. 350-1)

Samoa was fragmented into a large number of basically self-sufficient economic and social units comprising individual villages, or in some cases groups of two or three neighbouring villages. Contact between the villages was largely at the social and political level as indicated in the following passage:

> Goods and services which pass beyond the village are virtually wholly ceremonial, pertaining to elite integration, such as supplying pigs and other 'feast foods' or 'gift exchanges' of finely woven mats. Even selective and increasing penetration of the modern commercial economy, in which wanted trade goods and money are obtained mainly by selling copra . . ., has not disturbed this essential pattern. (Keesing and Keesing 1957, p. 17)

Two further observations from La Perouse show that the facilities for transporting goods in quantity between villages were poorly developed. 'Their villages are all situated in creeks by the sea-side, and have no paths except to penetrate into the interior of the country' (p. 117). While most inter-village travel was by sea even here it would have been difficult to transport goods in quantity: 'Their canoes have outriggers, are very small, and generally contain only five or six persons: some few, however, may contain as many as fourteen' (p. 117). It appeared fairly clear from the literature that the Samoan villages approached, in all essential respects, the Fisk ideal of a subsistence unit before a foreign-dominated market sector developed in Western Samoa.

The assessment of market incentive is a difficult and complicated process which is not likely to be achieved adequately even with detailed knowledge of village conditions. But it is assumed that certain factors which operate to link the village economy with the market sector—such as transport facilities and costs, location of trade stores and prices for trade goods and village output—are particularly important elements in determining the overall level of market incentive, and that economic linkage can be used as a first and reasonably close approximation to the more abstract concept of incentive. An examination of a map of Western Samoa indicated that sufficient differences between the villages in terms of linkage with the market sector (based on the one port-town of Apia) would be found to give the study a reasonable chance of success in this respect.

Almost three hundred villages are listed in the *Western Samoa*

*Population Census 1961,* ranging in size from less than one hundred to well over one thousand persons. Most villages, however, were found to have populations of under six hundred and it was considered that villages of this size could be surveyed adequately with the resources and time available for fieldwork.

## The selection of case studies

While it was theoretically possible to select the villages for study to represent different levels of market incentive, in practice this could only be approximated. Selection was in fact based on a few known factors which contributed to the economic linkage between the village and the market sector. Those considered were as follows:

1. Communications—distance, measured by the time, effort and cash cost, of a journey from the village to the commercial centre of Apia;

2. Marketing and distribution services—(a) the facilities available in, and within easy reach of, each village for the sale of village output, and the prices offered, and (b) the range, variety and prices of goods and services available for purchase in, or within easy reach of, each village.

The two hundred or so villages with populations under 600 were ranked roughly according to these linkage factors and it was assumed that this would approximate a ranking based on a more complete assessment of the levels of incentive. The ranked list was used as a guide in selecting the study villages. At first it was intended to select two villages at the bottom and two at the top of the list. But it was found that there remained only one village which had obviously weak linkage—no road access—and this was selected as the sole extreme case. Another village was selected to represent the other extreme—a village close to Apia—and here there was a wide choice. Two further villages were selected as examples of intermediate positions largely on the basis of the number of years they had been accessible by road. This was essentially the same as the number of years each had been able to market bananas and had relatively easy access to Apia. A village on the south coast of Upolu Island, which had been connected to the Upolu road network in 1949 and was a district centre with a hospital, police station, and intermediate school, was selected first. Then a village on the south coast of Savai'i Island which was not accessible by road until 1960 was selected.

Before making the final selection I travelled around the two main islands. But the fleeting glimpses of the villages which I had on this journey did not influence the choice to any great extent.

The initial selection was based largely on the sort of secondary data outlined above, evaluated after discussions with a number of people in Apia who knew the villages well. Only one village was known to me first-hand before it was selected for the study. Utuali'i was only five minutes' walk from Malua where my wife was teaching and where we had been provided with a house. Because it was close, I used this village for a full-scale test of the field methods and survey schedules I was intending to use. But after an encouraging fortnight working in this village it was decided to retain Utuali'i in the the study programme rather than to select another village near Apia as was the original intention. The location of the villages selected[1]—Utuali'i (I) near Apia; Poutasi (II) which had direct road access to Apia in 1949; Taga (III) in Savai'i Island which had been connected to the road only in 1960; and Uafato (IV) the example of weak linkage—is shown in the endpaper map.

### The collection of data

The primary objective of the fieldwork in Western Samoa was to assemble the data needed to test Fisk's propositions about the way in which economic behaviour of the villages is related to the strength of the linkage between the village and the market sector. This meant, amongst other things, being able to quantify accurately for each village such economic parameters as (a) the level and composition of subsistence production, consumption and investment, (b) the level and sources of cash income, (c) the level and direction of cash consumption expenditure, investment and savings, and (d) some of the important linkage factors such as cash returns to labour in the production and sale of village output, and retail prices of goods available in village stores. As there were virtually no records or written material available on the villages most of the data presented were collected by conducting surveys, and by careful observation of village life, during about seven weeks spent in each village.

The main limitation on the study as a whole was that it had to be compressed in scale to what could be handled by one person in the space of a year. The selection of villages, testing of schedules and questionnaires and other preparatory work, as well as various unexpected delays, in fact limited the actual survey time in the villages to about seven months. Recorders were employed in each village to carry out some of the routine survey work but these needed constant supervision and their work required careful

---

[1] The Roman numerals I to IV, which correspond to the initial ranking in terms of certain linkage factors, will be used to identify the villages where it seems useful.

checking. This effectively ruled out any possibility of collecting important data in all villages at the same time, and therefore limited severely the actual survey time that could be given to each village. Further, there were few persons available in each village who could be trained as recorders and this meant that most of the detailed data had to be drawn from a sample of households rather than from the whole village.

## The design of the survey

A solution to the problem of surveying *four* villages was found in a survey design suggested by Oram (1963). He was concerned with an age-old survey problem of reconciling a need for accurate and detailed data collected daily from a sample of households, with a requirement that these data span a period of several months. Clearly, intensive daily questioning would increasingly tax the patience and co-operation of respondents and recorders alike, and this could lead to rapid deterioration in the quality of the data collected. Oram's compromise offered to preserve the accuracy of the data and the overall time span of the survey by reducing the monotonous daily questioning to a series of one or two week-long periods interspersed with similar periods when the respondents would be left completely alone. The number and length of the survey and rest periods could be arranged to suit circumstances and the particular needs of the study.

Since there was no need to fit the survey to cover major seasonal changes in Samoa, this general survey design allowed me to supervise the collection of data in all four villages, and at the same time run the four surveys more or less concurrently. Each village was visited in turn for one or two weeks during which data were collected daily from a sample of households. It was then revisited four times in turn until five survey rounds had been completed, giving in all about seven weeks of intensive study in each village during the seven months available. The rest period for village A consisted of the time taken to carry out the survey in villages B, C and D; the rest period for village B consisted of the weeks spent in villages C, D and A, and so on. Since essentially the same data were collected in each of the villages, it was a distinct advantage to have the four surveys progress at about the same pace and span the same time period. For example, when a new line of inquiry was suggested by an experience in one of the villages it could be followed up without much delay in each of the others in turn.

There was an additional advantage of the rotation system which was totally unexpected, but as it turned out, very welcome. The first round, consisting of a fortnight in each village, had just been

C

completed when a hurricane struck Western Samoa. Thereafter things were far from normal in the villages. If the plan had been to study the villages seriatim, in all probability only one would have been completed at the time of the hurricane and much of the basis for comparing it with the three villages studied later would have been lost. Because of the rotation system the study was able to continue as planned, and it was possible to observe closely (over the following five months) the response of each village to the hurricane emergency.

The survey design also achieved Oram's original objective which was to reduce the monotony of a long survey involving a routine set of questions. An attempt was made to disguise the routine to some extent by adding in each round some new line of inquiry to the standard daily questionnaire, but on the whole a week of daily questioning seemed to be enough for most households and village recorders. After a break of five or six weeks they continued the routine as if it was something fresh and new, and the survey probably could have continued in this way for several more months before the participants would have become stale and disinterested. As it was, our visits and daily questioning seemed to give many of the participants a welcome break in the routine of village life.

*Household sampling*

As mentioned earlier, it was necessary to rely on a sample of households for much of the detailed data. Before the sample could be selected, however, a decision had to be taken on the type of household which would best suit the purposes of the study. In social and economic terms the Samoan village consists of a number of local lineages or *'āiga*, each of which is represented by its elected leader (*matai*) in the village council and controls land in the village area through customary and legal rights vested in its *matai*. Each *'āiga* is largely self-sufficient in the goods and services produced in the village. Each traces its origins back to the foundation of the village or farther, and sees its life stretching unbroken into the future. The *'āiga* forms the primary economic and social unit of the village community. For these reasons it was clear that the *'āiga* would have to be the 'household' for the purposes of the survey.

But *'āiga* vary a great deal in size, in the composition of their membership, in the effective role played by the *matai*, and in the organization of their economic activities. The largest *'āiga* in the four villages had fifty-two members, while the smallest consisted of only a *matai* and his brother. *Matai* vary considerably in their ability to organize the economic affairs of their *'āiga*, and in the resources available to them. At one extreme are those who directly control and supervise all the economic activities of their members. At the other are those who allocate areas of land to individual members who thereby gain a certain amount of economic freedom, although they are always subject to demands on their time and resources by the *matai*. This variation did not affect the need to take the *'āiga* as the household unit in the survey, but it did present certain problems of data collection, since in the latter type of organization, several semi-independent households had to be canvassed in order to build up a complete record of the activities of the whole *'āiga*. For example, one *'āiga* selected in Utuali'i consisted of six semi-independent nuclear families. Each worked a piece of land allocated by the *matai*, and provided him with food, labour and money either regularly or on demand. In the Utuali'i survey each of these families was treated as a separate respondent or household, and only later were these data collected together to present a complete record of the activities of the *'āiga* as a single economic unit. This method was adopted where necessary in each of the villages studied with the result that in Utuali'i sixteen sets of records were needed to cover eight *'āiga*, seventeen sets were required for the nine selected in Poutasi, and eleven sets were required for the nine Uafato *'āiga* included in the sample. In Taga there were fewer large *'āiga* and only one of those selected in the sample needed more than one set of records. These and related details are shown in Table 1.

Table 1   Sample Households and Village Populations

|  | Utuali'i (I) | Poutasi (II) | Taga (III) | Uafato (IV) |
|---|---|---|---|---|
| Village population[a] | 251 | 382 | 468 | 281 |
| Sample households (*'āiga*) population | 110 | 198 | 223 | 171 |
| Per cent of village population contained in the sample | 44 | 52 | 48 | 61 |
| Number of village households (*'āiga*) | 17 | 16 | 40 | 17 |
| Number of sample households (*'āiga*) | 8 | 9 | 15 | 9 |
| Per cent of village households (*'āiga*) contained in the sample | 47 | 56 | 38 | 53 |
| Number of family groups contained in the sample households[b] | 16 | 17 | 16 | 11 |

NOTES:   [a] The population and *'āiga* numbers excluded families which lie outside the traditional social organization of the villages, such as those of the pastors, teachers and traders.
[b] Several sample *'āiga* comprised two or more family groups each of which was included in the survey as a separate unit for purposes of data collection.

In selecting the '*āiga* in each village a compromise had to be reached between what was considered to be an ideal sample and what was possible and practicable under the circumstances. The ideal sample would have been randomly selected from a complete list of all '*āiga* stratified according to the level of '*āiga* cash income per head. But this was not possible. In the first place '*āiga* cash incomes per head were not known, and only with the well-informed help of the village pastor was an approximate ranking of '*āiga* possible. Second, it was considered advisable to comply with Samoan custom and etiquette and to include in the sample the '*āiga* of the high chief and the *pulenu'u*. Third, a few changes were made to the initial random selection where serious illness, absence, or some other factor would have prevented the '*āiga* from co-operating at the critical time. Finally, the number which could be included in the sample depended on a combination of three factors: (1) the number of recorders available in the villages; (2) a stipulation that each recorder should not be expected to complete more than six household schedules a day; and (3) the incidence of semi-independent families requiring full independent treatment in the selected '*āiga*. Because of these limitations and the possibility of serious error in the selection of the sample, it was decided to take the largest number possible in each village sample, even though this meant that the samples did not represent a consistent proportion of village populations.

The sample of '*āiga* in each village was obtained by working through the following five steps:

1. With the pastor's assistance the '*āiga* were listed and ranked according to rough estimates of total cash incomes.

2. After obtaining fairly accurate figures of membership the ranking was adjusted to represent '*āiga* cash incomes per head.

3. Information about probable numbers of semi-independent households requiring separate treatment was then obtained and entered against the appropriate names in the ranked list for later reference, and the '*āiga* of the high chief and *pulenu'u* were identified for certain selection.

4. The list was then divided into three sections corresponding to high, medium and low incomes per head.

5. The sample was drawn from this list to represent as far as possible the range and distribution of '*āiga* cash incomes per head found in the village. Even where there was a certain amount of juggling to fit in the two pre-selected '*āiga*, to replace those found to be unsuitable, and to accommodate semi-independent families

found in selected 'āiga, the sample retained this representative quality as far as could be judged at the time. It was anticipated that some changes might have to be made to the samples in the light of new knowledge and understanding of the villages, but only in one village was any change felt to be necessary, and all this involved was a slight reduction in the size of the sample when one 'āiga was dropped and not replaced.

Three main types of data were collected in the villages during the survey visits. The first was information of a general nature relating to the village as a whole, such as population, land use and control, transport facilities and costs, and various facets of the economic, social, political and religious life of the village community. The second covered the facilities and activities of stores and other commercial ventures in the village, and the general arrangements for buying and selling in the village and other centres such as Apia. Some data in these two categories were found outside the village, for example, from records of government marketing authorities, trading companies and church offices, but for the most part they were collected in the villages. The detailed data collected from the sample of 'āiga formed the third category. Population, land holdings and land use, capital assets and consumer durables, subsistence production, consumption and exchange, cash income, expenditure and savings/debts, work and leisure formed the main items in this category. There is no need to go farther into the collection of data in the first two categories, but some details about the third may be useful.

Information for each 'āiga on land use and holdings, capital assets, and consumer durables were collected systematically during the first round in each village, and again during the final round when changes were noted and explanations obtained if needed. Much of this information took the form of an inventory in a schedule which also contained demographic and other background material for each 'āiga.

A short questionnaire (Appendix Table 6) in the Samoan language was used to collect details of the daily activities of the sample 'āiga. This was completed by the village recorders each evening when most members of the 'āiga were assembled together for family prayers and the main meal of the day. The questionnaire was used during all five week-long working visits to each village as indicated in the fieldwork timetable shown as Table 2. Considerable detail was obtained by recording activities at the close of each day. Most activities formed a fairly regular pattern and this was assumed to continue during the unobserved weeks between visits. But there were other activities of an erratic nature which, because they were

## Table 2   Fieldwork Timetable

| Dates | Villages | Visit | A | B | C | D | E |
|---|---|---|---|---|---|---|---|
| 25 Oct.–8 Nov. 65 | Utuali'i (I)(a) | Test | x | x | | | |
| 15–28 Nov. | Poutasi (II) | 1 | x | x | | | |
| 13–26 Dec. | Uafato (IV) | 1 | x | x | | | |
| 3–17 Jan. 66 | Taga (III) | 1 | x | x | | | |
| 24–30 Jan. | Utuali'i (I)(b) | 1 | | x | | | |
| 7–15 Feb. | Poutasi (II) | 2 | | x | x | x | |
| 21–8 Feb. | Uafato (IV) | 2 | | x | x | x | |
| 7–14 Mar. | Utuali'i (I) | 2 | | x | x | x | |
| 15–21 Mar. | Poutasi (II)(c) | 3 | | x | x | x | x |
| 22–8 Mar. | Taga (III)(c) | 2 | | x | x | x | |
| 4–10 Apr. | Uafato (IV) | 3 | | x | x | x | x |
| 11–17 Apr. | Utuali'i (I) | 3 | | x | x | x | x |
| 18–24 Apr. | Taga (II) | 3 | | x | x | x | x |
| 25 Apr.–1 May | Poutasi (III) | 4 | | x | x | x | x |
| 3–11 May | Uafato (IV) | 4 | | x | x | x | x |
| 16–22 May | Utuali'i (I) | 4 | | x | x | x | x |
| 24–30 May | Taga (III) | 4 | | x | x | x | x |
| 10–17 June | Poutasi (II) | 5 | x(d) | x | x | x | x |
| 20–7 June | Uafato (IV) | 5 | x(d) | x | x | x | x |
| 28 June–4 July | Utuali'i (I) | 5 | x(d) | x | x | x | x |
| 6–13 July | Taga (III) | 5 | x(d) | x | x | x | x |

Schedules:  A — Household possessions—Appendix Table 6 (c)
B — Daily income and expenditure etc.—Appendix Table 6 (a)
C — Income and expenditure etc. between rounds
D — Production and distribution of output—Appendix Table 6 (b)
E — Labour (sub-sample of households only)

NOTES:    (a) Practice fortnight used to test schedules and methods. Daily schedule material was not used farther but Household possessions schedule was satisfactory and was not repeated in visit 1.
(b) Hurricane during the afternoon and night of Saturday 29 January.
(c) The village and visit had to be altered to fit in with accommodation arrangements in Taga village.
(d) Household possessions schedules were checked and revised during the final visit in each village.

often important in the economic life of the 'āiga or village, had to be recorded for the unobserved as well as the observed weeks. It was found that the respondents could usually recall these departures from the norm, particularly the more important ones like the periodic preparation and sale of copra, or a purchase of some durable or semi-durable article, several weeks after the event. Consequently, early in each visit the 'āiga were questioned closely about the preceding weeks and relevant information was recorded. Often it was found that more than one 'āiga had been involved in, or had knowledge of these more erratic activities, and they provided useful checks. Sales and purchases of a substantial kind could usually be checked with the stores.

During three of the five weeks information on the daily work activities of the men was collected from most of the sample 'āiga. There were two main objectives here: to get an approximate idea of the number of hours spent in the main productive tasks of village economic life; and to time certain common tasks such as the collection of coconuts and the preparation of copra. In order to get consistent data this survey was carried out in all villages by my research assistant.

This completes the description of the formal parts of the survey in each village. It remains only to say that the data collected in the various questionnaires and schedules were supplemented to an important extent by careful observation of the sample 'āiga and the village as a whole, by casual questioning, and with data collected from stores, church records and government officials. On the whole the data assembled during the survey were adequate for the purpose of testing Fisk's propositions. It was a distinct advantage of the general method, which treated each village as a case study and each of the sample 'āiga as a miniature case study, and allowed close observation of these over the whole survey period, that the limitations of the data being collected were known. Where the daily questionnaire data were weak it was often possible to find other means to strengthen them. Rarely did figures have to be accepted at their face value alone. But it would have been extremely valuable if a more thorough study could have been made of the relationship between the social and economic aspects of village life, and if a more knowledgeable assessment of land use and agricultural methods could have been completed. In both these fields I was an amateur.

Chapter 3

# THE SAMOAN ECONOMY
# AND SOCIETY

My first view of Samoa was from the deck of the M.V. *Matua*, one of the two small passenger-freight vessels which provide a regular fortnightly service between New Zealand, Fiji, Tonga, Niue and American and Western Samoa. First the peak of Silisili appeared, towering over 6,000 feet above Savai'i Island, then the lesser Savai'i peaks, Te'elagi, Siope, and Maugaafi all over 5,000 feet, and finally the 3,600-feet Fito, the highest point in Upolu Island. We passed between the black lava cliffs of Savai'i and the two small islands of Apolima and Manono which guard the approaches to Upolu, then along the north coast of Upolu with its many villages of thatched houses, large white churches and dark green backdrop of coconut palms. Absorbed in the natural splendour of the island it came as something of a surprise to round Mulinu'u point and see freighters from Yokohama, San Francisco and London anchored in the harbour, the shore lined with substantial buildings, red roofs filling the valley, and as our anchor splashed into the still sea, to watch the street lights come on.

A voyager arriving at this same harbour 130 years earlier would have found only the small village of Apia on its shores. Now Apia town has a population of about 25,000 people; it is the capital, the administrative centre and commercial *entrepôt* for Western Samoa. The growth of Apia began a few years after John Williams of the London Missionary Society established the first regular contact between Samoans and Europeans in 1830.[1] He was followed in 1836 by the first large party of missionaries to take up residence in the Islands and by 1845 a theological seminary had been established at Malua, on land of Utuali'i village, for the training of Samoan pastors. With missionaries in permanent residence in Samoa, whalers and traders began to use Apia harbour as a regular port of call.

[1] The following brief historical outline is based on a number of secondary sources of which the following were the most helpful: Davidson 1967, Fox and Cumberland 1962, Keesing 1934, Pirie 1964, Fairbairn 1963.

In 1846 seventy-two vessels called at Apia . . . and many stayed for a
substantial time. For the whalers, which constituted the bulk of the
callers till the mid-'fifties, a visit of several weeks or more offered the
opportunity of resting the crew and making repairs to the ship, as well
as of obtaining fresh supplies of provisions, water and firewood. . . .
Samoans and Europeans were brought into day-to-day contact with one
another; and the necessary conditions were created for the establishment
of organized commerce. . . . By 1860 over a hundred Europeans were
permanently settled around the shores of Apia harbour, running various
types of businesses—such as general stores, boarding-houses, and grog-
shops—and practising a variety of trades. Others had settled on the land
near by and were producing foodstuffs for the trade with visiting ships.
And still others had established themselves as traders in the outer districts.
. . . The most important of these European enterprises was the branch
of the Hamburg firm of Johann Cesar Godeffroy and Sohn which was
established at Apia in 1857. . . . The firm came to Samoa because it had
decided to concentrate its efforts in the islands upon supplying the
rapidly expanding world market for coconut oil; and Apia seemed an
ideal base for the development of this trade. Agents were appointed
throughout Polynesia and Micronesia; and a fleet of small vessels was
built up to bring the oil back to Apia for trans-shipment to Europe.
In these various ways, Samoa was first linked substantially with the money
economy of the Western world. The Samoan people themselves produced
coconut oil both to sell to the traders and as contributions to the funds of
the missions. Some supplied foodstuffs to the merchants and to visiting
ships. Some entered the employment of European residents or were
engaged as sailors on local or overseas vessels. And they developed, at the
same time, a demand for the manufactured goods that the merchants
imported. All these developments, like the commercial ventures of the
European residents, constituted a major break from the wholly self-
sufficient, non-monetary economy of former times. (Davidson 1967,
pp. 37-9)

During the nineteenth century, while European commercial
interests in the Samoan islands were strengthening, the Samoans
themselves were becoming politically weaker and torn by periodic
factional warfare. The Europeans were quick to take advantage of
this, offering advice and arms in return for copra and land. In
1900, after agreement with the European powers with interests in
Samoa—Germany, Britain and the United States—a German
colonial administration was established over the Samoan islands
west of the 171st meridian—Upolu, Manono, Apolima and Savai'i.
For the first time in many decades these islands had internal peace
and a strong central administration. European claims to Samoan
lands were evaluated and those which could not be adequately
substantiated were rejected. Thereafter Samoans were prevented
from selling their land except to the Administration, and the

mechanism by which Samoan lands were controlled and used was based on Samoan custom and tradition. The Administration set about improving facilities such as roads and the Apia harbour for the European-owned plantations on the north-west coast of Upolu and around the harbour, and allowed the plantations to import Chinese labour. It also began to interfere directly in village economic life; Samoan producers, for example, were protected against false weights and measures, an existing poll tax was enforced, and every Samoan land holder was required to plant fifty coconut palms on his own land each year.

In 1914 a New Zealand administration took over from the German and continued until 1962 when Western Samoa became an independent state. From 1918 until the Second World War the conditions for village commercial development were little better than they had been during the second half of the nineteenth century. In 1918 an influenza epidemic took the lives of about twenty per cent of the people. A little later an ambitious programme of economic and social reform initiated by the Administrator, Richardson (1923-8), earned the strong opposition of the Samoans, part-Samoans and traders and led to a mass movement of disobedience and non-co-operation with the Administration (the Mau movement) which lasted in one form or another until about 1945.

The war, particularly the American involvement, brought some changes in Western Samoa. Hundreds of Western Samoans found wage employment with the American forces. The Americans built an airfield at Faleolo at the north-western end of Upolu, improved the road from Faleolo to Apia, and built a new road across the island to the south coast. Samoan interest in cash cropping, which had been at a low level during the Mau, began to revive. After the war a fast refrigerated vessel, the *Matua*, began a regular service between Samoa and New Zealand and this allowed the banana export industry to develop on a more systematic basis than had been possible earlier. The Administration continued the road-building programme started by the Americans and by 1960 most villages in Upolu and Savai'i could be reached by road. As roads reached the villages they were admitted into the 'Banana [marketing] Scheme' run by the Department of Agriculture, and in most districts the coming of the road and a banana planting boom went hand in hand (Ward 1959).

Buses, many of which were owned by local villagers, began to serve those villages accessible by road. As travel to Apia became easier a few Chinese and Samoans opened retail and trade stores in their villages in competition with the trading stations owned by Burns Philp, Morris Hedstrom, O. F. Nelson and other large Apia firms. Earlier, these firms had a virtual monopoly of village trade because they owned the launch facilities needed to supply their stores and to ship village-produced copra and cacao beans back to Apia. Once buses started running from the outer districts to Apia anyone in a village could build a small store and buy stock from Apia. In 1966 many of the older trading stations were being closed down. Apia firms always had a great deal of trouble on the village retail side, with their traders consuming or giving away stocks (or liberal credit), but in order to capture the village copra and cacao they had been forced to accept such losses as an inevitable part of the game. Once villagers started running trade stores, or marketing their copra directly in Apia, the usefulness of the district trade stores declined and the Apia firms were, on the whole, happy to transfer their retailing problems and losses to the villagers.

The population of Western Samoa in 1961 was 114,427 (*Census* 1961). It had been increasing rapidly since the war—by an average of 3·1 per cent a year since 1951—and with 50·2 per cent under the age of fifteen years in 1961 had prospects of an even greater rate of increase in the future. The Apia urban area had experienced a twenty per cent average annual growth rate since 1956 and in 1961 had a population of 21,699, or about nineteen per cent of the total population. Apia is the only town or urban area in Western Samoa and the rest of the population lives in the 250 or so villages strung along the shores of the islands. Many of the villages close to Apia are much influenced by Apia, while some in the more isolated districts have changed relatively little from the days of John Williams. Samoans constituted 88·5 per cent of the population of Western Samoa in 1961 with Part-Samoans making up 10·3 per cent, Europeans 0·5 per cent (668 persons) and Others 0·6 per cent (including 108 Chinese). A large proportion of the Part-Samoans, Europeans and Chinese lived in or near Apia.

Apia was, of course, where most of the wage and salary jobs were located. The 1961 Census recorded 10,128 persons in full-time wage and salary employment (Tables 3 and 4) and of these roughly twenty per cent were employed by the government. About half of the employed were labourers or held semi-skilled jobs, thirty-five per cent held administrative, professional and clerical jobs in government, commerce, plantations and the churches and only fifteen per cent held jobs requiring technical skills.

The rest of the population, roughly eighty per cent of all adults, depended in the main on village agriculture for its income—both cash and subsistence. Village cash cropping and subsistence activities demanded no special skills which could not be easily acquired by the slowest learner. Being brought up in a village was sufficient

Table 3   Sources of Employment in Western Samoa in 1961

| | Male | Female | Total | Per cent of wage & salary earners | Per cent of population |
|---|---|---|---|---|---|
| Wages & salary employment: | | | | | |
| primary industry | 1,335 | 397 | 1,732 | 16 | 1·5 |
| secondary industry | 1,611 | 105 | 1,716 | 16 | 1·5 |
| tertiary industry and government | 4,537 | 2,143 | 6,680 | 64 | 5·8 |
| unemployed | 317 | 80 | 397 | 4 | ·3 |
| total wage and salary earners and unemployed | 7,800 | 2,725 | 10,525 | 100 | 9·2 |
| Village agriculture and home duties | 17,416 | 22,454 | 39,870 | | 34·8 |
| Not economically active[a] | 33,569 | 30,463 | 64,032 | | 55·9 |
| Total population | 58,785 | 55,642 | 114,427 | | 100·0 |

SOURCE: *Census* 1961

NOTE:   [a] children attending school and other students, children under 15 years not attending school, persons in hospitals and gaol, pensioners, etc.

apprenticeship for all the tasks normally performed in a village. The only agricultural implements in general use were the bush knife or machete, the axe, and the *oso* or digging stick, and little skill was required to handle these with reasonable efficiency. Even toddlers were often expected to be able to cut the grass in front of the *fale*[2] with a foot-long knife. Most men could build the simple type of *fale* in common use and most women could weave the thatches and the floor and sleeping mats. Specialist skills were required only when a large elaborate guest *fale*, a European-style house, a church, or one of the larger canoes was to be built; such occasions were rare in any one village and generally the services of a traditional 'guild' of carpenters were employed.

Wage and salary jobs are much prized in Samoa and with few opportunities at home many Samoans have sought them in American Samoa and in New Zealand (Fairbairn 1961, E.D.P. 1966-70). There has been an average annual net emigration from Western Samoa of 936 persons over the years 1955-66 giving a total net emigration of over ten thousand persons. By 1966 over eight per cent of all Western Samoans were living abroad. In Western Samoa there is tangible evidence of this, and the close ties which bind members of a Samoan *'āiga*, in the volume of New Zealand bank

[2] Traditional thatched dwelling

Table 4   Principal Occupations of Wage and Salary Earners in Western
Samoa in 1961

| Type of employment | Number of persons employed[a] | | |
| --- | --- | --- | --- |
| | males | females | total |
| Primary industry: | | | |
| labourer | 1,037 | 388 | 1,425 |
| foreman, overseer, planter, proprietor, manager | 166 | | 166 |
| Secondary industry: | | | |
| labourer | 233 | | 233 |
| carpenter, bricklayer, plumber, painter, electrician | 830 | | 830 |
| mechanic, boat-builder, ship's carpenter, sailmaker, blacksmith | 340 | | 340 |
| tailor, dressmaker | | 65 | 65 |
| Tertiary industry and government: | | | |
| labourer | 481 | | 481 |
| bus, truck, taxi driver | 487 | | 487 |
| domestic servant, gardener, laundress, cook | | 541 | 541 |
| sales, shop assistant | 401 | 317 | 718 |
| accountant, cashier, clerk, typist | 545 | 89 | 634 |
| proprietor, manager, foreman | 205 | | 205 |
| police and gaol personnel | 162 | | 162 |
| teacher | 499 | 572 | 1,071 |
| nurse | | 270 | 270 |
| clergyman, pastor, catechist, mission personnel | 617 | 106 | 723 |

SOURCE: *Census* 1961

NOTE:     [a] 8,351 persons, or 80% of the wage and salary employees recorded in
the 1961 Census, are included in this table.

notes remitted through the post each week. In 1965 some £255,000
entered Western Samoa unofficially through the post and with
returning migrants. During the first six months of 1967, after the
effects of the January hurricane had been publicized in the New
Zealand press, and Samoans in New Zealand had received letters
from home giving the most dire predictions of famine, about
£200,000 had been received.[3] The importance of this source of
cash income is obvious when one realizes that in 1965 it amounted
to nearly ten per cent of the total cash income from the three major
export crops—copra, cacao beans, and bananas.

From a total land area of about 700,000 acres, only about 156,000
acres (twenty-two per cent) was in agricultural use (including
fallow land) in 1955 (Table 5). Almost eighty per cent of this
'occupied' land was controlled by the villages and their *matai*, who

[3] Personal communication, Bank of Western Samoa

also controlled about the same proportion of the total land area including forest, mountain and lava field. Commercial plantations took about fifteen per cent of the 'occupied' land and the remaining five per cent was in other, mainly non-agricultural, use such as in the Apia urban area and the Faleolo airfield.

Table 5    Disposition of Land in Western Samoa in 1955

|  | Occupied village land[a] | Commercial plantations | Other uses[b] | Forest & lava field | Total land area |
|---|---|---|---|---|---|
|  | (per cent of total land area) | | | | ('000 acres) |
| Upolu | 24·6 | 7·9 | 2·8 | 64·7 | 276 |
| Savai'i | 13·3 | ·4 | ·1 | 86·2 | 423 |
| W. Samoa | 17·8 | 3·4 | 1·2 | 77·6 | 699 |

SOURCE: Fox and Cumberland, 1962, p. 186

NOTES:    [a] Land in agricultural use (including fallow)
              [b] Urban, church and government land other than plantations

The main foodcrops grown for village consumption have not changed since the 1840s nor have the methods of cultivation. (Watters 1958a, Barrau 1961). The main staple foods are taro (*colocasia* sp.), *ta'amū* (*alocasia* sp.), banana, plantain, breadfruit (*artocarpus* sp.), yam (*dioscorea* sp.) and coconut, all of which are grown in a number of known varieties. The rather dull staple diet is varied with a great number of other vegetables, fruit and plants such as pineapple, papaya, oranges, limes, mangoes, sugar-cane, tomatoes, Chinese cabbage, beans and other European vegetables. Since the banana variety Gross Michel began to be exported from Western Samoa (1928) this variety has been grown almost to the exclusion of others in the villages and has become a staple subsistence food. Other introduced food plants such as various European vegetables have not so far been a great success in the villages, although with the spread of cacao as a cash crop the Samoans developed a liking for the strong cocoa drink which they could then make for themselves.

Copra, cacao and bananas are the principal export, and therefore cash, crops. Village lands supply about eighty per cent of the copra, about half the cacao beans and virtually all the bananas (Stace 1965). Copra, cacao, and bananas earned Western Samoa an average income between 1960 and 1964 of just under £2,393,000[4]

[4] The value of the Samoan £ is linked with that of New Zealand at par.

a year, or ninety-seven per cent of the total value of exports (Table 6).

Table 6    Western Samoa's Principal Exports: Five-year Annual Averages
1915-64

|  | Quantities exported | | | Value of export | | | |
|---|---|---|---|---|---|---|---|
|  | copra | cacao | bananas | copra | cacao | bananas | other[a] |
|  | ('000 tons) | | | (£ '000) | | | |
| 1915-19 | 9·8 | ·9 | none | 252 | 66 | none | |
| 1920-4 | 10·8 | ·7 | none | 272 | 48 | none | |
| 1925-9 | 11·4 | ·7 | ·6[b] | 275 | 45 | 7 | |
| 1930-4 | 13·6 | ·9 | 3·4 | 109 | 44 | 35 | |
| 1935-9 | 11·0 | 1·0 | 6·7 | 135 | 44 | 62 | |
| 1940-4 | 12·6 | 1·5 | 4·7 | 136 | 94 | 46 | |
| 1945-9 | 8·8 | 2·2 | 4·2 | 555 | 318 | 72 | |
| 1950-4 | 15·4 | 2·7 | 6·1 | 848 | 741 | 151 | |
| 1955-9 | 14·2 | 3·6 | 17·9 | 950 | 889 | 610 | |
| 1960-4 | 14·2 | 4·4 | 21·0 | 822 | 808 | 763 | 70 |

SOURCE: Collector of Customs 1965

NOTES: [a] Available for the years 1962-5 only from *Western Samoa's Economic Development Programme 1966-70*, 1966, p. 188.

[b] Bananas were first exported in 1928.

The quantity of copra exported from Western Samoa has not increased significantly since about 1930. There has been little expansion of village coconut lands since about 1918 and little systematic replanting of existing lands. Much of the village coconut land has been neglected, and the village small-holdings are typically a mixture of old palms, self-sown young palms, bearing and unproductive palms, trees, bush, and a dense ground cover. The village copra industry seems to have gone through three main stages; first, a period of expansion from about 1880, through the German colonial period, and up to the influenza epidemic and the start of the Mau; second, a period of neglect due largely to the political troubles of the 1920s and '30s and low prices in the early 1930s; and third, the period since the Second World War when most villages have concentrated on bananas for export. During the second two stages the nuts have been harvested, and the copra prepared and sold, but there has been little expansion and often very poor maintenance of existing coconut lands.

Cacao became an important village cash crop after the war but due to falling and unstable prices there has been little expansion of this crop in the villages since about 1960. In 1963 village banana crops were infected with an aphid-carried virus (bunchytop), and by the end of 1965 this industry was in serious decline. The hurricane of 29 January 1966 temporarily destroyed what remained of the banana crops as well as the 1966 cacao bean harvest. As a result in 1966 the villages were largely forced back on copra as their main source of cash income. A new cash crop possibility did emerge in 1965, however. Some villages had begun to transfer their efforts from the rapidly declining banana plots into taro for export to New Zealand and American Samoa.

Little detailed information of imports into Western Samoa is available except for 1965 but it appears that the 1965 situation (Table 7) was little different from that of the preceding five or six years. A brief examination of the value of imports in 1965 gives a somewhat surprising result in view of Samoa's agricultural subsistence-based economy. Thirty-one per cent of the value of imports consisted of foodstuffs, and over half of this expenditure was on

Table 7    Western Samoa: Imports by Commodity Groups in 1965

|  | Value of imports | Per cent of imports |
|---|---|---|
|  | (£'000) |  |
| Foodstuffs |  |  |
| meat | 293 |  |
| fish | 156 |  |
| flour | 135 |  |
| rice | 54 |  |
| sugar | 109 |  |
| milk, cream, butter | 59 |  |
| biscuits (cabin & ship's bread) | 193 |  |
|  | 1,017 | 30·9 |
| Textiles, drapery, clothing | 319 | 9·7 |
| Soap and detergents | 67 | 2·0 |
| Alcoholic beverages, tobacco & matches | 179 | 5·4 |
| Drugs, chemicals, medical & scientific apparatus[a] | 69 | 2·1 |
| Mineral fuels, lubricants, kerosene | 107 | 3·3 |
| Machinery, equipment, tools | 468 | 14·2 |
| Transport equipment | 149 | 4·5 |
| Raw materials: |  |  |
| shooks for bananas & other fruit cases | 183 |  |
| cement | 32 |  |
| corrugated iron | 39 |  |
| all other items | 129 |  |
|  | 383 | 11·6 |
| Other manufactured goods | 532 | 16·3 |
| Total | 3,290 | 100·0 |

SOURCE: Collector of Customs, 1965

NOTE:        [a] Includes expenditure on manures and fertilizers of £684.

tinned fish, flour, rice and biscuits, which are fairly close substitutes for the foods produced in the villages. Food and other consumption goods accounted for nearly sixty-five per cent of all imports. The range of food and manufactured goods available in Apia stores was considerable and approached that of any country town in New Zealand, Australia or even the United States. In 1965 government imports accounted for about £750,000 (twenty-three per cent) of the total value of imports, a direct result of the construction of the Apia wharf and other harbour development, and the purchase of diesel generators.

Two further points may be noted here: first, imports of fertilizer in 1965 amounted to only about £680, not much more than would be used on experimental plots run by the Department of Agriculture, and second, about thirty-two per cent of the total receipts from export bananas was spent on imported wooden cases, wire and nails, used for shipping the bananas out. While Western Samoa appears to have considerable timber resources in its forests, timber suitable for banana cases has not been found. Little was known, however, of the economic potential of Samoa's forests and little had been done to improve this situation, as a plaintive note in *Western Samoa's Economic Plan for 1965* indicates: 'The Department of Agriculture is attempting to recruit a Forester but inability to pay an adequate salary has prevented recruitment' (p. 115).

This brief introduction to the Western Samoan economy is intended to be no more than a general background for the four case-study villages. But village economic life cannot be understood without reference to the social organization within which most economic and social behaviour is confined. While there have been great changes in the village economy since the 1830s with the development of a monetized trade sector and the church, there has been very much less change in the organization of village society and the control and use of village productive resources.

In social terms the Samoan village consists of a number of local lineage or extended family groups ('*āiga*), each with its own elected leader (*matai*). When a person is elected to this rank he takes the '*āiga* name and the *pule* (authority, responsibility, privilege) and the *mamalu* (dignity, respect, honour) associated with the title, which includes control over the '*āiga* lands. It is the duty of the members to support, and if possible enhance, the *pule* and *mamalu* of their *matai*. In choosing a new *matai* on the death of the old, the assembled '*āiga* looks for someone who has, over the years, given diligent service; one who has demonstrated by consistent hard work that he has their interests at heart. In more recent times, however, there have been many cases where titles have been given

D

to persons who have passed through the school system to wage and salary jobs. Most Samoan doctors and public servants and many teachers and clerks have been elected to *matai* status even though they have little intention of returning to their village and taking up the day-to-day responsibilities of their title. There have also been many cases where two or more persons have been elected to hold a title jointly. This is not a new idea in Samoa but it has been much more widely practised in recent years as, with a rapidly increasing population, it is an acceptable way by which the increasing number of contenders for *matai* rank can be accommodated. Most young men expect to be given a title before they reach forty-five or so and if they hold a salaried position they may expect it much earlier.

A *matai*'s control over land associated with his title is based on tradition and is recognized in law. It was and remains the responsibility of the *matai* to ensure that the land is used in the best interests of the *'āiga* as a whole and under this system there is no provision for individual use and development of land. By custom also the authority of the *matai* extends to the distribution of the proceeds of all work performed on the lands under his control. But this hard line is becoming increasingly softened in practice. Many *matai* now allow their *taulele'a* (untitled males) to use blocks of land as they please, to earn and spend their own money, and to live apart from the rest of the *'āiga*. They are still required to serve (*tautua*) the *matai* and *'āiga* but they are also allowed considerable freedom of action. Even so, under this system of land control no one, not even a *matai*, has security of tenure (a *matai* can be voted out), and no one, for example, can develop a block of land, put in fences and so on, and be certain that he and his immediate family will be allowed to receive the full benefits of this labour and investment, or even to continue to use the particular piece of land for very long.

The village *fono* (assembly of *matai*) is the highest authority in the village—it holds the *pule* and *mamalu* of the whole community. It is responsible for the social and economic welfare of the villagers and has wide powers to enforce its wishes on individual *matai*, *'āiga* and individuals. All *matai* of a village are members of the *fono* but all do not have equal status. The village titles are ranked according to genealogical evidence, and the status associated with each title is expressed openly in the fixed seating plan at *fono* meetings, by the order in which the ceremonial drink *kava* is distributed and by the village *fa'alupega*, a set of honorific phrases which is recited at all *fono* meetings and other formal occasions.

Corresponding with the *fono* there are other associations, such as the wives of the *matai* (*potopotoga'o faletua ma tausi*), the untitled men (*'aumāga*) and the wives of the untitled men. Members of these groups take the status of their *matai* in the *fono*. It is the duty of the *'aumāga*, commonly called the 'strength of the village'—a polite phrase for 'village workforce'—to wait on the *fono* and to carry out its instructions. As a general rule the *fono* and *'aumāga* hold their meetings at the same time and in adjoining *fale*. It has become the practice for these meetings to be held each Monday.

One of the responsibilities of the *fono* is to ensure that the food supplies of the village are maintained at an adequate level. In the past the *fono* instructed the *'aumāga* to clear forest and plant food crops, but in recent years it more often sets planting quotas for each individual to be carried out on the land of his *'āiga*. The *matai* inspect these plantings and fine individuals who fail to complete their quotas. The *fono* still instructs the *'aumāga* to carry out various village capital or maintenance works, such as the building or maintenance of a road, a bridge, a water pipeline, a latrine and so on. Instructions are still issued to weed footpaths, to clear land and food plots and to build fish traps.

Today the two women's groups are usually combined for certain purposes into one Women's Committee (*Komiti a Tinā*), but the relationship between the wives of *matai* and the other women is much the same as that between the *fono* and *'aumāga*. The committee concerns itself with maintaining certain standards among the village households. It carries out regular inspections of pandanus floor and sleeping mats ensuring a continuous supply of new mats; it inspects household linen and utensils; it assists the district nurse in her various duties; it keeps the bathing and washing pools clean and so on. Like the *fono* the committee has the power to enforce its decisions on its members and to fine offenders.

The social system outlined so far has its roots deep in tradition and custom, and it has not changed in any essential way since the establishment of European-Samoan contact. The church, on the other hand, does not originate in the distant Samoan past. The pastor often has considerable influence but he has no traditional social or political status. While the church plays an important role in the social and economic life of the village it is foreign to the traditional social system on which the village is based—it is an imposition and is formally treated as such. The pastor is accorded the status of an important guest in the village. It is not *matai* status and even after many years of residence he is not given the right to sit in the *fono*. He is not allowed to put down permanent roots in the village: his house belongs to the village; he may be allowed to cultivate certain plots of land but these belong to the village or an individual *matai*; he is provided with food, pandanus mats and other handicrafts, and with many of his household goods; he is given a monthly sum of money. He is kept dependent on the village for his livelihood.

The material support of the pastor (and his family) is often a fairly heavy charge on the village, particularly when the standard of upkeep becomes a subject of village pride and inter-village rivalry. Villages tend to compete with each other in the standard of housing provided for the pastor, in the impressiveness and size of the church building, in the generosity of their cash donations to various church funds. Within the village, cash and commodity 'gifts' to the pastor and church are made publicly and by '*āiga* rather than by individuals and this often becomes a matter of inter-'*āiga* rivalry.

*To'ona'i* is the Samoan name for Saturday. It means the day when food is collected and prepared for a special occasion, in this case for the *Aso Sā* or Holy Day which follows. Much of the work done in the village on Saturday is in preparation for Sunday, a day of rest and worship. The church is cleaned and the pastor goes his rounds of the village dressed in his formal white *lāvalava*, shirt and coat, and his black tie and umbrella. Taro and other food is harvested and carried down to the village. Many men go out fishing. Tinned corned beef and fish, the two main prestige-luxury foods, are bought at the stores. Last ditch efforts are made to find money for some special collection which will be made on the following day. And the special Sunday church-going clothes—white *lāvalava*, shirts and dresses, bras and black ties, coats and hats—are brought out from their boxes and are washed, starched, ironed and aired.

Sunday is a day of comparative peace and quiet, of church-going and feasting. Before the morning service the men of each '*āiga* prepare the *umu* (earth ovens), arrange bundles of taro, bananas, fish and *lu'au* or *palusami* (taro leaves and coconut cream) amongst the hot stones, and cover the lot with banana leaves. After the service the *umu* are opened and there is a great deal of coming and going with bundles of steaming food. Each '*āiga* sends a basket of choice food to the pastor's house, '*āiga* exchange with '*āiga*, and food is taken to the big *fale* where the *matai* will feast together, to another *fale* where the '*aumāga* is gathered, to another where the *faletua ma tausi* will share the meal, and to the various *fale* where the children and those not taking part in the group *to'ana'i* will eat. After the feast the groups gradually break up. There is probably an hour or two for a sleep, or perhaps a walk along the foreshore, or a talk with friends, before the bell heralds the evening service.

Early on Monday morning the *matai* assemble in *fono*, the '*aumāga* prepares the *kava* and the two groups settle down to their meetings.

Government business, if any, is first on the agenda and this is despatched as quickly as possible by the *pulenu'u*. Once this is out of the way the real business of the meetings is discussed in long formal speeches liberally sprinkled with biblical quotations and references to the past traditions and custom of the village and Samoan society. No matter how long the *fono* meeting lasts it will be served by a number of *taulele'a* and watched from the sidelines by others. In this way the *taulele'a* are prepared for the day when they will be elected to *matai* rank and will sit in the *fono*; they listen and learn the oral traditions of the village and the skills of oratory; they learn in fact how to perpetuate a social system which has withstood the pressures for change which came with John Williams in 1830 and the traders, administrators, advisers and other foreigners who followed him.

# PART II:
# FOUR VILLAGES

Chapter 4

# UAFATO

UAFATO (IV) was ranked fourth in terms of the strength of linkage with the market sector but will be presented first as the village which has changed the least from the pure subsistence situation. Following a brief introduction to the village, the chapter describes the productive resources available to the Uafato producers, the levels of subsistence and marketed output, the levels of subsistence and cash incomes and, finally, the use to which the cash income of the village is put.

Uafato is a small village in the Fagaloa District at the north-east end of Upolu Island, the geologically oldest and most heavily eroded area of Western Samoa. Original volcanic cone and flow surfaces here have been dissected into a tortuous pattern of sharp peaks, rock walls, short steep-sided valleys and long ridges. The sea bed drops away sharply from a cliffed and rocky coastline and the deep water close inshore has prevented the development of a reef and lagoon system such as is found along most of the Upolu coast. There are nine villages in the district, all on the coast. Six encircle Fagaloa Bay, a drowned river valley extending about two miles inland, two are located on a smaller bay to the west, and Uafato village is situated at another bay about two miles to the east.

Because of the mountains the Fagaloa District was the last part of Upolu Island to be connected by road. Only in 1960 were the Bay villages linked with the Upolu road network, thus ending their dependence on the sea for transport and communications. By 1966 the only village in the district which still could not be reached by road was Uafato—the only village still dependent on the whaleboat and canoe for transporting heavy and bulky produce and stores. The nearest bus was at Fagaloa Bay, only about two hours' walk away and the service was regular. Two buses left Fagaloa Bay each day for Apia between 5 and 6 a.m., and returned in the mid-afternoon. Of course Uafato people had to leave their village very early, about 2 a.m., to catch the bus, and if they were to take copra and other heavy produce, they often preferred to row it around the day before and stay the night with relatives at Fagaloa

39

Bay. The situation had been a great deal worse before 1960 when
the nearest bus was at Falefā, the best part of a day's walk away
or four or five hours by sea.

The foot track linking Uafato with its nearest neighbour,
Samamea village at Fagaloa Bay, was for the most part narrow,
steep and slippery. It took about an hour and a half to cross over
between the villages, and with heavy loads it was a laborious
business. The bus left from a village a further half-hour walk from
Samamea. The track was much used by both villages; it was the
only land link between them, and it passed across important parts
of their lands.

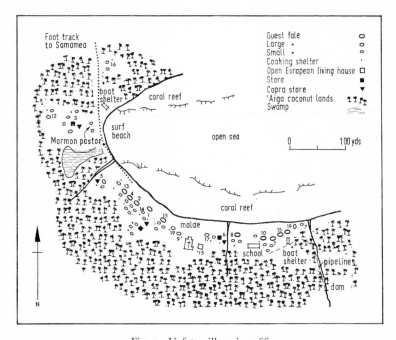

Fig. 1   Uafato village in 1966

Uafato village occupied a narrow strip of flat land along the
southern shore of the bay.[1] The principal '*āiga* buildings, the
elaborately built and carefully preserved guest-*fale*, were set in a
row facing out across a narrow open area (*malae*) towards the bay.[2]

[1] See Fig. 1.

[2] *Fale* is the Samoan word for house and this term will be used throughout to
indicate a traditional thatched dwelling. Where used, 'house' will indicate a
non-traditional, European-type dwelling, either with open or closed sides.

Behind each guest-*fale* were smaller living and service *fale* and cooking shelters. In the centre of the village stood a very large white
church, built in the late 1940s. A hundred yards or so east of the
church was a school, built in 1962. Apart from the church and
school there were four other non-traditional buildings; a roughly
built open-house, consisting of a rectangular concrete floor, open
wooden framework and a pitched corrugated iron roof; and three
small stores. Amongst the *fale* (dwellings) were small kitchen
gardens containing most of the village breadfruit trees, a few
coconut palms, citrus, mango and kapok trees, a few pineapples,
small stands of sugar-cane, papaya plants, and small plots of taro,
*ta'amū* and bananas. The village coconut lands began immediately
behind the village and filled all the flat and moderately sloping
land up to the surrounding ridges and steep valley sides. Some of
the steeply sloping land was cleared and contained plots of taro,
*ta'amū* and bananas, but these crops were grown mainly in the most
recently cleared area over the ridge on the northern side of the
bay.

With a population of 286 in 1966 Uafato was a fairly small village.
But it was growing rapidly. Annual reports of resident population
submitted since 1950 to the Congregational Church offices by the
village pastor[3] and a national Census taken in 1951, 1956 and 1961[4]
indicate that the average growth rate was about 3·5 per cent a
year. A Census of the resident population carried out during fieldwork corresponded closely with the pastor's count for that year.
One result of this high growth rate was the extreme youthfulness
of the Uafato population; nearly fifty-six per cent of the residents
were under the age of fifteen.

The residents were formally divided between eighteen *'āiga* and
the family of the pastor. In addition two teachers lived in the village
during school terms, although they usually left Uafato at weekends.
Two *matai* titles were temporarily unfilled but the *'āiga* retained
their independence. Two *matai* had left Uafato—one for another
village in Upolu where he held a second title, and the other for
American Samoa—and the *'āiga* members had become loosely
attached to two related *'āiga*. The net effect was that there were
fourteen *matai* and sixteen *'āiga*. The *'āiga* ranged from seven to

[3] See Appendix Table 1.
[4] The Census returns indicated a much lower population than did the report
of the pastor for corresponding years. The difference is partly explained by the
nature of the two sets of data; the pastor recorded resident population, while
the Census recorded those people who slept in Uafato on a specific night. It was
my observation that there was generally a number of Uafato residents temporarily
away from the village, and only rarely were there any visitors. The isolation of
the village tended to discourage visitors, but it encouraged residents to spend
time in Apia and other villages.

twenty-nine, and averaged sixteen persons. They were all of the extended family type and most consisted of two or more nuclear families.

PRODUCTIVE RESOURCES

Like most Samoan villages Uafato depended on agriculture for most of its livelihood and its two principal resources were therefore its land and labour. But the forest and sea also played an important role, particularly in the subsistence sector. The village had invested labour and money to improve its natural resources. Forest had been cleared, paths made, fences built and various items of productive equipment, such as agricultural tools, fishing gear, copra dryers and whaleboats had been made or bought.

1. *Land*

The total area which had been cleared of primary forest, and was either planted with coconuts and other tree crops, or cultivated under a system of bush fallow, was approximately 290 acres, or about one acre per head. Some steep land had been cleared but the reserve of cultivable land still under forest was small—only about twenty acres. There had already been small landslides on cleared steep slopes.

Soils were moderately fertile. Rainfall was over 200 inches a year.[5] Continuous erosion of the moderately fertile soils of the higher slopes helped maintain the natural fertility of much of the cultivated land on the lower slopes, and depletion of soil fertility through continuous agricultural use did not seem yet to have become a major problem. In the areas used for bush fallow cultivation— producing bananas, taro and *ta'amū*—plots were abandoned because of excessive weed growth rather than soil exhaustion. The extremely simple agricultural methods practised in Uafato, and the other villages studied, tended to encourage rather than discourage weed growth. A plot was cleared of trees and undergrowth, and holes, about a foot deep and about three feet apart, were pushed into the soil with a thick pointed stick (an *oso*). The crown (*tiapula*) of a previously harvested taro or *ta'amū*, or a banana rhizome or sucker, was then dropped in each hole. Rarely was any attempt made to disturb the soil around the holes. During the growing period, six to eight months for taro, eighteen to twenty months for *ta'amū*, and up to five years for bananas, the plot was usually visited once or twice and the weeds cut down with a long bush knife. Again no

[5] Information on soils and climate is drawn from two chapters, 'The soils' (A. C. S. Wright) and 'Weather and Climate' (Leslie Curry), in Fox and Cumberland (1962).

attempt was normally made to disturb the surface of the soil. When plots were on particularly steep slopes or remote from the village even this casual attention was often not forthcoming. The plots were used in this way until it was judged easier to clear a new area than to weed the old. The more conveniently located plots were usually kept in use for a longer continuous period than the remote ones, and the fallow period allowed was often shorter. Generally two or three crops of taro and one crop of *ta'amū* were taken from a plot before it was abandoned. Bananas were left to sucker and the plots were weeded only for as long as the plants remained productive. Areas abandoned to bush fallow were a tangled mass of weeds, creeper, unproductive banana, taro and *ta'amū* plants, and secondary bush and tree growth. Soil rejuvenation appeared to take five or six years, but this varied with location.

The coconut area, including a number of clearings which were occasionally used to produce food crops and bananas, covered

Table 8   Uafato: *Matai* Land Holdings and Land Use in 1966[a]

| 'Āiga | Number of blocks | House-land | Coconut planta-tion | Bananas | Taro & ta'amū | Pig com-pound | Bush fallow | Total area |
|---|---|---|---|---|---|---|---|---|
| | | | | | (acres) | | | |
| 1[b] | 11 | ·4 | 11·0 | 4·0 | 1·3 | | 2·6 | 20·5 |
| 2 | 6 | | | | | | | 19·4 |
| 3[b] | 7 | ·3 | 9·0 | 3·0 | 1·0 | | 5·9 | 19·3 |
| 4 | 4 | | | | | | | 7·2 |
| 5[b] | 10 | 1·0 | 19·0 | ·5 | ·4 | | 6·9 | 27·8 |
| 6[b] | 11 | ·4 | 11·0 | 2·6 | 1·1 | 1·0 | 2·0 | 18·1 |
| 7[b] | 5 | 1·0 | 7·0 | ·9 | ·8 | | 1·2 | 10·9 |
| 8[b] | 7 | ·2 | 15·0 | 2·9 | ·6 | ·5 | 2·6 | 21·8 |
| 9 | 3 | | | | | | | 6·0 |
| 10[b] | 5 | ·5 | 9·0 | 1·4 | ·3 | ·5 | 2·8 | 14·5 |
| 11 | 2 | | | | | | | 2·3 |
| 12 | 3 | | | | | | | 8·4 |
| 13 | 5 | | | | | | | 13·4 |
| 14[b] | 8 | ·2 | 8·0 | 1·3 | ·5 | | 5·7 | 15·7 |
| 15[b] | 5 | ·2 | 5·0 | 3·0 | 1·1 | | 3·9 | 13·2 |
| 16 | 7 | | | | | | | 23·0 |
| 17 | 6 | | | | | | | 19·8 |
| 18 | 5 | | | | | | | 9·7 |
| 19 | 7 | | | | | | | 19·0 |
| | 117 | 8·0 | 174·0 | 30·0 | 13·0 | 3·0 | 64·0 | 290·0 |
| Percentage of total area | | 2·8 | 60·0 | 10·3 | 4·5 | 1·0 | 21·4 | 100·0 |

NOTES:   [a] Estimated roughly from the Matai Land Holdings map (Fig. 3) and the Land Use map (Fig. 2).

[b] Sample *'āiga*

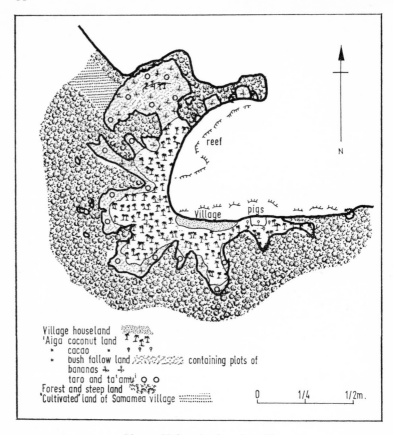

Village houseland
'Aiga coconut land
    "    cacao
    "    bush fallow land            containing plots of
         bananas
         taro and ta'amu'
Forest and steep land
'Cultivated' land of Samamea village

0        1/4        1/2m.

Fig. 2   Uafato: land use in 1966

about 174 acres, or sixty per cent of the cleared land. Most of this
area was planted between the 1880s and about 1920[6] and in the
last forty to fifty years it appears to have received very little attention
other than the harvesting of coconuts. During the period of expansion, coconut seedlings were often interplanted with the food crops.
When the plots were abandoned in the usual way they became
part of the increasing area under palm, and the food plots moved
farther from the village and eventually on to steep slopes. Little
care was taken to plant the coconut seedlings in rows, or to adopt
any particular spacing. As the coconut area matured, self-sown
seedlings were allowed to grow. Many areas carried well over 100

[6] The severe influenza epidemic of 1918 probably marks the end of the period
of coconut expansion.

palms to the acre—a mixture of younger self-sown palms, dead and otherwise unproductive palms, and a majority of fifty- to sixty-year-old productive palms. There had been no replanting except that performed by nature, and ground cover and bush growth was fairly dense.

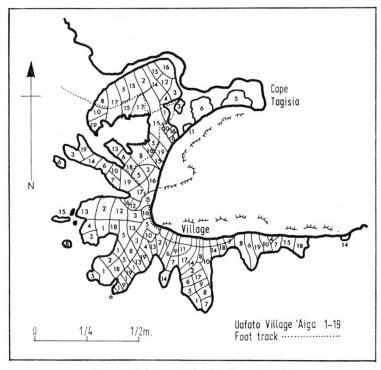

Fig. 3   Uafato: *matai* land holdings in 1966

The village houselands along the shore of the bay occupied about eight acres. This area produced an important part of the village food, including most of its breadfruit, and other crops such as pandanus, kapok, citrus, papaya and mango. The village houseland and the coconut land (a total of 192 acres, or sixty-six per cent of the cleared land) was kept in continuous agricultural use mainly under tree and palm crops. This left about ninety-eight acres (thirty-four per cent) in periodic use under the system of bush fallow cultivation, producing bananas, taro and *ta'amū*. In May 1966, after the emergency post-hurricane planting, about thirteen acres were planted in taro and *ta'amū*, and there were about thirty acres under bananas although only about ten appeared likely to recover from the hurricane and the spreading bunchytop disease. These crops were in small plots scattered throughout the area. Banana planting had ceased during 1965 as growers were pessimistic about their ability to halt the spread of bunchytop—their pessimism in fact appeared to stop them doing anything about it even though they knew the Agriculture Department recommendations. The extremely steep slopes cleared for bananas over the past few years, particularly on the village side of the promontory, indicated that there may have been some pressure on the available land for cultivation under the bush fallow system. But this did not appear to have limited output yet to any significant extent. There were some slopes still under primary forest which were little different from plots already in use.

The pattern of land use in Uafato is shown in Figure 2. Estimates of areas planted in the main crops, and somewhat more detailed estimates of land use made for the sample *'āiga*, are shown in Table 8.

The 290 acres (approximately) of Uafato cleared arable land were divided into 117 blocks representing the holdings (*pule*) in the different areas, of the eighteen Uafato *matai* titles. The block boundaries are illustrated in Figure 3 and the number of blocks and estimates of total area controlled by each *matai* are given in Table 8.[7] The average block size was 2·5 acres and the average holding consisted of 6·5 blocks or a little over sixteen acres. Land is not normally transferred from one title to another but is passed from the holder of a title to his successor. That is, the control (*pule*) of land, usually gained by clearing forest and planting crops in the clearing, remains with the title, and is exercised by the individual who currently holds the title. A *matai*'s prestige depends in great measure on the quantity of land he controls, and one of his important responsibilities as a title-holder is to know and defend his block boundaries. These are usually marked by natural features, coconut palms, tracks and streams. There were no fences on the Uafato lands but in several places, for example around the pig compound, stone walls had been built. Most blocks were named. The area controlled by a *matai* is therefore the accumulation of generations. It is not evenly distributed between *'āiga* nor does it correspond to

[7] Figure 3 was prepared with the help of several *matai* and *taulele'a* and a scale map of the village lands on which I marked recognizable features such as ridges, streams, paths and *fale*. It was then checked by each *matai* in the village. The map is not accurate for areas, particularly at the fringes of the cleared area where steep blocks were difficult to estimate; the boundaries between blocks are reasonable approximations, however, and the overall division of the land into 117 blocks, and the way these were divided between the *'āiga*, are accurate. The estimates of areas controlled by the *matai* (Table 9) are based on Fig. 3 and are no more accurate than this map.

the present labour supply of each *'āiga*. Among the sample *'āiga* coconut land per man varied from 5·6 acres to 1·5 acres, and the total area varied from 8·4 acres to 2·4 acres. The largest holding was nearly twenty-eight acres; the smallest was only six. But each *matai* controlled some land in each of the main crop areas.

The natural resources of the forest and sea contributed in important ways to the village economy. The forest supplied timber, ranging from firewood to the heavy centre-posts of the guest-*fale* and the trees selected for canoes. Poorer grades were easy to find near the village but the more accessible areas of the forest had been exploited over a long period for quality timber and this was much more difficult to locate and extract. Some of the timber used in the non-traditional buildings, the church, school, open house and the stores, had been bought in Apia and shipped to the village by launch and whaleboat. But all the timber put to traditional use came from the surrounding forest.

The forest was also a minor source of food. Pigeon-shooting was a popular pastime and the usually meagre bag added some variety to a fairly monotonous diet. In times of food shortage the forest was searched for wild taro (*pula'a*) and yams. It was also the source of sweet-scented *moso'oi* flowers and *laumaile* leaves. *Moso'oi* is an important ingredient in the scented coconut oil which is always much in demand—ten bottles of this oil were included in the formal payment to the school builder.

The sea was an important source of food, as well as the main transport route. Although Uafato did not have a lagoon, fishing was generally well rewarded and more fish was eaten here than in the other villages studied. The more skilled fishermen occasionally spent up to eight hours at a stretch about a mile out to sea in their small canoes, using long bamboo poles and carefully made shell lures to troll for *atu* (bonito). During March, April and May, large schools of *atule* (horse mackerel) came into Uafato Bay and when this happened every available canoe was out at daybreak circling around at the head of the bay. At low tide the women and children harvested the inshore reef of shellfish, crabs, small fish and octopus.

## 2. *Labour*

Few tasks performed in the normal course of village life required particularly difficult skills, and there was little opportunity for specialization. But labour was divided in two important ways: (1) between the sexes, and (2) between the social *élite*, the *matai* and their wives, and the untitled villagers. Generally speaking, men were responsible for the production and preparation of food, that is, for most tasks associated with agriculture, fishing and the prepara-

E

tion of the *umu* (earth oven). They also built *fale* and canoes.
Women were responsible for raising children, for production of the
various mats and items of clothing, for *fale* thatches and coconut-
leaf blinds, and for harvesting the lagoon and reef. This division
of labour may once have been strictly observed but the edges have
become somewhat blurred. Women now weed food plots. They do
most of the cooking like boiling and frying, which involves the use
of imported metal utensils. Men still prepare the *umu*, but in most
*'āiga* this is now only on Sundays and for special feasts. The men
have probably got the best of the changes, but they have additional
work in cash cropping.

The second division is between 'management' and 'labour'. The
*matai* is the embodiment of the authority and dignity of the *'āiga*
and as such 'he has to manage and direct the affairs of his adherent
group relating to land tenure and use, work effort, deaths, marriage
and other crises, negotiation with other groups, and many problems
of importance concerning which his followers share responsibility'
(Keesing and Keesing 1956, p. 40). The *taulele'a* are the work force.
A similar division on the women's side is between the wife of the
*matai* and the other women. At the village level this division is
between the *fono* and *'aumāga* and between the wives of *matai* and
other women in the Women's Committee.

A fairly uniform level of productive skill and knowledge is
acquired by all village Samoans, and in school education also there
was a certain uniform level which is achieved by most and exceeded
by few. All children in Uafato between the ages of five and eight
attended the village elementary school, and there was no adult
illiteracy. But few had gone beyond the elementary school level.
Only one *matai* had attended secondary school, and this was in
order to train as a pastor. Only five *taulele'a* living in Uafato in
1966 had attended secondary school, and only one had reached
Form Four. Four had been employed earlier in Apia, but in the
village they worked at the normal tasks of their group, and two
had additional responsibilities for the stores. Six other Uafato
*taulele'a* had been to mission secondary schools but they had left
the village to take up wage jobs: three were living in Apia, two had
emigrated to New Zealand and one was a policeman in American
Samoa. Only one had continued at school long enough to complete
professional or trade training, in this case as a teacher, and she was
the first from Uafato to emigrate to New Zealand.

Schooling has always cost money in Western Samoa. All secondary schools charge fees, and in addition the mission schools are
supported by funds raised in the villages. In recent years the government has staffed village (elementary) and district (intermediate)

schools, but the villages provide classrooms, furniture and equipment. The villages also provided housing and subsistence foods for the teachers. The new school built in Uafato in 1966 cost the village £600 plus labour.[8] Uafato had also helped to pay for the district school in Fagaloa Bay. During the 1966 school year Uafato *'āiga* spent about £247, or nine per cent of the cash income of the village, on schooling, in addition to gifts of food and housing made to the two teachers stationed in the village. £45 supported a young man at the Malua Theological College, about £40 was collected from village school pupils, £14 went to the district school as a contribution to running costs, £6 as fees, and £142 was paid for fees, books, uniforms and other expenses of children at mission schools.

This investment in education was not without its returns. If they can be assumed roughly to be the village cash income from wages and remittances, they amounted to £787, or twenty-nine per cent of the total village cash income over the twelve months from December 1965 to November 1966.[9] For individuals with secondary education to obtain wage employment they usually have to leave the village, and in some cases, the country. Only three wage-earners lived in the village—the district nurse, the *pulenu'u*, and one *taule'ale'a* who commuted weekly to Apia—and they earned £430 during the year which was fifty-five per cent of the village total from wages and remittances. Only a small proportion of the money earned by Uafato people living in Apia and New Zealand came back to the village. Remittances from abroad in particular were usually irregular, and rarely substantial. One Uafato *matai* expected that his son who was a policeman in American Samoa would one day return home with enough money to build an open-house in the village. Money brought by expatriates visiting their home village was often channelled into European-style housing. In very many cases it was expected of them, and they visited Samoa for this specific purpose. It had not yet happened in Uafato however.

### 3. *Producers' capital*

I am concerned here with a specific and limited type of capital—goods used to produce additional income. These, mainly tools and equipment for agricultural and fishing purposes, are the result of investment of money and subsistence resources (mainly labour) and are used to earn additional cash and subsistence income. Where possible, values have been imputed for these goods for two purposes: (1) to estimate the proportion of investment in producers'

[8] See Table 12.
[9] See Table 14.

capital from the monetized sector, and the total level,[10] and (2) to
impute the subsistence income derived from the use of these goods.[11]
The method used to impute values for producers' capital had been
consistently applied to the four villages so that inter-village comparisons can be made.

The following items of producers' capital are described below:
canoes and fishing gear, agricultural implements and copra dryers,
carpentry tools and sewing machines, whaleboats, and stores and
store equipment.[12]

The outrigger canoe is an important item of productive equipment used for fishing and, in Uafato, for transporting produce to
and from the Fagaloa Bay villages. There were twenty-six serviceable canoes in Uafato. Most had been made by the 'āiga which
owned them. Six were a simple type of open dug-out canoe called
a *paopao* which was more suited to the calm waters of a lagoon
than the usually rough waters of Uafato Bay. The others were small
single-seater canoes called *va'aniue* which, with covered fore and aft
sections, were often taken as far as a mile out to sea by the more
skilled fishermen in their search for bonito. The *paopao* generally
had no purchased parts, and it took only a few days to make.
Occasionally one could be bought in the villages near Apia for
from £3 to £5. The *va'aniue* was more difficult to make and a
craftsman might be engaged. *Va'aniue* were usually painted and
nails were used in their construction. One could sometimes be
bought near Apia for £5 but if it were well made it would fetch

[10] Where it has been possible to give cash or imputed values to producers'
capital the following principles have been used: (1) for bought items, such as
carpentry tools and certain fishing gear, one-quarter of the cash cost of replacement with new items at Apia prices has been used. There was no second-hand
market which could indicate the market value for used goods.

(2) For items resulting completely from investment of subsistence resources,
and with no market price, such as canoes and certain fishing gear, the labour cost
of production (hours) has been estimated and valued at the current wage rate
for unskilled labour in Apia—1s 6d an hour.

(3) For items which include components of cash and subsistence investment,
such as whaleboats and copra dryers, a combination of (1) and (2) has been used.
Some items were found to be occasionally sold for money in the market sector
and where there was firm evidence of something approaching a market price
this was used to modify the values imputed in the manner described above. I
attempted to finish with a set of values for individual items which approximated
a market price, but as there was no regular market for most of the items considered
this was difficult and was only partly achieved. Exactly the same sets of values
were used for each of the villages so that the results are directly comparable.

[11] Many of the items included here, such as carpentry tools, have resulted
partly or entirely from the investment of money. Their rental value is not strictly
a component of subsistence (non-monetized) income, but for convenience, and
because these items are used mainly for subsistence' production, the income derived
from their use has been included as a component of subsistence income.

[12] Social and village capital, such as dwellings, church and school buildings,
household furniture and equipment etc., will be described later in the chapter.

£10 or two '*ietōga*.[13] The labour cost involved in extracting suitable timber from the forest and making the twenty-six Uafato canoes is estimated roughly at 1,440 hours (£108) and the cash components at £12.

The fishing gear was simple and most items required only a small investment of labour and money. There were bought items such as hooks, nylon lines, steel rods sharpened to form spear points and a few nets. Equipment produced in the village included bamboo rods, shanghais (used as underwater fishing guns) and carefully made and highly valued shell lures. The total investment in canoes and fishing gear in Uafato is valued at £155 of which £120 represented the investment of labour and other subsistence resources and £35 the investment of money (Table 9).

Table 9   Uafato: Producers' Capital[a]

|  | Total | Cash component | Subsistence component |
|---|---|---|---|
|  | £ | % | % |
| Fishing gear and canoes | 155 | 23 | 77 |
| Agricultural tools | 35 | 86 | 14 |
| Copra dryers | 60 | 58 | 42 |
| Carpentry tools | 136 | 96 | 4 |
| Guns | 110 | 100 | — |
| Sewing machines | 100 | 100 | — |
| Whaleboats | 90 | 78 | 22 |
| Store buildings, equipment | 660 | 77 | 23 |
| Total investment[b] | 1,346 | 76 | 24 |
| Investment per consumption unit (£) | 7 | 5 | 2 |

NOTES:   [a] The method by which values have been imputed has been described on page 50.

[b] An imputed rent for the use of this equipment has been included as an item of subsistence income (see Table 14). This is based on the above values and estimates of the useful life of the various items.

[13] The '*ietōga* (fine mat) was the most important traditional valuable. The common type had a cash market value and could be bought in a number of stores in Apia, and occasionally in the villages. Prices varied with age and quality but £5 appeared to be about the average and this price has been used throughout the study where it has been found necessary to value these items. '*Ietōga* circulated through the subsistence sector as formal ceremonial gifts at funerals, weddings, title dedications etc. and formed the most important part of formal payments to carpenters and canoe builders etc. In certain traditional exchanges '*ietōga* had some of the attributes of money and it was fairly common to find money being used as a substitute for '*ietōga*. Keesing reported a Samoan as saying 'A chief's dignity and importance *fa'āSamoa* is his wealth in fine mats. A person of high title who has few mats is thought worthless and improvident' (Keesing 1934, p. 295). But generally speaking the exchange in which '*ietōga* were used were not market exchanges—'*ietōga* were given to create social obligations rather than to pay a debt for goods or services received.

Agricultural tools and implements were extremely simple. The main items were long knives (machete), and axes, both of which were bought, and the *oso* (digging stick), *amo* (wooden shoulder yoke), and various coconut-leaf baskets, which were made in the village. There were a few non-traditional tools such as picks and shovels. The total stock of these implements and tools in Uafato is valued at only £35 of which £30 represented the value of the bought items and components.

There were four copra dryers. The first was built in 1958 by an 'āiga which at that time also owned a whaleboat and a small store. The other three were built between 1960 and 1964 by the 'āiga which owned currently functioning stores. The dryer has an important bought component—one or two forty-four-gallon drums used as the furnace. Around the horizontally placed drum a box-like hot air chamber is built, with a slatted top to hold the copra. The structure is roofed, generally with coconut-leaf thatch. The hot air chamber is sometimes enclosed with roofing iron, sometimes with rocks and cement and sometimes with wood. The cash components of the four Uafato dryers are valued at £35 altogether, and the labour and other subsistence costs at £25.

Most 'āiga owned a collection of carpentry tools, a gun, and a sewing machine. Generally they were old, the accumulation of years; but most were serviceable and useful to their owners. They are valued at £346 for the village as a whole, of which £340 represents the value of the cash components and items.

In 1966 there were three whaleboats in Uafato. Two had been acquired from Fagaloa Bay villages after the need for them ended there with the opening of the road in 1960. One *matai* bought his in 1962 for £25, and a *taule'ale'a* who set up a store in 1964 obtained an old whaleboat from a relative in exchange for £5 plus one 'ietōga. The third whaleboat was built in Uafato in 1964 by a store-owning 'āiga at a cash cost of about £35 plus a considerable labour cost. The total cash cost of the three whaleboats appears to have been about £70 and the subsistence contribution is estimated roughly at £20.

There were three small stores. Each was a rectangular wooden building with a flat iron roof and cement floor. Customers were served through a hatch at the front. Equipment consisted of wooden shelves, a set of kitchen scales and a simple kerosene pump. One storekeeper bought a set of copra scales during the survey. These buildings and the equipment represented a total cash investment of about £450 and a labour investment valued at £150. Initial stock is estimated to have cost £60.

The total value of producers' capital described so far, and

summarized in Table 9, is estimated at £1,346 of which £1,020, or seventy-six per cent, consists of items or components which were bought in the market sector. The balance, £326, represented the contribution of the subsistence sector to this investment.

But the subsistence sector had contributed a great deal of additional productive capital for which it has not been possible to impute values. This includes the labour used to clear forest, to establish tree and palm crops, the labour put into making the paths and the Uafato-Samamea foot track, the labour used to make the rock-walled pig compound, and the labour invested in 1966 in the road from Samamea to Uafato. Uafato labour also contributed to the construction of the Fagaloa Bay road. By 1965 the roadhead was only about six miles from Uafato and in March 1966 work started on a regular basis to push the road through to Uafato. Half the men walked across to Samamea each Tuesday and Thursday for this work. Samamea labour was available for the first part of the road which ran through Samamea lands and the Department of Works contributed a truck and driver and assistance with surveying and blasting. Uafato investment in the road consisted entirely of labour. The six mile road was opened late in 1967 after twenty months' work. It was a substantial achievement for Uafato.

PRODUCTION

There are two main components to total village production of goods and services, that which was intended for village subsistence consumption and use, and that which was intended for market sale. These are dealt with separately in this section. Subsistence production is valued consistently in money terms so that its level and composition in each of the four villages can be compared. These values are based as closely as possible on market prices, although the commodities themselves do not enter the market sector, and where this is not possible the valuation is based on the three principles described earlier (page 50). Solely for the purpose of comparing the levels of monetization in the four villages, the imputed value of subsistence production is added to the cash income from market produce and other sources to give measures of total income and the extent of monetization.

1. *Subsistence*

All production of goods and services which is not sold in the market sector is assumed to be for subsistence consumption and use. Included, therefore, in the estimates of subsistence production, is a proportion of output which is not consumed but is wasted or given away as gifts and in traditional non-market exchanges. Non-market exchanges beyond village boundaries were quantitatively small and generally speaking they tended to cancel out in the long run. For this reason, and because it was difficult to record these exchanges satisfactorily, they are not dealt with in detail. The services available in the subsistence sector covered a wide range and were also difficult to record satisfactorily. But as they were similar in the four villages their exclusion from detailed consideration and from calculations of subsistence income does not affect the results of the study. Three main components of subsistence production are examined in this section: (1) food, (2) housing and (3) household durables. Village 'non-productive' capital works, such as the school and church, are described in a later section.

### (a) *Food*

The production of food is the principal task of the men. It takes precedence over all other activities in the long run.

Taro is the most important food staple, but breadfruit, bananas and *ta'amū* are important secondary staples. Fish is the main source of protein, but pork, chicken, pigeon, flying fox and shellfish and other seafoods supplement this at irregular intervals. Coconut is the most important supplementary food, consumed in some form each day. Minor additions to the village-produced food supply came from citrus, mango, papaya, pineapple and sugar-cane and, during the food shortage which followed the hurricane, wild taro and yams from the forest.[14]

Of the staples, taro is generally preferred, and supplies are maintained all the year round. Perhaps because of the fairly uniform flavour of the starchy staples, however, the Samoans seem to appreciate variety in the texture of their food and most meals consisted of a mixture of taro, *ta'amū*, bananas and, when in season, breadfruit. Consequently taro is not grown in sufficient quantity to rely on if the banana and breadfruit crops fail, as they did at the end of January 1966. With the expansion of bananas as a cash crop in Uafato after 1954 some *'āiga* had let their taro planting slip somewhat because bananas, even though intended for sale, were plentiful. As a consequence the total loss of bananas and breadfruit in the hurricane caused a serious food shortage in some *'āiga* almost immediately, and in the village generally after three months. This led to considerable post-hurricane efforts to plant taro, the quickest maturing of the food staples. Before the hurricane, taro, bananas and breadfruit were eaten in comparable quantities

---

[14] Supplementary foods were also bought in the stores and issued free by the Hurricane Relief Committee, but I am concerned here only with subsistence foods. Purchased foods are discussed later in the chapter.

totalling approximately thirty pounds harvest weight per week per consumption unit.[15] By July the supply was down to about ten pounds (mainly *uli*, a small corm which grows under the sucker of a taro plant and in normal times is discarded), but thereafter the quantity increased slowly as some of the taro planted immediately after the hurricane was harvested, and a few breadfruit began to mature. Rough estimates of the supply of starchy staple foods in Uafato during the survey period are given in Appendix Table 2. Averaged over the twelve months from December 1965 to November 1966, about 22·5 pounds of starchy staple foods were supplied per week per consumption unit.

The consumption of coconuts was not affected by the hurricane.[16] An average of 5·7 mature nuts per consumption unit per week was used to make the sweet or salty relish served with the starchy foods and to cook with other foods such as taro leaves. In addition, mature and immature (drinking) nuts were used by people working on the plantations; this is estimated at about two nuts per consumption unit per week. On average two nuts per consumption unit per week, mainly fallen immature nuts, were fed to pigs and chickens. In all some twenty-three per cent of the output of the Uafato coconut lands was consumed in the village (Appendix Table 3).

Fish was the only other important subsistence food and it was more plentiful in Uafato than in the other three villages. Pork and chicken were generally reserved for special feasts and guests.

The imputed value of subsistence food supplies for the twelve months from December 1965 to November 1966 is £5,685, or £28·51 per cent consumption unit. The details are set out in Table 14.

[15] In order to simplify the measurement of consumption of goods and services so that *'āiga* and villages can be compared without the complication of different age compositions and populations, I have used the concept of a consumption unit. The number of consumption units per *'āiga* and village is calculated from a simple table based on observation of village life.

Consumption Unit Coefficients

| Age group | Consumption units (male and female) |
|-----------|-------------------------------------|
| under 1   | 0·0 |
| 1– 4      | 0·5 |
| 5– 9      | 0·7 |
| 10–14     | 0·8 |
| 15–50     | 1·0 |
| over 50   | 0·8 |

[16] There was, of course, a loss of immature nuts in the hurricane, but this did not cause any apparent reduction in the consumption of coconuts. The loss may have been transferred to the sale of nuts and copra but in Uafato the coconut lands were not carefully harvested for consumption or sale, even after the hurricane.

An attempt was made during the third, fourth and fifth visits to the villages to measure labour costs of subsistence (and cash) production in terms of hours worked. This was difficult for several reasons; first, few village Samoans owned watches and could accurately record the time spent at various tasks; second, many important activities were irregular and in three weeks it was almost impossible to get a fair cover; third, the period was unusual since it included the post-hurricane emergency efforts to plant food crops. In spite of these difficulties some useful data were obtained and these will be referred to as needed.

In Uafato the men averaged 8·8 hours and the women 2·8 hours a week in the production of taro and *ta'amū*. The men did most of the clearing and planting, and the women did much of the weeding. This was certainly a much higher level of activity than would normally be found; not only was there more planting, but more time was spent also in harvesting which, at this time, involved the search for *uli* and taro in abandoned plots. Most men took about two hours fifty minutes to clear undergrowth from a bush fallow plot and plant 100 taro (or *a'amū*). During the survey each man averaged about five hours a week at this task. Records were obtained of the numbers of taro and *ta'amū* planted by the sample *'āiga* from September 1965 to May 1966 and, over these nine months, each man need have averaged only about one hour a week preparing plots and planting taro and *ta'amū*. This is probably closer to the normal labour input in this task than the survey estimate. The survey estimates for the other tasks associated with taro and *ta'amū* production were not affected much by the hurricane and are assumed to be reasonably close to the normal level. An average of five hours a week from the men plus 2·8 hours a week from the women produced the village supplies of taro and *ta'amū* in a normal year.

But in a normal year bananas and breadfruit were at least as important quantitatively as taro and *ta'amū*. Breadfruit needed very little labour since the trees were planted close to the *fale*, they received no attention, and bore fruit for up to fifty years. Harvesting was simply a matter of climbing the tree, or knocking down the fruit with a long pole—a task usually performed by the children. This virtually labour-free staple accounted for about one-quarter of the village subsistence food supply in a normal year. Bananas required much the same attention as taro. Banana planting, although not harvesting, had stopped before my first visit and this activity was not observed. Two hours a week is a reasonable estimate, however, for the time normally given by the men to the production of bananas and breadfruit for subsistence food needs.

The minor food crops were all grown in the village area and the time spent on them was small. Livestock (pigs and chickens only in Uafato) were fed fairly regularly with coconuts and food scraps, usually by the children. The coconuts gathered for food took the men an average of half an hour a week. Again this was often a task for the children.

Fishing was the only other important food-producing activity. The labour survey indicated that an average of 7·5 hours a week was spent by the men in this activity, and the main daily household schedule indicated an average of five hours and an average catch of two pounds of fish an hour. Fishing was to some extent seasonal and also depended on the weather, particularly in the villages like Uafato which did not have a sheltered lagoon. The time spent harvesting the reef by the women and children was not recorded, but from observation it could have averaged an hour a week. This was as much a leisure activity as a work chore, as indeed was much of the fishing done by the men.

In summary, each man put in an average of thirteen hours a week, and each woman about four hours a week in the production of subsistence foods. This includes the time needed to walk between the food plots and the village but not that needed to prepare meals.

### (b) *Housing*

All '*āiga* but one in Uafato were housed in traditional oval thatched *fale*. These required a certain amount of maintenance, particularly keeping the thatches waterproof. The labour survey indicated that the women spent about two hours a week on *fale* maintenance, mainly the production of thatches, while the men spent only 0·4 hours. There were many small jobs which were not recorded, however, and these are certainly under-estimates. Three new buildings were constructed during the survey period—two small crudely built *fale* (*fale o'o*) and a long coconut-leaf thatched shelter for one of the whaleboats. Three men took about forty-eight hours to build the boat shelter. The *fale o'o* were built between survey visits and the labour costs were not recorded.

The *fale* (dwellings) were of two types: craftsman-built guest-*fale* (*fale tali malo*) and the less elaborate living and service *fale* and shelters. The guest-*fale* stood as a class apart but the living *fale* ranged in size and quality from a less elaborate version of the guest-*fale* to small and often crudely built *fale o'o* and rough thatched shelters over the cooking fires and *umu* (earth oven). Another class apart were the latrines, built on stilts at the lower-tide mark and reached by plank or coconut palm catwalks.

There were nine guest-*fale* in Uafato. Foundations, some containing heavy centre posts, showed where five others had stood in the past. Guest-*fale* were ceremonially important buildings indicating the rank and status of the *matai* and '*āiga* who owned them. They were intended as meeting places for the *matai* and various village groups, and as suitable dwellings for important visitors. Five of these were being used as dwellings during the survey, but when they were needed for ceremonial or social purposes the occupants temporarily moved out. The construction of a new guest-*fale* involved a great deal of traditional ceremonial and cost. It was an event of considerable importance, not only to the '*āiga* concerned, but to the village as a whole and to relatives in other villages who were usually called on to provide sennet ('*afa*) for bindings, and traditional valuables ('*ietōga*, *siapo* and pandanus sleeping-mats) and money for the carpenter.

As an example of what was involved in a decision to build a guest-*fale* we will take the most recent one in Utuali'i. It was not particularly large, but nevertheless it was a structure of considerable social significance for the *matai* and his '*āiga*.

In February 1961 the *matai* Vaili formally requested the *matai* Lavea a *tufuga* (craftsman carpenter) to build a guest-*fale*. The request was accompanied by a gift of £5 which, once accepted by Lavea pledged his services. Traditionally the pledge gift (*tāuga*) consisted of one or more '*ietōga* (fine mat) but in this case cash was accepted as a substitute. Once the commission was accepted, Vaili set about collecting and preparing the necessary building material. In the forest about two hours' walk from the village, large trees were selected for the eight interior posts (about ten feet long and a foot thick), and other trees were cut for the roofing timbers and the twenty-eight matched outside posts. Rocks were carried from the shore for the foundations and the raised floor platform. Vaili began to visit his relatives in Uafato and other villages to ask for sennet which would bind together the structural timbers, roof frame and thatches. About 1,000 fathoms were used. He then approached the Uafato Women's Committee with a gift of £10 and a request that they make the 1,800 sugar-cane thatches he would need. By October the material was ready and Lavea supervised the construction. By December the building was finished. Between October and Christmas Lavea and his family were supplied with food by Vaili, including bought foods such as sugar and tinned fish and meat. Just before Christmas the guest-*fale* was ceremonially opened and a feast given for the Uafato *matai* and relatives from other villages. From his relatives Vaili collected together most of the items he presented to the carpenter—eight '*ietōga*, one finely woven mat decorated with coloured wool (*fala lau'ie*), fifty sleeping-mats, ten pieces of tapa cloth (*siapo*) and £10 in cash.

It is very difficult to estimate the full cost of this guest-*fale*. The '*āiga* was occupied on and off for ten months preparing the building material, growing extra food, and serving the carpenter. The remembered cash costs—for the carpenter, thatches, and a small quantity of nails and paint—amounted to £27, but the actual cash cost was certainly much higher. Some of the cash and most of the traditional items given to the carpenter, and most of the sennet, were provided by relatives, but the labour came from Vaili's '*āiga*. By any count the actual costs of this quite small guest-*fale* (it measured twenty-eight feet by ten feet) were considerable and no *matai* could enter on such a project lightly or without the support of his '*āiga*. Only two guest-*fale* had been built in Uafato since 1950.

Social status was the motive for building a guest-*fale*, but ordinary dwellings and other buildings owned by the '*āiga* were built as they were needed. There were eleven well built *fale* in Uafato occupied by the *matai* and pastor, and thirty-four *fale o'o* provided living and sleeping accommodation for the rest of the village. There was only one non-traditional dwelling—a poorly built open-house constructed in 1961 by the *matai* who afterwards left the village to live in American Samoa. After his departure in 1964 it housed a daughter married to another Uafato *matai*. Most of the material, the cement, roofing iron, nails and much of the timber, had been bought in Apia and shipped to Uafato by whaleboat.

The '*āiga* dwellings in Uafato are valued at £2,935, of which £2,649 (ninety per cent) represented the investment of subsistence resources, labour and material.[17] The average yearly contribution

[17] In order to impute values for dwellings I estimated the construction costs (cash and subsistence) of average examples of dwelling types. These are as follows:

| Dwelling type | Construction costs | | |
| --- | --- | --- | --- |
| | cash component | subsistence component | total |
| | £ | £ | £ |
| Guest-*fale* | 2·5 | 140·0 | 142·5 |
| Large *fale* | 1·0 | 100·0 | 101·0 |
| Small *fale* | 0·2 | 20·0 | 20·2 |
| Cooking shelter | 0·2 | 2·0 | 2·2 |
| Latrine | 0·2 | 2·0 | 2·2 |
| Large *fale* with cement floor and iron roof etc. | 200·0 | 80·0 | 280·0 |
| Open house (average) | 250·0 | 80·0 | 330·0 |
| Closed house | various | | |

These cost estimates have been used for each village. Although there was little variation between villages in the construction and sizes of the different types of *fale*, there was some variation in the quality of materials used and workmanship which are excluded by this standard procedure. If anything, this exclusion damps

to the construction of dwellings, which is taken to represent the
subsistence income from dwellings, is estimated to be £146, or
£0·7 per consumption unit.[18]

### (c)  *Household durables*

There was very little European-style furniture in Uafato. A
wooden box or chest was the most common item and most adults
owned one for their personal belongings. Most chests had been
bought in Apia where they were made, and cost about £5 each.[19]
Most *'āiga* owned a bed, one or two wood-and-flywire foodsafes
and several roughly made tables and chairs.[20]

Woven pandanus and coconut-leaf mats of various kinds are the
basic items of household furniture. They range from coarse floor-
mats (*papa*) to finely woven sleeping-mats (*tu'ulaufala*, *afiafi*); from
small food-mats (*laulau*) to the finely woven and elaborately decorated *falalau'ie* which usually hung from the beds to conceal the
boxes of household utensils stored underneath. The manufacture of
these mats is one of the principal productive tasks of the women.
Apart from the weaving, mat making involves planting and tending
groves of pandanus, and harvesting, drying and preparing the leaves.
All women take part in these activities, both individually and as a
group.

Sleeping-mats are decorated with a fringe of bought wool; on
the long edges of the smaller *afiafi*, and on all four edges of the large
*tu'ulaufala*. The all-over decoration of the *falalau'ie* is often also of
wool. The wool decorations on the stock of mats in Uafato cost
about £96. The 'mat' with the highest ceremonial value is the
*'ietōga* and several of the older women in Uafato occasionally spent

---

down the differences between the villages which in general conformed to the
ranking of the villages in terms of market linkage. Uafato not only had the lowest
imputed income from dwellings per consumption unit, but its dwellings were also
the poorest built and maintained. The standard of building improved from
Uafato (IV) to Taga (III), from Taga to Poutasi (II), and Utuali'i (I). There
were more obvious differences in the size, standard of workmanship and materials
in the non-traditional houses and where possible these differences have been
included in the estimates.

[18] Subsistence income from dwellings is estimated from the cost figures divided
by the average lifespan of dwelling type.

[19] Prices varied with size and quality but £5 is a reasonable average on 1966
prices.

[20] No Samoan in Uafato slept on a bed. When the Women's Committee was
preparing for my first visit to Uafato some difficulty was experienced in finding a
bed which was suitable (no European visitor could possibly be allowed to sleep
on mats although this would have been cooler and more comfortable). The beds
were normally used as storage units: mats were stacked on top under a village-
made kapok mattress covered by a brightly coloured cotton or satin bedspread,
and various household utensils were stored underneath.

an afternoon working on these.[21] Sleeping-mats also have some ceremonial value. They normally form a part of the traditional payments to carpenters, and are often given as gifts. At the Women's Committee's 'weaving circles' sleeping mats were the most common item produced.

A few other household items are made in the village. Several *matai* owned carved wooden kava bowls which were made in Uafato, but the best examples had all come from Savai'i Island. Each *'āiga* had one or two carved wooden food bowls (*'umete*) and large wooden mortars used to crush roasted cacao beans, and most of these were made in Uafato. While most tools were bought in the stores, a few, such as the digging-sticks (*oso*) and the sometimes carefully carved shoulder-yokes (*amo*), were made in the village, as were the canoes and some of the fishing gear.

Each *'āiga* had accumulated a sizeable stock of purchased household utensils such as mugs, plates, cutlery, trays, bowls, pots and pans, and various items of household equipment, such as lamps, charcoal irons, primus stoves and radios. The estimated value of these items for the village is £206, based on a cash expenditure over the past ten years or so of £800.[22] There were also other bought household items, such as cotton sheets, mattresses and pillows (filled with village-produced kapok), mosquito nets, cotton drapes, etc., and personal items such as clothing, which were not recorded satisfactorily as the quality, size and range varied greatly. In general the stocks of these items varied between the villages in a way consistent with the ranking based on linkage with the market sector. Their exclusion tends to dampen the recorded differences between the villages but does not bias the results of the survey.

## 2. *Market*

The main commodities produced for market sale in Uafato were copra, bananas, pandanus tablemats and baskets, kava, taro and fish. The first three were by far the most important.

### (a) *Copra*

Copra was probably the first commodity to be sold from Uafato and, from the 1880s when it was first produced to 1954[23] it was the

[21] Of the four villages studied, only in Taga (III) in Savai'i Island were *'ietōga* made in quantity. It was generally recognized that the weaving of *'ietōga* had almost died out in the Upolu Island villages and in this respect Uafato was something of an exception, but an exception which fitted the relative isolation of the village. Much the same was true for the manufacture of *siapo* (tapa cloth) which was again found mainly in Savai'i villages; but a number of Uafato women made *siapo* during the survey period.

[22] The imputed value is taken as one-quarter of the replacement cost.

[23] In 1954 Uafato was admitted to the government-controlled 'Banana [marketing] Scheme'.

only important source of cash income. There were no trade-store records of Uafato copra sales but on the basis of data collected during the survey I estimated that the production and sale of copra was between 50,000 and 60,000 pounds a year. During the seven months of the survey about 25,000 pounds of copra were sold, and returned about £500.

Copra production in Uafato appeared to have declined in recent years. Population had been rising by nearly four per cent a year since 1950 and this inevitably led to a rise in the quantity of coconuts consumed. There had been little expansion of the coconut lands after about 1920, and little effort was made to clear undergrowth and secondary forest growth, to remove dead and otherwise unproductive palms, or to replant. Even so, the output of the coconut small-holdings was not harvested fully and almost forty per cent of the coconuts were left to rot or seed under the palms.[24] Subsistence food needs for coconuts were always fully satisfied, but the production of copra for sale did not use the balance of the output. The main deterrent to copra making for most Uafato 'āiga was the high labour costs of marketing.

The labour costs of marketing copra have always been high for Uafato producers. The village was isolated and small and had not attracted an Apia-based trading-station. Until the 1920s the nearest trade store was at Falefā, four or five hours away by whaleboat. In the 1920s a trading-station was established in the Fagaloa Bay village of Lona, only about two hours away by whaleboat, but Falefā remained a preferred market because the stores there were better stocked and paid higher prices for copra. Falefā also had bus access to Apia after about 1950 which was not the case for the Fagaloa Bay villages until after 1960. Even in 1966, when the nearest bus was at Fagaloa Bay, a Uafato whaleboat was occasionally taken on to Falefā.

At least after 1950 there were sound economic reasons why Uafato people preferred to sell their copra in Apia rather than in Fagaloa Bay or Falefā. In 1948 the Copra Board of Western Samoa was established with powers to regulate the buying price of copra. A uniform price has been set for all districts and a margin of about eighteen per cent over this was paid for copra delivered to registered exporters' sheds in Apia.[25] In 1965-6 the regulation price was paid at the Fagaloa Bay stores[26] (£1 18s 6d per 100 pounds of hot-air

---

[24] See Appendix Table 3.

[25] The regulation prices in force during 1965-6 are shown in Appendix Table 4.

[26] These were trading-stations of Apia companies and they normally observed the price regulations closely.

dried copra), generally about £2 could be obtained at Falefā,[27] and the Apia rate was about £2 4s.

The three small stores in Uafato did not buy copra. Instead they bought mature coconuts or exchanged them for store goods. Each store had a dryer and two had whaleboats. Most of the copra sold from Uafato came from the two *'āiga* which had invested in the store-dryer-whaleboat combination.

*Mamea's store.* Mamea was a *matai* and the village *pulenu'u*. The store was an *'āiga* enterprise under his supervision. It was built in 1962 at a cash investment in the store building and initial stocks of about £70, and in the following year a further £5 was invested in a copra dryer and about £35 in a whaleboat. The store, dryer and whaleboat were built in the village by the *'āiga*[28] after buying the timber, nails, paint etc. in Apia. Mamea traded and bought mature coconuts from the village and with these and the nuts from his own small-holding he produced about 15,000 pounds of copra (£300), or sixty per cent of the village total, during the seven-month survey period. Coconuts were bought or traded for store goods at one shilling for eight mature nuts; this was the usual price in each of the villages. While most store goods were traded for nuts, one commodity was specifically designed for this; Mamea bought packets of tobacco in Apia and from these he rolled cigarettes which he traded, one for two coconuts. He was generally not prepared to sell whole packets of tobacco, and rarely had more than a packet or two in stock. About once a week an average of 200 pounds of copra, and other produce such as taro, fish, and handicrafts, were rowed around to Fagaloa Bay in the whaleboat, taking five or seven men about two hours each way. It was then taken on to Apia by bus, involving a journey of two hours each way, a cash fare for one person of eight shillings return, a freight charge on copra of two shillings a bag of 200 pounds, and a wait in Apia from about 8.00 a.m. to 2.30 p.m., during which time other business, such as buying stock for the store, was transacted.

*Taufuga's store.* Taufuga was a *taule'ale'a*, a son of one of the absentee *matai*. He liked to be called a 'trader' but in fact he was called on to perform the normal tasks of a *taule'ale'a* in the *'āiga* to which he had become attached and he, in turn, used the labour of this *'āiga* to help make copra. Taufuga had attended a mission school in Apia where he reached the secondary level Form Four. Then he took a job in an Apia store for about a year until he

[27] Independent traders, such as those at Falefā often paid higher than regulation prices.

[28] The non-cash component—labour—is estimated at £10 for the store and £4 for the dryer. No basis for an estimate for the whaleboat was available but the labour cost must have been considerable.

became involved in the theft of money and goods from the store
and served a sentence in the Apia gaol. This limited his opportunities for further employment in Apia, and barred him from emi-
grating to New Zealand. He returned to Uafato (where there was
no stigma attached to his Apia activities) and started growing
bananas. In 1962, after two years of this, he had saved enough
money to build the small store, similar in type and cost to that
built by Mamea. The following year he added a copra dryer and
in 1965 he acquired a fairly old whaleboat from Fagaloa Bay for
one 'ietōga plus £5. His total cash investment in the store, initial
stocks, dryer and whaleboat up to 1966 was around £80. In May
1966 he invested a further £15 in a set of copra scales, the first in
the village, and made it known that he would buy undried copra
as well as nuts which he bought and traded like Mamea. In addition Taufuga made 'pancakes'[29] for sale. Over the seven months
observed he produced about 10,000 pounds of copra (£200), or
thirty per cent of the village total.

*Ah Chong's store.* Ah Chong, a Chinese trader, married a sister
of a Uafato *matai* and in 1962 moved to Uafato and set up a store
on the houseland of his brother-in-law. It was similar to those of
Mamea and Taufaga, and Ah Chong engaged in the same sort of
trade. But neither he nor his wife's '*āiga* owned a serviceable whaleboat, which made it difficult to transport his copra out, and he
had been too liberal in giving credit to the members of the '*āiga*
to make a success of his store. As a result he owed money to several
Apia stores from which he bought stocks. In 1966 he was served
with a Court injunction for these debts and left the village to work
in Apia. His wife and children remained in the village and occasionally sold a few items such as sugar from the store, but the trade in
nuts virtually ceased.

During 1966 most of the Uafato copra was made by the two store-
owning '*āiga*. The rest of the village relied for their cash income
from their coconut small-holdings mainly on selling nuts to the
stores. For this they received a high return per hour of labour;
that is, for collecting the nuts and carrying them to the store.
About 230 mature nuts produced 100 pounds of hot-air dried copra
and to collect this number in the Uafato small-holdings took, on
the average, about five hours. For 230 nuts the villagers received
£1 8s 10d which gave them a return per hour of labour of about
5s 6d.[30]

---

[29] Dumplings of flour, baking powder, sugar and water fried in dripping.
[30] I have omitted reference to the labour costs of establishing the village coconut
lands for two reasons: first, there was no activity of this sort during the survey
and second, the main expansion period was between 1890 and 1918 and the present
generation had contributed virtually nothing to the establishment of the coconut

Table 10    Commodities Shipped in Mamea's Whaleboat to Fagaloa Bay

| | Cash received in Apia | | | | |
|---|---|---|---|---|---|
| | copra | taro & ta'amū | fish | tablemats & baskets | total per shipment |
| **1966** | | (shillings) | | | £ |
| March  7 | 265 | 50 | 26 | 72 | 20·7 |
| 10 | — | 167 | — | 108 | 13·8 |
| 15 | 20 | 54 | 28 | 44 | 7·3 |
| 19 | 74 | — | — | — | 3·7 |
| 23 | 25 | 50 | — | — | 3·8 |
| 31 | 55 | 50 | 30 | — | 6·7 |
| April  2 | 70 | 42 | — | — | 5·6 |
| 6 | 159 | — | — | 90 | 12·5 |
| 9 | 154 | — | — | 116 | 13·5 |
| 21 | 140 | — | — | — | 7·0 |
| May  19 | 66 | — | — | 46 | 5·6 |
| 21 | 38 | — | — | 110 | 7·4 |
| 24 | 40 | — | — | 40 | 4·0 |
| June  3 | 36 | — | — | — | 1·8 |
| 17 | 44 | — | — | 20 | 3·2 |
| | 1,186 | 413 | 84 | 646 | 116·6 |
| | | (per cent) | | | |
| | 50 | 18 | 4 | 28 | 100 |

It took an average of 4·1 hours to husk 230 nuts, remove the flesh and place it in the dryer, collect firewood, and tend to the copra while drying. The only processing cost other than labour was the depreciation of the dryer which, with a cash plus labour cost of about £15 was less than one penny per 100 pounds of copra dried.

In order to estimate the labour costs of marketing the following data were collected: (1) the occasions when Mamea's whaleboat was used to ship produce from the village, (2) the produce taken each time, and (3) the cash received for this produce in Apia. Altogether fifteen trips were recorded from March to early June (Table 10). An average of about 200 pounds of copra was taken on each trip and this represented half the cash value of all produce shipped. Half the labour costs of rowing around to Fagaloa Bay, plus half the time involved for one person to take the produce to Apia by bus and sell it, represented the labour cost of marketing

lands they harvested. The Uafato 'āiga in fact put little effort during the survey into the maintenance of the coconut lands. Much of the clearing and weeding which did take place is included in the labour cost of harvesting, for it was often necessary to slash down undergrowth in the search for fallen nuts.

200 pounds of copra. The whaleboat trip to Fagaloa Bay took from five to seven men about two hours. The bus trip took about two hours, and another hour was needed to sell copra and the other commodities taken in at the same time. Thus the labour costs of marketing the 200 pounds of copra averaged fifteen hours, or half this for 100 pounds of copra.[31] The depreciation cost of the use of the whaleboat is estimated at 4s a round trip, or 6d per 100 pounds of copra.[32]

The subsistence, or non-monetary component of the cost of producing and marketing 100 pounds of copra in Apia is therefore roughly 9·1 hours production, plus 7·5 hours marketing—a total of 16·6 hours; plus a depreciation allowance for the use of the dryer and whaleboat of 4s 1d.

There were also cash costs which reduced the actual return from 100 pounds of copra from 44s to about 41s. The single fare for one person from Fagaloa Bay to Apia was 4s, and the freight charged on 100 pounds of copra was about 2s. Assuming that the return fare could be charged against other business transacted in Apia, and that 100 pounds of copra contributed only one-quarter of the value of the produce taken in to Apia for sale, the cash cost of marketing 100 pounds of copra is therefore 3s.

Disregarding the depreciation charges, which were certainly not considered by the Uafato producers, the net cash return of 41s for 100 pounds of copra sold in Apia gave a cash return to labour in production and marketing of only about 2s 5d an hour. This was exceeded by most Uafato 'āiga which simply gathered the nuts from their small-holdings and sold them to the stores, receiving about 5s 6d an hour for the limited number of hours they were able to fill with this task.[33] The cash return to labour in the store-owning

---

[31] 100 pounds of copra was one-quarter of the cash value of all commodities taken into Apia on average per whaleboat trip. The cash and labour costs of the return journey I have allocated to the other activities usually carried out on a trip to Apia, such as buying stock from the store and transporting it to Uafato, and other business and social activities. It may be argued that the labour and cash costs of marketing copra were higher than these estimates but it certainly cannot be argued that the estimates are too high.

[32] This is extremely difficult to calculate since the cash, labour and other costs of the three whaleboats varied. Estimates of useful life were also difficult to make since it was certain that when the road from Samamea was completed the whaleboats would have reached the end of their useful lives in Uafato. Since no other villages in this part of Samoa have use for them, they will probably have little resale value. Mamea's whaleboat cost £35 cash plus a considerable investment of labour in 1963 and it was probably useless and worthless by the end of 1968. It was used on average about once a week. Assuming an initial cash plus labour cost of £50, a depreciation cost of about 4s per trip was estimated.

[33] The stores bought only a limited quantity of nuts and there was always a limit, although it was not often reached, in the quantity of nuts produced by the coconut small-holdings.

'*āiga* from copra produced from bought nuts was very low. In order to gross 44s (100 pounds of copra) the stores had to pay out about 29s for the nuts plus 3s in fares and freight—a net cash return of 12s. Their contribution to the labour costs were 4·1 hours to husk the nuts and dry the copra, plus 7·5 hours to market it in Apia. Their actual cash return per hour was therefore only about 1s. By accepting this low return to labour the store-owning '*āiga* did tend towards maximizing their cash income from copra, while the other '*āiga*, when they simply sold nuts rather than copra, received the lowest cash income from their coconut resources.

### (b) *Bananas*

Bananas were marketed through the 'Banana Scheme', a division of the Department of Agriculture. It collected cases of bananas from Uafato by launch, and from most other villages by truck, and paid the same price to all growers in all villages. This removed the disadvantage Uafato growers would otherwise have had of high marketing costs. The only restriction was a quota on the quantity which could be shipped from Uafato based largely on the capacity of the launch, which made only one trip each time bananas were being assembled in Apia for shipment to New Zealand: about once a fortnight. However, an examination of the Uafato records indicated that the village quota was not often filled.

One way for an '*āiga* to increase its share of the village quota was to register more than one grower. Examples were found where the names of small children were registered in this way. But in most '*āiga* with more than one registered grower, the names were those of the *matai* and one or more *taulele'a*. *Taulele'a* could register as growers with or without the *matai*'s consent and were treated equally by the 'Banana Scheme', which paid them direct rather than through their *matai*. Banana production gave many *taulele'a* their first taste of independent action in village agriculture, independent, that is, of *matai* control. Quotas and harvesting and packing timetables were controlled by the 'Banana Scheme', not by the *matai*. Most *matai* did not appear to resist demands by *taulele'a* that they produce bananas for sale. After all, the cash income of the '*āiga* would rise as a result, and the *matai* would gain an additional source of money for '*āiga* purposes. Several cases were recorded where *taulele'a* left a *matai* who had either prevented them from producing bananas on their own account or had demanded the full cash payments as they were made by the 'Banana Scheme' officers.

I was able to watch the work involved in harvesting, nailing together the wooden boxes supplied by the 'Banana Scheme', packing the bananas, and taking the boxes to the launch in canoes, only once before the hurricane halted the export of bananas from Western Samoa. No attempt was made to record details of labour inputs at that time as it was expected to be only the first of several occasions when this could be done. As a result, I am able to make only a very rough estimate of the labour costs involved. However, I discussed this with the *matai* and *taulele'a* and with officers of the Department of Agriculture—the best that could be done under the circumstances—and it appeared that to produce one box of bananas, packed and delivered to the launch, took an average of about two hours twenty minutes. Eleven shillings a box was paid to growers in 1965-6 which gave a cash return to labour of about 5s an hour. This was a high return compared with that from copra in Uafato, and the main reason was the very low labour costs of marketing. There were no cash costs of marketing bananas in so far as the producers were concerned.

An average of 2,980 cases of bananas (217,500 pounds) a year was produced for sale in Uafato from 1959 to 1965[34] which was roughly twice the quantity consumed in the village.

(c) *Handicrafts*

The Uafato women made an important contribution to the cash income of the village by manufacturing and selling small pandanus tablemats and baskets. Much of this work was done to fill orders from four Apia stores which exported handicrafts and sold them to tourists. But the women often produced more than they needed to fill their orders. They usually tried to sell the surplus to the same stores, but were often forced to hawk them around Apia. The stores generally demanded a certain minimum quality and anything which did not meet their standards had to be sold to tourists and others around the town. The products were standardized by size, type, weave and material. Tablemats, of which there were four sizes, were sold in bundles of twelve and the baskets in sets of three. Often the women took their handicrafts to Apia themselves after carrying them over the foot track to Fagaloa Bay. It was often a welcome opportunity to leave the village and visit relatives, to shop, or to go to the cinema. Just before Christmas I accompanied nine women and about sixty dozen tablemats to Apia. We left the village at 2 a.m. and caught the bus at about 5.30. On this morning there were many more people waiting in the Fagaloa villages than the bus could take, so the driver took the first load only to Falefā and returned for the rest. We meanwhile caught another bus in Falefā and arrived in Apia at 8.15. It had taken about six hours from Uafato. In April a Department of Agriculture bunchytop

[34] Appendix Table 5.

control team visited Uafato and when the team left (after a week of fishing, according to several Uafato *matai*) six women and 100 dozen tablemats accompanied them to Fagaloa Bay to take advantage of a free ride to Apia in the Department truck. On this occasion the tablemats were all sold at 12s a dozen; sixty-eight dozen to the four Apia stores, twenty dozen to the wife of the Head of State, and twelve dozen to tourists from the s.s. *Matua* from New Zealand. They earned £60 gross, and incurred the following costs: (1) labour time—about 100 hours to prepare the raw material, 350 hours to weave the tablemats, and ninety-six hours to take the tablemats to Apia and sell them—a total of 546 hours, and (2) 24s as the return bus fares. The net cash return was therefore £58 16s which meant that the women earned about 2s an hour. Of course some of the ninety-six hours and 24s shown as marketing costs should fairly be charged against other business and pleasure which were part and parcel of most journeys to Apia, and the return per hour could have been as high as 3s.

### (d) *Secondary crops and fish*

Prompted by high prices after the hurricane, two '*āiga* began to take taro and *ta'amū* to Apia for sale, but in April this was stopped by the *fono* in order to preserve food supplies in the village. Cooked taro was sometimes taken into the Apia market by people going to Apia for other purposes. Kava was sold in Apia by most '*āiga* occasionally, but only two did this regularly. Fish was also occasionally taken into the Apia market, and during the survey two '*āiga* did this fairly often. The sale of fish and secondary crops took two forms: (a) anyone going to Apia from the village might take in a small bundle of fish etc. to cover his fare, and (b) the two store-owning '*āiga* (especially those of Mamea), often took in small quantities of fish and secondary crops along with their copra and weaving. Rarely was a trip made to Apia specifically to sell fish, taro or kava and for this reason marketing costs were low. About seven per cent of the village cash income came from the sale of fish and secondary crops.

### 3. *The effect of social and organizational institutions on production*

An important feature of the economic life of Uafato, and other Samoan villages, is the influence of social and organizational institutions on the direction and level of demand and production. A few instances will be given here in illustration but the significance of these factors will be discussed in the final chapter.

At the village level there are two institutions which play an important role in determining the level and composition of output;

the assembly of *matai* (*fono*) and the assembly of the wives of the *matai*. Each has the power to direct part of the village work force in the interests of the village as a whole; the first commands the labour resources of the *'aumāga* (association of untitled adult males) and the second commands the labour resources of the women. Generally the *fono 'aumāga* and Women's Committee[35] hold meetings once a week. Attendance at these meetings is usually compulsory and absentees are fined.

One responsibility of the *fono* is to ensure that village subsistence food supplies are maintained at an adequate level. Periodically the *fono* issues instructions to the *'aumāga* that each member plant a certain number of taro, *ta'amū*, bananas, breadfruit trees and so on. A specific period is usually set for this and at the end of it the *matai* inspect the work and fine those who have not filled their quotas. In the past the *fono* used to instruct the *'aumāga* to clear forest land and plant food crops as a group; today it is more usual for the members of the *'aumāga* to plant their quotas on the land of their *matai*. During the survey, three village inspections of food crop plantings were held, two in March and one in April, and for each the quotas of fifty taro per *matai* and 100 taro per *taule'ale'a* had to be filled in a fortnight. In May the *fono* also directed the *'aumāga* to weed their food plots, and this work was inspected at the end of the allotted time. In January, February, March and April the Women's Committee instructed its members to plant pandanus seedlings (fifty a month). At the end of January it organized the harvesting and drying of pandanus leaves from hurricane damaged plants. A considerable quantity of pandanus was being used to make tablemats for sale, and this had led to a shortage of the raw material for subsistence needs. The action of the Women's Committee was an attempt to ensure that supplies were adequate for both purposes. The Women's Committee also directed the type and quantity of subsistence handicrafts produced, such as mats. Periodically it set production quotas and held inspections. In this way adequate supplies of new mats were maintained in each *'āiga*, both for normal use and to form a stock of mats for gifts.

Another responsibility of the *fono* was to ensure that existing facilities, such as the paths, were maintained. During the survey the *'aumāga* was instructed to clear the path to Samamea on one occasion, and paths into the coconut lands on another. The Women's Committee had a similar responsibility to clean and otherwise maintain the bathing and laundry pools in the streams at each end of the village.

[35] The two groups of women together formed an organization called the *kalapu 'o tama'ita'i* (Women's Committee).

It was generally in the *fono* that decisions were made to invest at the village level in various capital works, such as the church, school and road. Two such projects were organized during the survey. In 1965 the village received a gift of galvanized water pipes from a European missionary. During 1965 the pipes were carried over from Fagaloa Bay, some by foot and some in the whaleboats, and when I first visited Uafato (December 1965) they were stacked on the *pulenu'u*'s houseland. In May 1966 the *fono* levied a cash subscription on the *'āiga* to raise £20 for cement to build a small dam on the eastern stream. The cement was bought in Apia, taken to Fagaloa Bay by bus and shipped around to Uafato in a whaleboat. The *pulenu'u* obtained the services of a Department of Works plumber, and the *matai*, *'aumāga* and Women's Committee spent the best part of three days building the dam and laying the pipes down to the village. The *matai* helped the plumber at the dam site and generally supervised the *'aumāga* which laid the pipes. The women carried sand from the beach to the dam site in coconut-leaf baskets. The plumber happened to hold a *matai* title and was treated as an honoured guest in the village; as well as being housed and fed with the best available he was given a gift of £5.

Table 11   Cash Subscriptions for the Uafato School 1961-2

| Month | Details[a] | Amount collected[b] |
|---|---|---|
| | | £ |
| September | £3 3s 6d per *matai* | 54 |
| October[a] | £1 per *matai* 10s per *taule'ale'a* | 40 |
| October[b] | £1 per *matai* 10s per *taule'ale'a* | 40 |
| November | £1 per *matai* 10s per *taule'ale'a* | 40 |
| December[a] | £2 per *matai* £1 per *taule'ale'a* | 79 |
| December[b] | £5 per *matai* | 85 |
| February | £4 per *matai* | 68 |
| March | £1 per *matai* 10s per *taule'ale'a* | 40 |
| April | £1 per *matai* 10s per *taule'ale'a* | 40 |
| June | £10 from Women's Committee £5 from teachers and children | 15 |
| | | 501 |

NOTES:  [a] Subscription details were obtained from the *matai* who served on the building committee.
[b] Records had not been kept and the figures given are only approximate.

At the instigation of the *fono* Uafato men helped periodically after 1958 to carve out the road down to Fagaloa Bay. In May 1966, with only the last stretch between Samamea and Uafato to be completed, this work was organized on a regular basis. The *matai* made several visits to Apia to obtain the help of the Department of Works, but with little early success. The *fono* decided that the village should start on its own and ordered each adult male to give one full day a week to this work. From May until my last visit to Uafato in August, half the men went across to Samamea on Tuesdays and the other half on Thursdays. By August, after roughly 4,500 hours of hard labour, the road had been pushed up the steep ridges behind Samamea.

Laying the pipeline and building the road were the two village capital projects under way during the survey and they were alike in that the investment was mainly from within the subsistence sector. In 1962, however, Uafato built a new school which required a considerable cash investment. While providing the necessary unskilled labour to construct the school and to bring building material around from Fagaloa Bay, the village raised about £500 by subscriptions on the *'āiga* to buy cement, roofing iron, timber, nails and paint, and to pay for the services of a skilled carpenter from Apia. The subscriptions are shown in Table 11. Three *matai* acted as a School Committee on behalf of the village. They hired the carpenter and arranged for the credit purchase of building material from an Apia store. Three separate orders were placed and the accounts for the first two, amounting to £370, were paid. The third, for £128, remained unpaid in 1966 and the village was taken to court to recover this money.

The carpenter received £91 altogether, as follows:

(1) on engaging the carpenter (*tāuga*)     —  £ 5
(2) on completion of the foundations        —  £ 1
(3) on completion of the framework          —  £ 5
(4) on completion of the building           —  £10
(5) on the opening of the school            —  £70

In addition he was given food and housing whilst working in the village, and a substantial gift of traditional valuables when the school was opened—twenty-seven *'ietōga*, thirty *siapo*, 100 pandanus sleeping-mats, and ten bottles of coconut oil scented with *moso'oi* flowers. The estimated total cost of the school is shown in Table 12. This building replaced a number of *fale* which had been built entirely with subsistence labour and material, and must have been a good deal cooler and more comfortable for the teachers and pupils.

Table 12   The Estimated Cost of the Uafato School

|  | Cash component | Subsistence component |
|---|---|---|
|  | £ |  |
| Building material | 498[a] |  |
| Carpenter | 102[b] | 270[c] |
| Village labour |  | 75[d] |
|  | 600 | 345 |

NOTES:   [a] This includes the amount of £128 which was still owed to the supplying company in 1966.

[b] Includes an amount of £11 as a rough estimate of cash spent on food for the carpenter while he lived in the village. He received £91 in cash.

[c] Imputed value of traditional payment valued as follows: 'ietōga—£5, siapo—6s, sleeping mat—£1, Samoan oil—2s; these came to a total of £245. A rough estimate of £25 has been given to subsistence food and services provided while the carpenter lived in the village.

[d] Roughly 1,000 hours at 1s 6d an hour

Much earlier, during the 1940s, the village invested heavily, both from the subsistence and cash sectors, in the church. No records had been kept and I was unable to find anyone who remembered the details with any accuracy, but judging from other known examples the cash cost of material and the services of the skilled carpenter could have been around £2,000. Again, the village provided all the necessary unskilled labour and provided food and housing for the skilled workers on what was customarily a lavish scale. Something like the scale of operations experienced in Uafato is illustrated by an example of church construction in 1953 at the village of Patamea in Savai'i Island.

In addition to the disadvantage of its small size (380 to 400 inhabitants, half under 16 years of age), Patamea was handicapped in that its only link with the coast was an 8½-mile foot-track running across a recent broken-surfaced lava flow. Over 1,000 bags of cement, all the timber and roofing-iron, etc., used in constructing and furnishing their impressively-large church, was carried over this route by the people themselves, mostly after darkness. In addition, they manhandled in baskets from nearby rivers all the sand needed in the construction of their 5,000 square-feet (115' × 45' approx.) concrete structure of unreinforced solid design. . . . Under the supervision of a Samoan tradesman from Apia, the people of Patamea provided the unskilled labour required for the construction period—April 1950 to August 1953, excluding all of 1951, when no work was done on the church. At the same time, their production of copra, cocoa and foodstuffs was maintained at a high level to provide a cash surplus for purchase of church building materials at a cost of over £4,000. In August 1953 the only outstanding sum due in respect of this church was an amount of £600 owing to the skilled foreman and his assistant. (Stace 1956, p. 57)

The Uafato pastor was housed in two large well-built *fale*. He was the only pastor in the Fagaloa district not to have a European-style house. In May 1966 the church committee of *matai* and the *fono* decided to rectify this deficiency and the first subscription (5s per *matai* plus 1s per man woman and child of Congregational Church affiliation), was announced in church by one of the deacons. It was expected that about £15 a month would be collected from this subscription but the *matai* intended to collect more when bananas were again marketed.

Village level social institutions, such as the *fono*, were responsible for initiating and organizing these large capital works and the motivation was very largely a matter of the social prestige of the village. This was true particularly of the scale of the projects—the Uafato church was as large and impressive as those in much larger villages and could have seated comfortably a congregation three or four times that of Uafato. The school children could have been as adequately, and certainly more comfortably, housed in a number of well-built *fale*, and the same applied to the pastor whose large *fale* were soon to be replaced with an open-house. At the 'āiga level social prestige motivated the construction of guest-*fale*, buildings which were rarely used but which stood as monuments in the *malae* to the status of the *matai* and the unity of the 'āiga. In Table 13 rough estimates of investment in social and village capital are given. This is investment of cash and subsistence resources in buildings, household furniture and equipment which does not play an active role in reducing costs of production or in increasing the level of normal subsistence and marketed output. Approximately sixty-two per cent of the total investment in social and village capital in Uafato came from the subsistence sector.

INCOME

The total income in Uafato for the twelve-month period, December 1965 to November 1966, is estimated to have been £8,949, or £44·9 per consumption unit. The total figure is calculated from the imputed value of subsistence income (£6,217) and the estimated cash income from all sources (£2,732). The purpose of adding these two together is strictly so that similar estimates for the four villages can be compared. Although subsistence income is valued in such a way as to approximate market values where possible, there is no real basis for assuming that this ideal is achieved. In adding the imputed value of subsistence income to cash income, two different units are being added giving a result that is useful

Table 13   Uafato: Social and Village Capital[a]

|  | Total | Cash component | Subsistence component |
|---|---|---|---|
|  | £ | % | % |
| *'Āiga* |  |  |  |
| Dwellings | 2,935 | 10 | 90 |
| Furniture | 110 | 40 | 60 |
| Mats etc. | 533 | 13 | 87 |
| Utensils and equipment | 206 | 100 |  |
| Total | 3,784 | 16 | 84 |
| Village | 1,102 | 59 | 41 |
| Church | 2,370 | 63 | 47 |
| Total investment | 7,256 | 48 | 62 |
| Investment per consumption unit | £40 | £15 | £25 |

NOTE:   [a] Estimated original costs of the social and village capital existing in 1966

for comparing the levels of income and the monetized proportions of income of the four villages, but has little value beyond that. Even this comparison is possible only because a standard method of valuing subsistence income is used consistently for each village. The monetized proportion of total income in Uafato is thirty-one per cent; this will be termed the *monetization factor*.

It is assumed that subsistence income is equal to subsistence production. The largest component of subsistence income is the supply of food, £5,685 for the village, or £28·5 per consumption unit. The much smaller contribution of housing, household durables, producers' capital and social and village capital results from the method used to impute income rather than the level of satisfaction derived from their ownership and use. This occurs also in the estimates of subsistence incomes for the other villages and does not distort the value of the estimate for purposes of inter-village comparison.

There were two main components of cash income: (1) the money earned from the sale of agricultural commodities, fish and handicrafts, and (2) wages, remittances from Apia and abroad, and cash gifts received from relatives and visitors through the traditional exchange system. £1,917, or seventy per cent, came from the sale of village produce. Copra was the most important commodity, earning fifty-seven per cent of the cash income from agriculture, fishing and handicrafts, but this was not a normal situation in Uafato because of the loss of income from bananas. In 1966 only £65 was earned from bananas (none being sold after January)

compared to an annual average of £1,556 over the seven years
1959-65.

Table 14    Uafato: Subsistence and Cash Incomes[a]

|  | | Village | Per consumption unit |
|---|---|---|---|
| SUBSISTENCE (non-monetary) INCOME | | £ | £ |
| Food | | 5,685 | 28·6 |
| coconuts[b] | 440 | | 2·2 |
| bananas & breadfruit[c] | 877 | | 4·4 |
| taro and ta'amū[c] | 3,968 | | 19·9 |
| fish | 308 | | 1·6 |
| pork and chicken[d] | 92 | | ·5 |
| Buildings | | 205 | 1·0 |
| 'āiga | 146 | | ·7 |
| village | 25 | | ·1 |
| church | 34 | | ·2 |
| Household durables | | 229 | 1·2 |
| Tools and equipment | | 98 | ·5 |
| Total subsistence income | | £6,217 | £31·3 |
| CASH INCOME | | | |
| Agriculture & fishing | | 1,496 | 7·5 |
| bananas | 186 | | ·9 |
| copra and coconuts | 1,092 | | 5·5 |
| kava | 123 | | ·6 |
| taro | 72 | | ·4 |
| fish | 23 | | ·1 |
| Handicrafts | | 421 | 2·1 |
| Wages | | 430 | 2·2 |
| Remittances from Apia | | 164 | ·8 |
| Remittances from abroad | | 193 | 1·0 |
| Gifts | | 28 | ·1 |
| Total cash income | | £2,732 | £13·7 |
| TOTAL INCOME[e] | | £8,949 | £45·0 |
| Monetization factor[f] | | 30% | |

NOTES:   [a] 12 months, December 1965 to November 1966

[b] Average per consumption unit a week of 5·7 coconuts as food plus
2·1 fed to pigs and chickens; valued at village store buying price of
1s for 8 nuts.

[c] Based on Appendix Table 2 with quantities valued at pre-hurricane
market prices in Apia: taro—6d per lb., ta'amū and breadfruit—4d
per lb. and bananas—3d per lb.

[d] A rough estimate of quantity based on observation and valued at 2s
per lb. for pork and 2s each for chickens.

[e] Aggregate of imputed value of subsistence income and cash income;
intended only for intervillage comparisons.

[f] Proportion of cash income in total income

Two Uafato residents received wages for work in the village: the *pulenu'u* (£10 a quarter), and the district nurse (£4 12s a week). One resident worked in Apia with the Department of Agriculture Bunchytop Control Team and commuted from the village weekly (about £3 a week). These three individuals earned £430 over the twelve-month period or sixteen per cent of the total cash income of the village. Several *taulele'a* lived in Apia where they had wage jobs, and their *matai* and relatives obtained money from them when they visited Apia. Roughly £164 was obtained from this source during the twelve-month period. A number of Uafato people had emigrated to New Zealand and American Samoa and sent money to their Uafato relatives through the post. This source of cash income yielded about £193 during the twelve-month period. My own visit to Uafato, and those of other outsiders, were minor sources of cash income, estimated at about £28. In all about £815, or thirty per cent of the total village cash income came from sources other than the sale of village output.

Details of subsistence and cash incomes for the village are summarized in Table 14.

OUTLAY

This final section will be concerned primarily with the monetized sector of the Uafato economy—the use to which the cash income of the village was put. It examines the following aspects of cash outlay: (1) expenditure on goods and services, (2) the range, variety and prices of goods and services supplied by the local stores, near-by stores and Apia, (3) the effect of social and organizational institutions on cash outlay, and (4) cash savings. The relevant survey data are summarized in Table 15.

Table 15    Uafato: Cash Outlay[a]

| | Village | | Per consumption unit | | Percentage | |
|---|---|---|---|---|---|---|
| | £ | £ | £ | £ | % | |
| 'Āiga | | 2,268 | | 11·3 | | 86 |
| food | 916 | | 4·6 | | 35 | |
| other commodities | 642 | | 3·2 | | 24 | |
| local fares | 288 | | 1·4 | | 11 | |
| schooling | 247 | | 1·2 | | 9 | |
| gifts | 95 | | ·5 | | 4 | |
| New Zealand fares | 80 | | ·4 | | 3 | |
| Church and pastor | | 214 | | 1·2 | | 8 |
| Village | | 162 | | ·8 | | 6 |
| Total | | 2,644 | | 13·3 | | 100 |

NOTE:    [a] 12 months, December 1965-November 1966

## 1. Cash expenditure on goods and services

The total cash income in Uafato, for the twelve months December 1965 to November 1966 is estimated at £2,732, or £13·7 per consumption unit (Table 14). Total cash outlay fell short of this by £88 or £0·4 per consumption unit and this is an indication of the level of apparent savings. Approximately eighty-six per cent of total cash outlay (£11·3 per consumption unit) went on various goods and services of which food (£4·6) and other commodities (£3·2) were the most important (Table 16).

Bought foods did not play an important role in the diet in quantity terms. The average consumption of purchased foods per consumption unit per week was only eleven ounces of sugar, seven ounces of flour and rice, and 0·3 ounces of tinned herrings. Bread was not available in the village or at Fagaloa Bay and the bakery products listed consisted mainly of pancakes made by a storekeeper in the village, hard sea biscuits, and bread which was occasionally brought back from Apia. Consumption of flour and rice was higher than shown in Table 16 as in June the village received ten bags of flour and fifteen bags of rice (about 2,340 pounds altogether) from the Hurricane Relief Committee and this raised the average consumption to about eleven ounces a week. This was still small, however, compared with the estimated average weekly consumption of 22·5 pounds of village-produced staple foods.

Sugar was the only bought food which was habitually used each day by all 'āiga, and generally bought each day in small quantities. Flour and rice, and the village-made pancakes, were used increasingly as the post-hurricane shortage of subsistence staples was felt. All the other food items, including the tinned fish, were bought occasionally to be served on Sundays and other special occasions.

Cash expenditure on commodities other than food is estimated at £642 or £3·2 per consumption unit. Kerosene and benzene for lamps was the most important single item, followed by soap and tobacco. The commodity groups shown as 'household' and 'individual' include a great variety of different items. Household commodities include purchases of cotton cloth for sheets and curtains, mosquito netting, cooking and eating utensils, and work tools such as bush knives. Individual commodities include expenditure on clothing, playing cards, hair oil, stationery and stamps, and an Apia cinema ticket.

There were no purchasable services available in the village except that of the school, for which small fees were levied (2s to 4s per child per term) to cover costs of maintenance, chalk, pencils and other supplies. School fees were also paid in Fagaloa Bay (the district school) and Apia (various mission schools). Altogether about £247 was spent on school expenses, or nine per cent of the total cash outlay. Local bus fares, mainly for journeys between Fagaloa Bay and Apia, cost the village about £288, or eleven per cent of the total cash outlay. The two store-owning *'āiga* accounted for about twenty per cent of this expenditure; for them it was a necessary business cost. During the survey a fare was paid for a *taule'ale'a* who planned to go to New Zealand (£80).

Table 16  Uafato: Commodity Purchases[a]

|  | Expenditure | | | Main shopping centres | | |
|---|---|---|---|---|---|---|
|  | Village | Per consumption unit | Percentage | Uafato | Fagaloa | Apia |
|  | £ | £ | % | % | % | % |
| Food: |  |  |  |  |  |  |
| sugar | 300 | 1·5 | 19 | 80 | 5 | 15 |
| flour, rice, bread | 273 | 1·4 | 18 | 59 | 5 | 36 |
| fish[b] | 184 | ·8 | 12 | 88 | 2 | 10 |
| dripping, salt etc. | 59 | ·3 | 4 | 75 | — | 25 |
| meat[c] | 44 | ·2 | 3 | 27 | — | 73 |
| tea, coffee, cocoa | 37 | ·2 | 2 | 64 | — | 36 |
| other foods | 39 | ·2 | 2 |  | 5 | 95 |
|  | 916 | 4·6 | 59 | 69 | 3 | 28 |
| Other: |  |  |  |  |  |  |
| household | 307 | 1·5 | 20 | — | — | 100 |
| individual | 145 | ·7 | 9 | 5 | — | 95 |
| kerosene, benzene | 77 | ·4 | 5 | 80 | — | 20 |
| soap | 57 | ·3 | 4 | 70 | — | 30 |
| tobacco | 56 | ·3 | 4 | 30 | — | 70 |
|  | 642 | 3·2 | 41 | 20 | — | 80 |
| All commodities | 1,558 | 7·8 | 100 | 49 | 1 | 50 |

NOTES:  [a] 12 months, December 1965-November 1966
[b] 100% tinned fish
[c] 59% tinned meat

## 2. *Shopping facilities and centres for Uafato buyers*

About forty-nine per cent of the £1,558 spent on food and other commodities went to the two small Uafato stores. They supplied most of the sugar, salt, dripping, soap, kerosene and benzene, and a good proportion of the tinned meat and fish, coffee and cocoa, flour and rice, and bakery products, but only twenty per cent of the non-food commodities (Table 16).

G

Table 17   Stock and Prices—Mamea's Store
April 1966

| Items in stock | Quantity | Price | Apia price |
|---|---|---|---|
| | | s d | s d |
| Corned beef (12 oz. tin) | 9 | 3 9 | 3 3 |
| Corned beef (1 lb. tin) | 11 | 4 9 | 4 3 |
| Herrings (tin) | 19 | 1 8 | 1 6 |
| Sugar | 30 lbs. | 1 0 lb. | 1 9 lb. |
| Flour | 22 lbs. | 0 9 lb. | 0 6 lb. |
| Rice | 6 lbs. | 1 6 lb. | 1 0 lb. |
| Salt | 4 lbs. | 0 8 lb. | 0 4 lb. |
| Laundry soap[a] | 18 bars | 3 0 bar | 2 6 lb. |
| Toilet soap | 8 | 1 0 | 1 0 |
| Hair oil | 12 | 2 0 | 1 9 |
| Combs | 4 | 1 0 | 0 6 |
| Matches | 20 | 0 8 | 0 3 |
| Razor blades | 7 | 0 6 | 0 3 |
| Chewing gum | 20 | 0 3 | 0 3 |
| Coleman lamp mantle | 13 | 1 3 | 1 0 |
| Kerosene[b] | 3 gall. | 1 0 pint | 0 9 pint |
| Benzene[b] | 2 gall. | 1 3 | 1 0 |
| Balloons | 21 | 0 3 | 0 2 |
| Instant coffee[c] | part jar | | |
| Cocoa | part jar | | |
| Cigarettes (home rolled)[d] | 4 | | |

NOTES:   [a] Bars of laundry soap were bought in Apia (2s 6d) and cut into six cakes which were sold at sixpence each.

[b] Kerosene and benzene were bought in 4-gallon lots and sold at 1s per beer-bottleful.

[c] Instant coffee and cocoa were bought by the jar and sold at 6d for two teaspoonsful.

[d] Uafato storekeepers rarely sold packets of tobacco but they rolled cigarettes which were sold at threepence or two coconuts.

One-third of the total sales of the two village stores was sugar; about eighty-five per cent of all sugar consumed in the village. Tinned fish comprised another nineteen per cent of their sales, and they supplied about eighty-nine per cent of the village purchases of this item. The total stock of the two stores rarely exceeded £40 and was often very much less. There were frequent shortages, even of sugar. Tinned corned beef was stocked only occasionally. Table 17 shows a stock-taking of Mamea's store at a time when it was well supplied. Even then, dripping, a frequently-bought item, was out of stock. Sugar, flour, rice, kerosene and benzene were all sold in shilling or sixpenny lots. Instant coffee and cocoa were sold by the spoonful. Bars of laundry soap were cut into six small cakes. Cigarettes were rolled by the storekeepers and sold singly. Razor blades were also sold singly. Coconuts were accepted in exchange for most commodities at the standard rate of eight mature nuts for 1s. Credit was given to most '*āiga* in small amounts.[36]

The local storekeepers bought most of their goods from the 'wholesale' counters of the larger Apia stores where between five and ten per cent discount was given on bulk orders. Some items were even bought at normal Apia retail prices. They were sold in the village at prices ranging from ten to thirty per cent higher than in Apia. Only one non-store-owning '*āiga* bought sugar, kerosene, flour, rice and dripping in bulk in Apia for its own use. It had a steady wage income in the village and two *taulele'a* working in Apia.

Some goods were bought from the trading-stations at Fagaloa Bay. During one visit to Uafato, neither of the local stores had any sugar. As a result several '*āiga* sent over to Fagaloa Bay for supplies and a *matai* sold some of his sugar to the Women's Committee for one of its meetings. Ah Chong's *matai* brother-in-law took advantage of the situation by sending to Apia for a bag of sugar and temporarily opening the Ah Chong store. It was two or three days before Mamea and Taufaga again had sugar for sale.

## 3. *The effect of social and organizational institutions on outlay*

The effect of social and organizational institutions such as the *fono*, '*aumāga*, Women's Committee and the '*āiga* on the level and composition of output was discussed earlier, with particular reference to subsistence production. The effects were similar on the cash side. By demanding money from the '*āiga* for the support of the pastor, donations to the church, and the construction of a school building, the level of marketed output probably rose above that motivated by the individual demand for money.

During the survey cash subscriptions were levied by the *fono* (Fagaloa Bay district school—£14; water pipeline—£10; village school fees—£40), and the Women's Committee (district hospital at Fagaloa Bay—£8), and all groups collected small amounts from members for sugar, tinned meat and tea for their meetings, and to entertain guests to the village. Subscriptions levied during the year totalled £162, or £0·8 per consumption unit. In the past subscriptions had been considerably higher, particularly when the church and school were built. They were probably higher also after the survey as money was being collected for the pastor's house.

About £95 was given to relations and others, compared with £28 received as gifts. Money was taken (along with subsistence

---

[36] During the survey period village debts to Mamea's store varied between £14 to £17 and to Taufaga's store between £40 and £50. About £150 was owed to Ah Chong mostly by his own '*āiga*.

goods such as *'ietōga*) to funerals, title-dedications, guest-*fale* dedications and other affairs involving related *'āiga*, but there was only
one occasion in Uafato during the survey where corresponding
gifts were received. The largest cash gift was £10 given by a *matai*
to his brother when he returned on furlough from missionary work
in Papua.

The church received nine per cent of the cash outlay of the
village. Uafato was predominantly a Congregational Church village
and all but one *'āiga* contributed regularly to its various funds. One
*'āiga* and several members of others, including a *matai*, belonged to
the Mormon church, to which they were expected to give ten
per cent of their income. There were no records of this, but as
church giving is a strongly held custom they probably contributed
as much on average as the Congregational Church *'āiga*.

All important church collections were made on an *'āiga* basis
and the *matai* or a representative publicly presented the *'āiga*
contribution in church. The performance was always the same—
after the service the deacons (village *matai*) would announce that a
certain collection was to be made. Then they would call out the
name of each *'āiga* whose representative would hand over the
money and wait while the amount was loudly announced. On the
first Sunday of each month money was collected for the pastor.
At other times during the year collections were made for the church
in Samoa—a major fund which generally reached close to the
amount paid to the pastor over the year, missions, the mission ship
*John Williams*, youth work and other small funds. Except for the
monthly gift to the pastor, the money went to the head office of
the church in Apia.

In 1965 the Uafato pastor received £166, in monthly instalments
from the village. In 1966 he received only £87. The other donations
totalled £283 in 1965 and £54 in 1966. The drastic fall in 1966
reflects a general shortage of money in the village after the hurricane,
and the increased purchases of food.

The Uafato *'āiga* gave similar amounts to the church funds so
that there was an inverse relationship between *'āiga* income and
the size of the contribution (Table 18).

In March 1966, despite the post-hurricane fall in village cash
income, the first of a series of subscriptions was levied on the
Congregational *'āiga* to raise money for a new house for the pastor.
The subscription was five shillings per *matai* plus one shilling for
each person in the *'āiga*. The same subscription was levied again
in April and it was planned to continue it each month until sufficient
money was in hand. The village needed about £300 altogether and
at this rate it could take about two years to collect.

Table 18    Uafato: Cash Donations by the Sample *'Āiga* to Congregational
Church and Pastor[a]

| *'Āiga* | Estimated cash income of the *'āiga* | Cash donated to church and pastor | Proportion of cash donations to cash income |
|---|---|---|---|
| | £ | £ | % |
| 1 | 235 | 14 | 6 |
| 2 | 148 | 12 | 8 |
| 3 & 4 | 136 | 24 | 17 |
| 5 | 85 | 10 | 12 |
| 6 | 77 | 11 | 14 |
| 7 | 57 | 13 | 23 |
| 8 | 46 | 12 | 25 |

NOTE:    [a]12 months, December 1965-November 1966

In many respects the pastor was treated as an honoured guest of the village. Not only did it provide him with housing and a cash income but he also received all the subsistence foods he required and supplies of other subsistence commodities such as mats. It was the practice in all villages for the women to weave a supply of mats each year specifically for the pastor. In January 1966 the Uafato pastor was presented with fifty *papa* (coarse floor mats), twelve *tu'ualaufala* (large sleeping-mats), twenty *afiafi* (medium sized sleeping-mats) and fifty *laulau* (small food-mats). At all times the pastor and his family were served by two or three young people who did much of the housework and food preparation. It was said commonly, although not entirely accurately, that the village pastors and their wives did not have to lift a finger to provide their consumption needs.

It was very difficult for an individual in Samoa to save money unless he held an important title or could become independent of his *'āiga* and relatives by holding a permanent well paid job. It was often a desire for independence that motivated individuals, particularly *taulele'a*, to migrate to New Zealand. Those with wage jobs in Western Samoa were expected to distribute their earnings among *'āiga* and relatives, close and distant. Any meeting with a relative could be the occasion for a request for money, always with good reason, of course, such as to pay a fare, to help the *matai* meet a subscription for the church, to buy food and so on. A refusal to meet such requests, at least partly, meant that the right to ask for reciprocal treatment in the future could be denied. Few Samoans were in a position where they could give up this right, that is, dependence on the *'āiga*. There were powerful social sanctions against the accumulation of material wealth of the kind which

could be easily transferred, such as money. This was observed to
be the case by Churchward in the 1880s:

> Amongst other curious Samoan customs is that of begging material for
> specific objects, and such applications are very rarely refused. There is no
> shame whatever felt about it; it is the custom of the country, and the
> persons solicited yield in obedience to that custom, and perhaps the very
> next week are at the same game themselves for some purpose or other.
> This custom they extend at times to foreigners, but unless they are in
> some way connected with them they rarely do this. At its worst however,
> it can hardly properly be termed begging in our acceptance of the term,
> for, from a Samoan point of view, a native, in begging anything that he
> may want, is only exercising a right that he might at any future time be
> required to accord to others. (1887, p. 116)

### 4. *Cash savings*

It is difficult to estimate the extent of cash savings in the village.
On one hand there is some evidence, in the balance between the
estimates of cash income and outlay, that about £88 may have been
saved from current income during the year. On the other hand
savings in bank and post-office accounts held by Uafato people
declined from about £200 at the beginning of the period, to about
£50 at the end. In two cases savings were withdrawn for specific
purposes: one *matai* was preparing to visit a sister in California
(mainly at her expense), and another *matai* paid the air fares to
New Zealand for one of his *taulele'a*. Only six people altogether
had savings accounts including the pastor, Mamea and Taufuga.
It was impossible to know the amounts of money kept in tin boxes
in the village but it was unlikely to have been much. When money
was being collected for some village or church purpose most *'āiga*
found it necessary to make copra or handicrafts, and to sell them
in Apia, before they could make their contributions. Often when
Uafato people took the bus to Apia they arranged with the driver
to pay the fare on the return journey after selling their produce in
Apia. It is considered unlikely that savings increased in the village
as a whole in the months following the hurricane although they
may have done so in one or two *'āiga* with wage incomes.

# Chapter 5

# TAGA

TAGA was ranked third in the initial assessment of linkage with the market sector. It was assumed to have stronger linkage than Uafato for two main reasons: two trading stations (Burns Philp and O. F. Nelson & Co.) were established in Taga in the 1920s or early 1930s; and with the completion of the Savai'i Island south-coast road in December 1960, dependence on the sea for transport and communications ended and buses provided a daily service with other Savai'i villages and the inter-island ferry terminal at Salelologa. Before 1960 'contact with Apia and other villages had been extremely limited' and Taga was 'not greatly disturbed by modern influences' (Fairbairn 1963, pp. 348-9).

This chapter follows the general outline of that on Uafato with sections on productive resources, production, income, and outlay. Comparisons will be drawn with Uafato where relevant and features of the economy which are similar to those already described for Uafato will not be dealt with in detail.

Taga is on the south coast of Savai'i Island at the head of a small indentation in one of the most forbidding stretches of coastline in Western Samoa. High forest-capped lava cliffs stretch some nine miles to the east to the nearest village, Gataivai. To the west a narrow sand-ridge planted in coconuts follows the coastline, separating the rock ledges and cliffs from the forest. Sala'ilua, the nearest village along this coastline, is eight miles away.

The small bay offers Taga no protection from the rough seas of the south coast of Savai'i. The ceremonial centre (*malae*) of the village is close to sea-level on a sand and pebble deposit which provides the only landing-place for canoes and boats along this dangerous coastline. But by no means is it a sheltered anchorage. Before 1960 when the Taga trading stations were served by motor launches, they had to stand off under power while the village copra and cacao and store supplies were transferred in whaleboats and canoes, a hazardous undertaking at the best of times. The church, the Burns Philp station, and dwellings of about one-third of the village '*āiga* are in this part of the village. The other '*āiga*, the Nelson

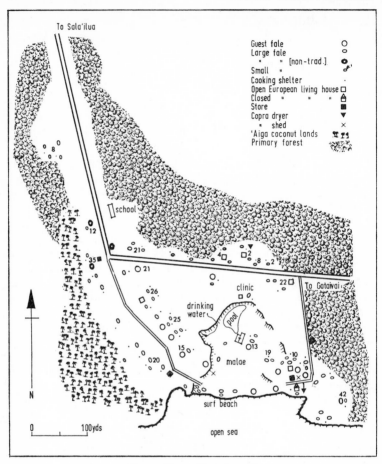

Fig. 4   Taga village in 1966

station, the clinic and school are located on higher ground at the
top of a cliff. The only source of fresh water for miles around is at
the base of this cliff in the lower village. Several families live more
or less permanently on agricultural blocks up to four miles from the
village. The church, the clinic and the first European house were
all built in 1952. During the 1950s several dwellings were built on
blocks away from the village but there was little other change. In
1960 a school was built near the new road at the north-west corner
of the upper village to replace three *fale* in the *malae*. Over the next
four or five years five 'open-houses', four large *fale* with cement
foundation-floors and iron roofs, two small stores, three copra

dryers, and a number of guest and large *fale* were built in the village, many on land fronting the new road.

Before 1960 communications were maintained with other villages and Apia either through the trading-station launches which called at irregular intervals, or by foot along a rocky track through the forest between Sala'ilua and Gataivai. This track was well known in Samoa. It had neither water nor coconut palms along most of its sixteen or so miles and this earned it the title *'auala mativa*—the way of poverty.

Communications were greatly improved after 1960 by a regular bus service. But a journey to Apia was still expensive and took a long time. Buses passed through Taga on their way to the inter-island ferry terminal at about 4 a.m. It took about two hours in the ferry to reach Upolu and another hour and a half to two hours in a bus to reach Apia. With no hold-ups, Apia could be reached by 8.30 or 9 a.m., about five hours after leaving Taga. The total fare was fifteen shillings. Usually the return journey could not be made until the following day. A bus left Apia at 3 a.m., to connect with the first ferry to Savai'i Island. If one was lucky a Savai'i bus would start back along the south coast when the ferry arrived. More often than not, however, the Savai'i buses would wait in Salelologa until mid-morning. It could be midday or later, ten hours after leaving Apia, before one could step down in Taga. The high fares and the time involved in a visit to Apia meant that most Taga people did not go very often, and usually only when they could visit relatives and stay for several days. But they did go often to Salelologa where there were three large stores, to the near-by Tuasivi government offices and Court, and to Sala'ilua which had the nearest hospital and post office and a store which was better stocked than those in Taga.

The resident population of Taga in January 1966 was 505.[1] As in Uafato, over fifty per cent of the population was under fifteen years of age. The pastors' reports of resident population for the years 1950 to 1965 and the Census returns for 1951, 1956 and 1961 indicate an average annual growth rate of four per cent between 1950 and 1959 and possibly a lower rate after 1959. The pastors' reports for several years enumerated only members of the Congregational Church and were not as informative as those for Uafato. The growth rate since about 1961 is therefore in doubt. Many Taga people, however, had emigrated to other villages, Apia and even New Zealand after the road opened, and this may have contributed to a decline in the growth rate.

Taga society was based on twenty *'āiga* titles which, in 1966,

[1] Appendix Table 1.

were held by over forty *matai*. One title was held jointly by seven
men and others had six, four, three and two joint holders. Only
ten titles had single holders. Most of this title-splitting had occurred
since 1955. During the early 1950s several *taulele'a* had cleared land
in the remote north-west corner of the Taga forest. When it became
known that the road would pass close by they demanded the *pule*
(control) of these blocks. Disputes in some *'āiga* over this land
eventually led to the splitting of their titles. Titles were also given
by some *'āiga* to men who had wage or salary jobs. In this way they
would be made more responsible for the financial well-being of the
*'āiga*. Most of these *matai* continued to live in Apia. I knew of only
one *matai* who voluntarily gave up a permanent government job
to return to Taga. There was a less voluntary case of a nineteen-
year-old youth who was made a *matai* on being appointed to a
government position. He eventually returned to Taga after a
conviction for theft and a spell in the Apia gaol. He claimed that
he had stolen because his *'āiga* made unreasonable demands on him.

In 1966 forty *'āiga* and *matai* were resident in Taga. Many *'āiga*
were close to nuclear families in size and composition. There were
still a few large *'āiga*, such as that of the Burns Philp trader[2] with

[2] This trader, Tialavea, had managed the Taga station for some twenty years.
Although he came originally from another Savai'i village and held a title of that
village he was admitted into the Taga *fono* in the early 1950s. Before this he had
shared the lands of a relative, a Taga *matai*, and in 1952 he started to clear land
some three miles inland from the village where he planted coconuts and cacao.
The *pule* over this land was secured when he was admitted to the *fono*. The block
was directly in the path of the road built six years later. Tialavea was a part-
Samoan and he had attended mission secondary school in Apia and spoke excellent
English. He was providing his children and a number of relatives with the best
schooling available in Western Samoa; in 1965-6 his eldest daughter and son were
working in New Zealand after completing their secondary schooling in Samoa;
his second son was completing his final year at the Malua Theological College;
his third son was a teacher at the Taga school; the fourth son completed his secondary education at Samoa College, the main government secondary school in
Apia, and was working in Taga while waiting for a visa for New Zealand; his
next two sons were at secondary schools in Apia; and other children were attending
mission and government intermediate and elementary schools in Taga, Apia and
other villages. All members of the nuclear family and several other members
of the *'āiga* spoke good English. In 1952 Tialavea built the first European house
in the village and in 1961 he built the first copra dryer. In 1964 he bought an old
one-ton truck at a government disposal sale. He was one of the most respected
and influential *matai* in Taga and was the leading *matai* behind the building of the
church and clinic in 1952 and the school in 1960. He had in fact been the carpenter
for the clinic and school. Tialavea was a church deacon and his cash and other
support for the pastor and church far exceeded that of any other Taga *matai*.
The pastor referred to Tialavea as his 'right arm'. While Tialavea was on a three-
month visit to New Zealand (December 1965 to February 1966) his *'āiga* mis-
managed the store and he returned to find a debt of about £500 to the head office.
Most of this he paid from his New Zealand earnings but at the end of 1966 the
station was closed down. In May 1966 Tialavea moved his European house from
the village to his inland block and by 1967 the whole *'āiga* had moved from the
village proper.

twenty-six members, but twelve was the average and fourteen *'āiga* had fewer than ten members.

PRODUCTIVE RESOURCES

The assessment of Taga's productive resources will take the same form as that adopted in the previous chapter on Uafato, where land, labour and producers' capital were described in turn.

1. *Land*

Taga land was extensive but generally of low quality. It sloped gently inland for about five miles before rising steeply to the 6,000-feet-high central mountain ridge of the island, about ten miles from the coast. Taga claimed control of over 50,000 acres, but less than two per cent had been brought into agricultural use. Most of this large area had very shallow, rocky and bouldery soils of low natural fertility, but there were two limited areas, about 400 acres altogether, with soils of high natural fertility.[3] The areas with a thin soil cover tended to lose their fertility rapidly after being cleared of forest. There was no permanent surface water, but two streams flowed intermittently and had built up ribbons of fertile sticky black alluvial clay soils. These two areas, and a long narrow sand-ridge along the coast to the west of the village, were the only areas cultivated until about 1950.[4]

(a) *The coastal sand-ridge*

The narrow sand-ridge extended some five miles along the coast west of the village, varying in width from about twenty to one hundred and fifty feet. It had been planted with coconuts, probably well before the turn of the century. Although most of the palms appeared to be over fifty years old they were generally healthy-looking except for those in the outer fringe which were damaged by salt spray. The palms had been closely planted and many fallen nuts had been allowed to seed. The ground was strewn with rat-damaged coconuts and at a rough guess some ten to fifteen per cent of the output of the area must have been lost in this way. A path followed the sand-ridge and it took about an hour to walk to the farthest blocks. Several *'āiga* had planted pandanus on their sand-ridge blocks but no other crops were grown in this area.

(b) *The eastern stream*

A stream flowing almost due south entered the sea about a

[3] Land Classification Map of Savai'i, Western Samoa, R. E. Owen, Government Printer, Wellington, New Zealand. The Uafato soils were classified as of high to moderate natural fertility.
[4] These areas have been described in some detail in Barrett 1959.

quarter of a mile east of the village. Alluvial soils along the banks
had been planted with coconuts for about two miles from the mouth
of the stream, mainly before 1920. A great deal of effort had been
put into removing rocks and boulders which were piled in large
heaps at the forest edge. The palms had been again closely planted
and as along the sand-ridge there was a good sprinkling of younger
self-sown palms. Little if any attempt had been made in either
area to remove dead or unproductive palms, or to replant. It took
about an hour to reach the blocks farthest from the village, along a
path through the forest. Cacao trees had been interplanted with
palms on some blocks during the 1930s but they were no longer
productive.

(c)  *The northern stream*

About a mile north of the village at a westward bend in a second
stream about 150 acres had been cleared, mainly for subsistence
food production under bush fallow methods. Land had also been
cleared along the banks of the stream to the north for a distance of
about a mile and a half. The most distant blocks were nearly three
miles from the village. In addition to food crops some '*āiga* had
planted cacao in the area.

After 1950 there appeared to have been sufficient pressure on the
land to force some growers to clear forest in much less fertile areas.
Fairbairn noted that 'the buoyant market for cocoa in the post-war
years encouraged many planters to establish large plantations on
land several miles inland from the village' (p. 350). Among the
first to expand into this poorer land were Tialavea, the Burns
Philp trader, and Kauli Long, a part-Chinese man who married a
Taga girl.[5] Both were permitted by the *fono* to clear forest in the
remote north-western corner of the Taga land. After 1955 many
others started to clear forest and plant cacao on land in the path
of the projected road and by 1958-60, when the road was pushed
through from Sala'ilua to Taga, all the land along it had been
cleared and claimed.[6] Many of the *taulele'a* who earlier had started
to clear blocks in this area found that their *matai* were exerting

[5] Kauli Long had taken up residence in Taga in about 1954. Through his
*matai* brother-in-law, he had been allowed to clear land deep in the forest and
plant coconut and cacao. The block was close to that of Tialavea and when the
road went through in 1960 he obtained a narrow frontage and built a short
access road into his block. In 1960 he also built a European house on the block
and in 1963 he bought a bus and began a daily service between Sala'ilua and
Salelologa. As the husband of a *matai*'s sister he was not expected to serve formally (*tautua*) the *matai* but in fact he did make fairly regular cash gifts and provided a free bus service for the '*āiga*.

[6] Only a relatively small area of this 'second grade' land had been cleared up
to 1954.

their rights and taking over. Disputes over the use of this land led to the splitting of several titles. By obtaining a title, the man who had earlier cleared the land obtained formal control over it and over the cacao crops which he had planted.

With the opening of the road Taga became a supply area for the Banana Scheme and after 1960 there was a rapid expansion along the road for banana production. Some bananas were grown in the old northern stream area but most were produced on land newly cleared near the road. As this land rapidly lost its natural fertility once the forest cover had been cut down and burnt, banana production was maintained by continuously clearing new land. Between 1960 and 1966 about 300 acres of this poorer land were cleared for banana production and in 1966 about two-thirds of this had already been abandoned to bush fallow. In 1965 the banana plots suffered badly from bunchytop disease and by the end of the year most growers had stopped planting, and most banana plots were abandoned. 1964 was the peak year for banana production when an average of 714 cases a month were sold. By the end of 1964 production had already started to be influenced by bunchytop[7] and output declined as follows:

| 1965 | Jan. | 347 cases exported |
|------|------|------|
|      | Feb. | 414 |
|      | Mar. | 502 |
|      | Apr. | 353 |
|      | May  | 382 |
|      | June | 440 |
|      | July | 250 |
|      | Aug. | 233 |
|      | Sept.| 215 |
|      | Oct. | 170 |
|      | Nov. | 246 |
|      | Dec. | 269 |
| 1966 | Jan. | 138 |

Even if there had been no hurricane in January most growers would probably have sold no bananas after June 1966.

In 1966 the coconut was the most important crop in terms of land use. About 325 acres, or thirty-six per cent of the productive

[7] Bunchytop was first 'found in Taga [in 1962] by the District Field Assistant who immediately carried out control work with his staff. Diseased plants were dug up, split and burnt. The whole of the Eastern district from Pu'apu'a to Gataivai is heavily infested and a combined effort of some co-operative growers with the department teams arrested the spreading . . . from Taga to (Salailua) Palapala'. (Dept. of Agric., Forests and Fisheries, Annual Report for 1962, pp. 13-14.)

area was under the palm.[8] About eighty acres were under cacao, mostly badly neglected and overgrown with creepers, although still being harvested until the hurricane. It was difficult to estimate the area under bananas, but there were roughly twenty acres which appeared to be recovering from the hurricane, although

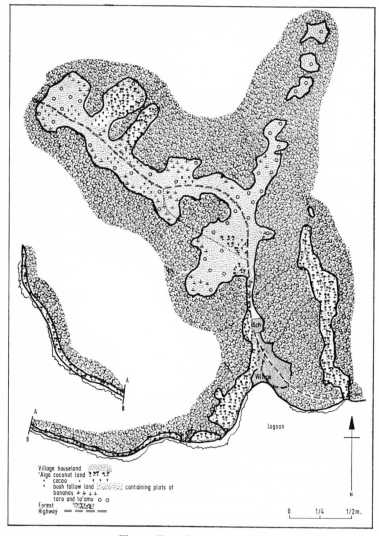

Fig. 5    Taga: land use in 1966

[8] See Table 19 and Figure 5.

Table 19   Taga: Land Use in 1966

| | Vill-age[a] | Coco-nuts | Cacao | Bana-nas | Taro and ta'amū | Pig com-pound | Fallow | Total |
|---|---|---|---|---|---|---|---|---|
| Estimated area (acres) | 59 | 325 | 80 | 20 | 60 | 20 | 336 | 900 |
| Percentage | 6·5 | 36·1 | 8·9 | 2·2 | 6·7 | 2·2 | 37·3 | 100·0 |

NOTE:      [a] Includes houseland, *malae* and school grounds.

not free of bunchytop. In May 1966, after much of the post-hurricane emergency food planting had been completed, about sixty acres were in taro and *ta'amū*. Many *'āiga* had planted taro in excess of their consumption needs and intended to sell the surplus through the Department of Agriculture. The fallow area, largely abandoned banana plots, was about 336 acres.

Table 20   Taga: *Matai* Land Holdings in 1966

| *Matai* | No. of blocks | No. of acres | *Matai* | No. of blocks | No. of acres |
|---|---|---|---|---|---|
| 1[a] | 10 | 67 | 22[a] | 5 | 16 |
| 2[a] | 11 | 26 | 23 | 1 | —[b] |
| 3 | 16 | 41 | 24 | 12 | 27 |
| 4[a] | 10 | 21 | 25[a] | 3 | 7 |
| 5 | 13 | 35 | 26[a] | 4 | 16 |
| 6 | 9 | 17 | 27 | 11 | 28 |
| 7 | 4 | 19 | 28 | 6 | 11 |
| 8[a] | 7 | 28 | 29 | 4 | 16 |
| 9 | 7 | 23 | 30 | 5 | 6 |
| 10[a] | 11 | 34 | 31 | 5 | 13 |
| 11 | 9 | 16 | 32 | 9 | 25 |
| 12[a] | 9 | 27 | 33 | 11 | 18 |
| 13[a] | 6 | 21 | 34 | 3 | 3 |
| 14 | 2 | 2 | 35 | 6 | 24 |
| 15[a] | 17 | 31 | 36[c] | 3 | 56 |
| 16 | 4 | 11 | 37[a] | 9 | 40 |
| 17 | 7 | 15 | 38 | 1 | —[b] |
| 18 | 10 | 19 | 39 | 9 | 15 |
| 19[a] | 10 | 39 | 40 | 2 | 22 |
| 20[a] | 6 | 12 | 41 | 7 | 16 |
| 21[a] | 7 | 24 | 42 | 7 | 13 |
| Total | 185 | 528 | Total | 308 | 900 |

NOTES:      [a] Sample *'āiga*
            [b] House land only
            [c] Kauli Long

The cleared land was divided into 308 recognized blocks,[9] and these were divided between the forty 'āiga in such a way that most

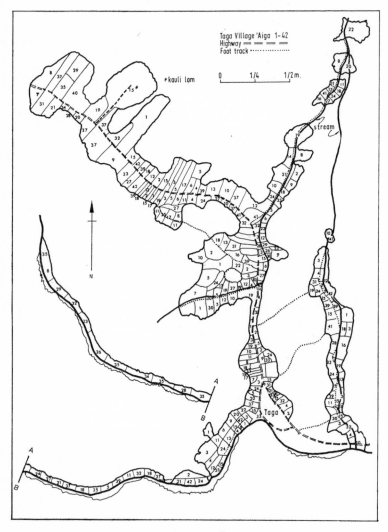

Fig. 6    Taga: *matai* land holdings in 1966

[9] Barrett counted only 145 blocks in 1958 but he apparently did not include houseland which would add another 40 or so. The increase in the number of blocks between 1958 and 1966 was due to the expansion of cleared land along the road and to the division of older blocks with the splitting of titles.

controlled land in the main areas.[10] The average *matai* holding
consisted of seven blocks and 22.5 acres, but the number of blocks
varied from one to sixteen and the areas from two to sixty-seven
acres.[11] There were several fairly large blocks, particularly along
the road three to four miles from the village. The largest, that of
Kauli Long, was almost fifty acres. Permanent dwellings had been
built on many of these larger blocks.

The forest was a valuable natural resource not only because it
was a vast reserve of potentially productive land, but also because
it provided timber and a certain amount of food. Local timber had
been used almost exclusively in the *fale* and houses, although much
of the timber in the church and school had been imported from
outside. Compared with Uafato it was relatively easy to extract
timber from the Taga forest as the forest wall was nowhere very
far from the village or agricultural lands. After 1960 quality timber
could be cut at the roadside and brought to the village by truck.
This very great reduction in the labour costs of extracting timber
partly explains the increased building activity in the village after
1960.

For most Samoan villages the sea is an important source of food.
But Taga was poorly endowed in this way. It was dangerous to
take a canoe out to sea and there were in fact very few canoes in
the village. Fishing consisted mainly of dangling a line on a long
bamboo pole from the top of the cliffs. Groups of young men
occasionally swam along the coast to the west of the village with
shanghais and short steel spears, and in rough weather attempts
were sometimes made to trap fish thrown up on to the rock ledges.
These methods were much less rewarding than the bay fishing at
Uafato and lagoon fishing at Poutasi and Utuali'i. However some
Taga men did a lot of fishing, and, like fishermen everywhere they
undoubtedly enjoyed it.

### 2. *Labour*

The organization of labour at the *'āiga* and village levels was
similar to that described for Uafato; the *matai* acted as managers
and the *taulele'a* as labourers. The *matai*'s wives supervised the work
of the other women. The same variety of commodities was produced, both for subsistence use and sale. Methods of production
and the knowledge and skills required from the producers were also
much the same, as was the division of tasks between men and
women.

[10] See Table 20 and Figure 6. The large block used by Kauli Long is shown
separately from that of the *matai* who held the formal *pule*.
[11] The average *'āiga* holding in Uafato (IV) was only sixteen acres divided
between 6·5 blocks.

H

But Taga was a larger village and had recently experienced a minor building boom. More men claimed to be skilled carpenters and builders,[12] although few of these were able to spend much time at their craft.

There were very few opportunities for unskilled wage labouring in or near Taga. In the early 1950s Tialavea and Kauli Long had employed casual labourers in establishing their small-holdings about three miles inland from the village. During the construction of the road in 1959-60 seventeen Taga men had been employed as labourers by the Public Works Department (Fairbairn 1963, p. 351). These were the only cases I could discover of wages paid for unskilled labour in Taga. But during the survey an interesting variation was discovered; one *matai*[13] made it known that he would pay £4 to anyone who would clear bush fallow land and plant one thousand taro for him. The scheme was initiated by an Apia relative with the intention of producing taro for export. Several men started planting in May and two months later two had completed a thousand each and three others were still working at theirs. It took about thirty-five hours to clear sufficient land and plant a thousand taro, so that they earned about 2s 3d an hour—a higher rate than the 1s 6d received by many unskilled labourers in Apia. The *matai* expected, on the basis of 1966 prices, to earn about £50 for each thousand taro. He would have to do some weeding, and harvest and pack the taro for delivery to Department of Agriculture trucks at the road.

There was another case of cash being paid by Taga *matai* for unskilled work on their lands. A group called the '*autalavou*—the Association of Congregational Church Youth—worked on most Wednesday mornings for any *matai* willing to pay ten shillings an hour. For this ten shillings he had the labour of between twenty and thirty strong young people. Most of the money earned by the

[12] For example, Tialavea, the Burns Philp trader had supervised the construction of his own house and the village clinic in 1952, the village school in 1960 and an 'open-house' for a related *matai* in 1963. Two *taulele'a* held Government permits to build European-style houses and several others had supervised the construction of open-houses in Taga. Two *matai* were known as skilled traditional carpenters and these had supervised the construction of a number of guest and other large *fale* in Taga, and during the survey one of them was away building a guest-*fale* in another village.

[13] This *matai* held a title which had been split between at least six *matai* (there were six in Taga). His '*āiga* was a young nuclear family plus his adult brother. His own '*āiga* labour resources would not have been sufficient to carry out the planting scheme envisaged, hence the novel method adopted. This *matai* was something of an oddity in Taga for other reasons also. He lent small sums of money to various Taga people (seven shillings was the largest sum recorded) and he expected this money to be repaid, contrary to the usual village custom. This lending rather than giving earned him the uncomplimentary nickname of *papalagi*—foreigner.

'*autalavou* went into a fund for the proposed new house for the pastor.
It appeared to be a fairly common fund-raising method amongst
church youth groups when money was needed for capital works of
this kind, although it had not been used in Uafato.

There was slightly more opportunity for skilled wage employment in Taga than in Uafato. Three Taga persons taught at the
village school, another commuted weekly to the Sala'ilua school,
and there was a district nurse, two traders and the *pulenu'u*.
Many other Taga people had jobs in Apia, in other villages where
they had been posted as teachers, or in New Zealand. I knew of
eight teachers, four nurses and ten other people with jobs away
from Taga, and this was certainly not a complete list. At least
five of these wage-earners held Taga titles. This contrasts markedly
with Uafato which had produced only one teacher and had only
a handful of men with jobs in Apia and New Zealand in 1966.

The number of skilled and professionally trained people from
Taga is evidence of considerable past cash investment in education.
Tialavea's '*āiga* is an extreme case in point, but by no means the
sole example. Many young people in Taga spoke reasonably good
English, many more in fact than in the other three villages. There
were good reasons why *matai* accepted the cost of keeping children
at school beyond the village school level—prestige was augmented,
or a son might want to be a pastor. But the main reason given by
most *matai* was the desire to have a wage-earner in the '*āiga*.

In 1966 twenty children attended the district (intermediate)
school, fourteen were at various mission schools, two were at the
main government secondary school in Apia (Samoa College), one
was completing his final year at the Malua Theological College
and two were trainee nurses at the Apia hospital. About £450 was
spent on school fees and related expenses in 1966. This was, however, only £1·24 per consumption unit, about the same amount
as in Uafato. Measured roughly as income from wages, remittances
from overseas and gifts, the returns to investment on schooling were
£5·9[14] per consumption unit in 1966. In Uafato this was only
£2·9.[15]

Taga *matai* were at a disadvantage compared with those of
Uafato, Poutasi and Utuali'i in reaping the cash harvest from their
children and relatives with wage jobs in Apia. For example, one
Uafato *matai* had two sons working in Apia. He visited them about

[14] See Table 25.
[15] They were higher still in Poutasi (II) £11·8, and Utuali'i (I) £20·1. These
figures include wages earned in labouring jobs and cash gifts which were unrelated
to the level of education or to the village investment in education but they serve
to indicate the sort of differences between the villages which resulted from different
levels of past investment in schooling.

once a week and was usually given part of their earnings. He did not make unduly heavy demands on his sons' money, but he could ask for it directly when he needed it. Poutasi *matai* were in much the same position and Utuali'i *matai* were even better placed since the wage-earners usually lived at home. But for Taga *matai* there were few opportunities for direct face-to-face requests for money from relatives employed in Apia, simply because it was too expensive to go to Apia very often. They had to rely on the strength of '*āiga* ties and on the postal services for remittances and gifts from Apia, just as all village *matai* did for remittances from New Zealand. The expense of travel to Apia probably reduced the cash returns to past investment in education.

### 3. *Producers' capital*

Most items of capital equipment in Taga were intended for use in the subsistence sector; they were mainly carpentry tools and fishing gear. Because there were few differences between Samoan villages in the methods of subsistence production, or in the goods and services produced for subsistence consumption, there were correspondingly few differences in the variety and quantities of items of productive equipment. The items of fishing gear and work-tools were almost identical in each of the villages studied, although there were differences in the quantities owned. Taga '*āiga* owned little fishing gear: £0·3 per consumption unit compared with Uafato (IV)—£0·8, Poutasi (II)—£0·8, and Utuali'i (I)—£0·6. Considering the poor natural conditions for fishing in Taga this was only to be expected. However, they owned more carpentry tools; £3·7 per consumption unit compared with Uafato—£2·0, Poutasi—£3·5, and Utuali'i—£1·9. There were three copra dryers; one owned by Tialavea and used as part of his trade-store business, one owned by Kauli Long and located on his inland block, and one other. The last two were small dryers like those in Uafato. They cost about £15 for drums and other components and about eight hours' labour. Tialavea's dryer, built in 1961 and the first in the village, was much larger and cost about £30 and at least twenty hours' labour. That only three of the forty Taga '*āiga* had built dryers is difficult to explain in economic terms as there was no shortage of timber for the fire; it took no longer to dry the copra in this way than in the sun. Hot-air-dried copra was worth two shillings more per hundred pounds. By contrast, all '*āiga* in Poutasi (II) had copra dryers and no sun-dried copra was sold in that village. Forty-four-gallon drums were available in Taga; the Burns Philp trading-station had ten in stock in May 1966. Social fragmentation in Taga with the break-up of several large '*āiga* and the division of land holdings may be a partial explanation. Many *matai* controlled only small areas of coconut land and they may have considered the use they would get from a dryer not worth the investment. But the larger '*āiga* had not built dryers either. Another reason may have been the demand made on the copra production of the village for village rather than '*āiga* capital works. For several months of the year copra production and sale was forbidden by the *fono* or the church committee so that coconuts could accumulate in the plantations to be collected by the '*aumāga* and processed into copra by the village as a whole, using the dryer of Tialavea.

When the road was opened Tialavea bought an old truck for £45 and an extra motor for another £30, and Kauli Long bought a bus for about £600. Investment of this kind was not possible in Uafato but it was matched in Poutasi and Utuali'i.

Total subsistence plus cash investment in producers' capital in Taga totalled £1,736 or £4·2 per consumption unit (Table 21), of which eighty-nine per cent represented investment from the monetized sector.

Table 21   Taga: Producers' Capital[a]

|  | Total | Cash component | Subsistence component |
|---|---|---|---|
|  | £ | % | % |
| Fishing gear and canoes | 116 | 18 | 82 |
| Agric. tools | 112 | 89 | 11 |
| Copra dryers | 60 | 58 | 42 |
| Carpentry tools | 233 | 97 | 3 |
| Guns | 110 | 100 | — |
| Sewing machines | 305 | 100 | — |
| Motor vehicles | 600 | 100 | — |
| Stores equipment and stock | 250 | 80 | 20 |
| Total investment[b] | 1,786 | 89 | 11 |
| Investment per consumption unit | £5 | £4 | £1 |

NOTES:   [a] The method by which values have been imputed has been described on p. 50.
   [b] An imputed rent for the use of this equipment has been included as an item of subsistence income (see Table 25). This is based on the above values and estimates of the useful life of the various items.

PRODUCTION

The commodities produced in the subsistence and cash sectors, and the methods of production, were similar to those described for Uafato. But Taga had almost twice the population of Uafato; it was differently endowed with natural resources; and it had stronger linkage with the market sector, and these factors did cause some significant differences between the two villages.

1. *Subsistence*

(a) *Food*

In general, the greater distances between Taga village and its food plots and coconut lands raised the effort-cost of subsistence food production to a slightly higher level than in Uafato. More time was needed to walk to and from the food plots, and more effort was needed to carry harvested food down to the village. A number of Taga *'āiga* built small *fale* near their food plots in the northern stream area so that the men could stay there for several days at a time, and cut out the long daily walk. The effort required to clear land, plant, weed and harvest food crops was not observably different from Uafato, except on the poorer quality Taga lands. But the more frequent shifting of plots on this land compensated to some extent for laborious weeding needed in the more fertile areas.

It was difficult to assess the subsistence food situation with any accuracy after the hurricane, but during 1965 the production of bananas for consumption and sale declined fairly rapidly due to bunchytop and by the end of the year most *'āiga* started to increase plantings of taro and *ta'amū* to substitute for failing banana supplies. Several *'āiga* planted taro in excess of this hoping to have a surplus which they could sell through the Department of Agriculture, and during 1965 some taro was sold in this way. After the hurricane the Government prohibited the export of taro and bananas from Western Samoa and the 'surplus' production of taro in Taga was used in the village to substitute partly for the complete loss of breadfruit and bananas. Consequently Taga had a better supply of taro after the hurricane than the other villages studied. The total supply of food staples—taro, *ta'amū*, breadfruit and bananas— before the hurricane appeared to be much the same as in Uafato, about thirty pounds harvest weight per consumption unit per week.

During the five months before the hurricane (September to January) each man in the sample *'āiga* planted an average of 140 taro and *ta'amū* a week. After the hurricane the average over the four months February to May was 330.[16] In Uafato the post-hurricane planting was intended solely to compensate for the loss of other subsistence food staples. In Taga (and Poutasi) the inten-

---

[16] The pre-hurricane average numbers of taro and *ta'amū* planted each week per man in the other villages were as follows: Uafato—60, Poutasi—100, Utuali'i— 60. The post-hurricane averages were: Uafato—180, Poutasi—600, Utuali'i—260.

tion was partly this and partly to produce a surplus for sale. With this complication of an intended market surplus in Taga it was more difficult to calculate the labour costs of subsistence food production in this village, but the labour survey provided a basis for a limited comparison of subsistence food production costs. It was found that in Uafato one man took about two hours fifty minutes to plant 100 taro or *ta'amū*. This included the time taken walking between the village and the plot. The same task in Taga required an average of three hours twenty minutes. These higher labour costs were due partly to the greater distances between the plots and the village, and partly to greater difficulties of clearing and planting in the poorer areas near the road.

About thirty per cent of the taro and *ta'amū* planted between September 1965 and May 1966 would have been sold rather than consumed. To produce the subsistence food component the Taga men averaged 6·1 hours a week and the women about 1·7 hours. This yielded about eighteen pounds of taro and *ta'amū* per consumption unit each week.

At the beginning of the survey bananas contributed roughly twenty per cent and breadfruit roughly seventeen per cent of the supply of subsistence staple foods. These were lower proportions than in Uafato, where bunchytop had come later and where bread-fruit trees were more easily grown on the houselands. At this time about seven pounds of bananas and five pounds of breadfruit were being produced each week. The men averaged about two hours a week at this task, about the same as in Uafato, although smaller quantities were produced.

The labour costs of supplying coconuts for village use were also slightly higher than in Uafato and, in addition, the average rate of consumption of coconuts was higher.[17] In Uafato the coconuts could be gathered on the way to and from the staple food plots but in Taga the coconut and staple food areas were in different directions from the village and the gathering of coconuts was a separate and largely additional task from harvesting and carrying down the taro. It was a task usually given to the children after school, but if each man had put in one hour a week he could have satisfied the average requirement of fifteen nuts a week per consumption unit.

Although it was not very rewarding the Taga men averaged

[17] An average per consumption unit of 6·9 nuts was used as food and 4·1 nuts as livestock food, per week. This was the highest rate of consumption of coconuts recorded in the four villages—Uafato 7·8 nuts per consumption unit per week, Poutasi 5·8 nuts and Utuali'i 4·8 nuts. One reason for this was the greater number of pigs kept in Taga and another was the better supply of taro which was usually eaten with coconut cream.

about four hours each week fishing from the cliffs or swimming along the shore with goggles and spears. Their average catch was only half a pound of fish an hour. Only once did I see a canoe taken out and although the sea looked calm, the canoe overturned and the men had to swim back to shore. The canoe was lost.

The imputed value of the actual subsistence food supplies for the twelve months from December 1965 to November 1966 is £11,143 or £30·6 per consumption unit. The details are given in Table 25.

### (b) *Housing*

Most of the *fale* in Taga were similar to those described for Uafato. Both villages had good supplies of timber on their lands, but the labour costs of extracting it were undoubtedly lower in Taga, particularly after the road improved access to the Taga forest.

In contrast with Uafato, where there had been little recent building activity, there was a great deal in Taga after 1960. With the opening of the road, access was improved not only to forest timber supplies but also to supplies of building materials in the market sector, such as cement, roofing-iron, timber etc.[18] The road also allowed Taga '*āiga* to market bananas and thus to increase their cash incomes. At the same time it made it easier to visit other villages and Apia, and for visitors to reach Taga. Thus access to building material improved, cash incomes increased, and there was a social motivation for investing in new and often non-traditional '*āiga* buildings. Between 1960 and 1966, eight new large *fale* (including three guest-*fale*), four large oval *fale* with concrete floors and roofed completely or partly with corrugated iron,[19] and five open-houses with rectangular concrete floors and iron roofs, were built in the village. A number of other *fale* and houses were built along the road. Some of the later ones pre-dated the road as they were built when their owners started to clear land in preparation for the expected market outlet for bananas.

This building boom represented a large cash and subsistence investment at the '*āiga* level. It is interesting to note here that after the new school was built in 1959-60 there were no large village-level capital works until 1967 (after the survey) when a new house was built for the pastor. The period 1960 to 1965 was one in which there was a rapid expansion of '*āiga* capital works in the form of large *fale* and houses—it appeared to be a post-road phenomenon

---

[18] Mainly at the large stores at Salelologa near the inter-island ferry wharf at the eastern end of Savai'i Island.

[19] Two of these were of two storeys and one had been closed in with timber and fitted with doors and windows.

Table 22  The Estimated Cash and Subsistence Costs of Five Open-Houses in Taga

| | | I | II | III | IV | V(b) |
|---|---|---|---|---|---|---|
| Year built | | 1962-5 | 1963(a) | 1960 | 1961-4 | 1962 |
| Approx. size | (feet) | 36 x 20 | 34 x 20 | 38 x 23 | 36 x 20 | 25 x 18 |
| *Cash payment*: (£) | | | | | | |
| material | | 200 | 250 | 300 | 200 | 250 |
| carpenter(e) | | | 3 | | | 10 |
| village(f) | | | | 20 | 2 | |
| *Subsistence payments to carpenter*: (nos) | | | | | | |
| '*ietōga* | | 12 | 1 | (d) | 7 | 6 |
| *siapo* | | 20 | | | | 20 |
| sleeping-mats | | | | | 20 | 40 |
| *to village*(f) | | | | | | |
| '*ietōga* | | | | 35 | 10 | |
| *Unskilled* '*āiga labour*: | (hrs) | 1200 | 670 | 1130 | 1200 | 600 |
| *Total cost*: (£) | | | | | | |
| cash | | 200 | 253 | 320 | 202 | 260 |
| Imputed value of subsistence payments(c) | | 80 | 5 | 175 | 105 | 76 |
| Imputed value of unskilled labour(g) | | 90 | 50 | 85 | 90 | 45 |
| Total | | 370 | 308 | 580 | 397 | 381 |

NOTES:  (a) The house and payments had not been completed.
(b) Five related *matai* shared this house.
(c) Imputed values: '*ietōga*—£5; *siapo* (tapa cloth)—6s; sleeping-mats —£1
(d) The carpenter was related and received no payment.
(e) Formal payment only. Money was usually given to the carpenter on request throughout the work period for a variety of purposes, such as for cigarettes, fares etc.
(f) Formal distribution of money and '*ietōga* to the village *matai* and pastor
(g) Unskilled labour valued at 1s 6d an hour. The estimates of hours are very rough.

and it apparently had come to an end by the time of the survey. It was extremely difficult to obtain reasonably accurate data on the costs of this '*āiga* investment as records were not kept and the various costs and payments were, in most cases, spread over two or three years. Several of the large *fale* and houses were not yet finished and the owners had but vague plans for completion. Very rough estimates of the cash and subsistence costs of the five open-houses built in Taga since 1960, based on the recollected cash and subsistence payments made, and an informed guess at the quantity of unskilled '*āiga* labour used, are given in Table 22. The

usual sort of open-house contained purchased materials, such as
cement, roofing iron and timber, costing between £200 and £300.
This, of course, varied with the size and finish of the building as
did the investment of subsistence labour. The quantity of subsistence
valuables given to the carpenter and village varied on a completely
different basis. It was related more to the social ambitions of the
*matai* and '*āiga* than to the size and quality of the dwelling.

Only one of the five open-houses appeared to have been financed
largely from cash cropping. The cash earnings of the '*āiga* concerned
over the four years when its house was being built was roughly
£1,350 (copra—£1,000; bananas—£350) and the open-house
represented an investment of about fifteen per cent of this plus the
labour and other subsistence resources involved. Probably a small
open-house built for five related '*āiga* (a split title) was also financed
largely from copra and bananas but there was also money coming
in from New Zealand. The other three had been financed largely
from wages and remittances from New Zealand. One was built
with money earned during the years when the *matai* served as the
district representative in the Legislative Assembly; another was
financed largely with money sent from New Zealand, and the
third was financed largely by two men who held wage jobs in Samoa.

Then there were two large two-storey non-traditional *fale*. One
was built in 1964 by a teacher after he received a Taga title. It
was financed entirely from his salary. After the building was completed he worked in New Zealand for six months and, on his
return, he invested part of his New Zealand savings in a small shop.
The other two-storey non-traditional *fale* (1964-) was also financed
largely from wage earnings.

While there were exceptions, it was clear that a large proportion
of the money invested in '*āiga* buildings in Taga since 1960 came
from sources other than village cash cropping.[20] In each case, of
course, there was also a substantial investment from the subsistence
sector in the form of labour, food and traditional valuables. The
relatively high cash cost of these buildings was not typical of '*āiga*
buildings as a whole, but only of the larger dwellings built in recent
years. Many traditional *fale* were built in the same period, almost
entirely with subsistence resources.

The '*āiga* dwellings in Taga are valued at £8,700, of which
£5,986 (sixty-nine per cent) represented the investment of sub-

[20] This pattern, in which non-traditional '*āiga* buildings with large cash components in their total costs were financed largely by income from wages and
remittances from abroad, was observed also in the other villages studied. One
example already described was the sole open-house in Uafato which had been
financed by remittances from American Samoa.

sistence resources—labour and materials.[21] The use or 'rental'
value of these dwellings is estimated to be £396, or £0·8 per
consumption unit a year.[22]

### (c) *Household durables*

Most Taga '*āiga* owned wooden chests, foodsafes, beds and other
items described earlier for Uafato, and in much the same quantities.
In Taga, however, the pastor and Tialavea (the Burns Philp
trader) had furnished their dwellings in the European style and
several other '*āiga* also owned various items of western furniture,
such as wardrobes, sideboards and chests of drawers, which were
not found in Uafato at all. Usually those '*āiga* with non-traditional
dwellings also owned pieces of non-traditional furniture. As with
the non-traditional dwellings, the accumulation of non-traditional
furniture represented the investment of money rather than subsistence resources. Tialavea spent four months in New Zealand
at the beginning of the survey and he brought back a second-hand
dining-room suite and a bedroom suite.

In most '*āiga* pandanus and coconut-leaf mats formed the basic
items of household furniture, as in Uafato. Compared with Uafato,
however, the supply was considerably greater.[23] Two factors partly
explain this difference: (1) in Uafato much of the pandanus raw
material available was used to produce tablemats and baskets for
sale rather than to produce mats for village use; and (2) Taga
received many more visitors than did Uafato and there was greater
need to maintain stocks of sleeping-mats for the visitors and for
gifts. Over the New-Year week the Taga Women's Committee
went on a *picnic*, that is, they arranged to take Kauli Long's bus
for the day to drive to Asaga on the east coast of the island. For
this service each woman gave Kauli Long 2s plus one sleeping-mat.
The use of the sleeping-mat in the traditional payment to carpenters
and other craftsmen was described earlier and this was an interesting
variation since a bus ride was hardly a traditional service. Altogether
there was more opportunity to use mats in traditional payments in
Taga than in the still isolated Uafato.

[21] The Taga '*āiga* buildings have been valued on the same basis as those of
Uafato and set out on p. 59. There was a significant increase in the proportion
of the value of dwellings which originated in the monetized sector between Uafato
and Taga—from 10% in Uafato to 31% in Taga. This increased contribution to
the value of dwellings from the monetized sector makes it less realistic to consider
the 'rental' value of dwellings as a component of subsistence income; but this
method has been used for convenience.

[22] This is close to the estimate for Uafato of £0·7 per consumption unit.

[23] The estimated stock of mats etc., held in Taga is valued at £1,711, or £4·82
per consumption unit. The values per consumption unit in the other villages
studied were as follows: Uafato—£2·73; Poutasi—£5·31; and Utuali'i—£2·34.

Taga was the only village of the four studied where *'ietōga* were still made by most women. This practice had virtually died out in Upolu but was still found in most Savai'i villages where people were considered to be more traditionally minded. Certainly the linkage between many Savai'i villages and the market sector, particularly with Apia, was generally weaker than that of the Upolu villages and the construction of roads, which made the populations of the villages much more mobile, was more recent in Savai'i. But five years after the Taga road was opened the women staged a *fuataga*, a village display of newly-made *'ietōga* (about 200), and the Women's Committee planned another one in 1967. With constant work, a fast weaver can finish an *'ietōga* of the coarsest type in three or four weeks. When the job is taken up in 'spare moments' it might take three or four months. Between 200 and 300 hours were needed to complete one *'ietōga* and the 200 displayed in Taga in January 1965 represented between 40,000 and 60,000 hours' work over six months by about ninety women—roughly twenty hours a week each. The weaver's reward for her effort was her satisfaction when her *'āiga* would present an *'ietōga*, the most highly valued of the Samoan ceremonial items, at some important occasion such as a funeral or the granting of a *matai* title. During the survey most women were making *'ietōga*, but the stocks in the village were small.[24] As soon as a new *'ietōga* was finished there would usually be some occasion for it to be presented by the *matai* as a gift, or it would be requested by some other *matai* who had need for one.

Taga *'āiga* owned household utensils and other purchased goods similar to those described for Uafato. The estimated value of these commodities is £682, which, in per consumption unit terms is almost double that recorded for Uafato.[25] As many of these goods were used only when there were guests, and the Taga *'āiga* had ready access to trading-stations which stocked a wide range of such items, it was not surprising that this difference between Taga and Uafato was found.

## 2. Market

Copra and cacao were the two main cash crops in Taga before 1960. With the opening of the road in that year a third crop,

---

[24] At one count during the survey the stocks of *'ietōga* held by the sample *'āiga* were as follows: Taga—42; Poutasi—17; Uafato—9; and Utuali'i—4. Valued at £5 each this gave a value per consumption unit of £1·35 in Taga, £0·50 in Poutasi, £0·39 in Uafato, and £0·24 in Utuali'i. Although the stocks were small in Taga they were still considerably larger than those of the other villages studied—a situation undoubtedly due to the continued manufacture of these valuables in Taga.

[25] The value of these items per consumption unit in Uafato was £1·06.

bananas, was added, and in 1965 the facilities of the Banana Scheme were used by the Marketing Division of the Department of Agriculture to provide an export marketing outlet for taro. Taga was the only village of the four studied which had been encouraged to produce taro for export through these facilities.

There was a small internal market for village produce. Fish was the commodity most frequently sold, but the survey recorded occasional sales of other commodities in the village, such as crabs, crayfish, octopus, pigs, tomatoes, eggs, chickens, sleeping-mats, fishing-goggles,[26] *siapo*, *lau'ie*,[27] and a Samoan cricket bat. Commercial transactions between individuals and *'āiga* were uncommon, and quantitatively they were very small, but they were found more frequently in Taga than in the other villages surveyed. This appeared to be related to the growing social fragmentation of the village as evidenced by the splitting of titles, the movement of a fairly large part of the population to houseland along the road, the division of the Women's Committee between the upper and lower village, and dissension in the *fono* and *'aumāga*.

(a) *Copra and cacao*

Before the 1920s Taga copra was sold at Sala'ilua after an eight-mile trip by canoe or whaleboat, usually in rough and dangerous seas. In the 1920s two trading-stations were established in Taga— O. F. Nelson and Burns Philp—giving Taga producers their first local marketing facilities. The stations were serviced by launches owned by the parent companies and, in addition to supplying the stations with stock and shipping village copra and cacao out, these improved communication between Taga and Apia. Taga continued to rely on the launch service until 1960 when the road was opened and a daily bus service was established.

Records kept at the Apia offices of O. F. Nelson and Burns Philp show that the average annual production over the five years 1948-52 was 278,562 pounds of copra (sun-dried) and 47,589 pounds of cacao beans. This gave the village an average annual cash income of £6,294, or approximately £20 per head. The only other period for which complete records were found were the years 1961 to 1965. There had been a considerable fall in the quantities of copra and cacao bought by the two trading-stations, to an average of 87,096 pounds of copra, and 17,258 pounds of cacao a year, giving an average annual income of £2,689, or approximately £5 per head (Table 23).

[26] Made for sale by one *matai* who sold three or four pairs a year at 4s each.
[27] Dried leaves of a variety of pandanus used to make *'ietōga*. The process of preparing the *lau'ie* was complicated and time-consuming.

Table 23    Copra and Cacao Purchased by the Two Taga
Trading-Stations 1948-52 and 1961-5

| | COPRA | | CACAO | | Total cash paid to village |
|---|---|---|---|---|---|
| | Quantity | Cash paid[a] | Quantity | Cash paid[a] | |
| | (lbs) | (£) | (lbs) | (£) | (£) |
| 1948 | 291,889 | 3,211 | 27,426 | 1,310 | 4,521 |
| 49 | 351,368 | 3,874 | 42,742 | 1,496 | 5,370 |
| 50 | 366,995 | 4,154 | 51,595 | 3,779 | 7,933 |
| 51 | 238,462 | 3,156 | 85,045 | 6,740 | 9,896 |
| 52 | 144,098 | 2,286 | 21,137 | 1,464 | 3,750 |
| Annual average | | | | | |
| 1948-52 | 278,562 | 3,336 | 47,589 | 2,958 | 6,294 |
| 1961[b] | 120,925 | 1,478 | 6,952 | 440 | 1,918 |
| 62 | 81,425 | 892 | 41,909 | 3,001 | 3,893 |
| 63 | 60,842 | 814 | 15,205 | 684 | 1,498 |
| 64 | 104,436 | 3,290 | 12,962 | 447 | 3,737 |
| 65 | 67,854 | 2,198 | 9,262 | 204 | 2,402 |
| Annual average | | | | | |
| 1948-52 | 87,096 | 1,734 | 17,258 | 955 | 2,690 |

SOURCE:  O. F. Nelson & Co. Ltd., Burns Philp (South-Sea) Co. Ltd., Apia
NOTES:    [a] Includes commission paid to the two Taga traders.
          [b] After 1960 a proportion of Taga copra and cacao was sold in other
          villages. This was not possible earlier and the 1945-52 figures
          represent total production in those years.

The decline in the business of the two village stores does not measure a decline in village output although cacao production did fall off. After 1960, with regular bus services to other parts of Savai'i, Taga producers started to sell their copra and cacao in other villages. After 1963 Kauli Long could sell his copra and cacao, and that of his father-in-law and probably of other *matai* as well in Salelologa, at no cost apart from the effort needed to load and unload his bus. Other *matai* were able to take their copra and cacao by bus when travelling to Salelologa on business. Copra prices at the ferry terminal were slightly higher than in Taga[28] and this at least covered the cash freight cost of about 2s a bag of 200-300 pounds, although not the bus fare of eight to ten shillings return, or the labour cost of over four hours on the bus and two to five hours at Salelologa. There was no cash cost involved in selling copra in the village. Except in the special case of Kauli Long (and his relatives and friends), it did not appear at first sight to be an economic proposition for Taga producers to take copra to Salelologa unless

[28] £1 18s 6d in Taga and £2 in Salelologa per 100 lbs hot-air dried No. 1 copra, in 1965-6.

they could 'charge' the costs of the journey to some other necessary business. Nevertheless, after 1960 a large proportion of Taga copra was sold in Salelologa.

One reason for this was the not infrequent practice of placing a ban on '*āiga* production and sale of copra so that money could be raised for various village and church purposes.[29] In 1958 this method was used to collect money for a Congregational Church fund—the *Taulaga mo Samoa*. The *Taulaga mo Samoa* was an annual collection of funds for the Samoan church and the average Taga contribution between 1950 and 1965 was under £250. But a special effort was made in 1958 to compete with other villages in the district and Taga raised £1,000. There was usually some such project under way and in each year since 1948 copra production and sale was banned from four to six months. After 1960 the '*āiga* were able partly to contravene the ban by producing small quantities of copra and selling it at Salelologa. It was after 1960 also that the *matai* changed the method of collecting the nuts and making the copra at the conclusion of each ban period. Earlier this had been a community effort using the '*aumāga* and Women's Committee, but under the new system each '*āiga* was made responsible for its own lands. Each was expected to contribute the full value of the copra resulting from the nuts which had accumulated during the period of the ban. It was difficult to avoid this if it were all sold in Taga, but it could be avoided partly by selling the copra in Salelologa. So the Taga '*āiga* were prepared to accept high cash and labour costs to market copra so that they could retain a larger part of the proceeds. For the '*āiga* concerned it was a sound economic proposition.

Much of the cement, roofing iron and other material used in Taga non-traditional dwellings after 1960 were bought at Salelologa where stocks were held in the three large stores. Some of this was bought on credit and copra was taken to Salelologa to repay debts. Regular sales of copra to the Salelologa stores could have meant more liberal credit arrangements and most *matai* liked to spread

[29] For several months during each year the production and sale of copra by the '*āiga* was banned. At the end of each one or two months period of the ban, the '*aumāga* was instructed to collect all fallen coconuts and to heap them in the *malae*. These would then be husked (mainly by the women) and the flesh dried and sold. In this way the whole copra output of the Taga coconut lands for several months in the year would be diverted from '*āiga* use to village use. After 1960 this rigid system was broken down by a decision of the *fono* in keeping with the general tendency towards greater '*āiga* independence. Henceforth the '*āiga* would collect and process the nuts from their own small-holding at the end of each period of the ban on copra production and they would contribute the cash proceeds to the village. This, of course, made it easy for the '*āiga* to retain part of the proceeds for their own use. When money was being raised for the school (under the old system), each two-month ban yielded between £300 and £400. In 1965, under the new method, a two-month ban realized only £175.

their sales between various stores so that their total credit allowance could be maximized.

A third reason for selling produce in Salelologa was that the stores there stocked a greater variety of goods than those in Taga and prices for some goods were lower. Salelologa was the nearest centre where the stores were appreciably better than those in the village and most Taga shoppers went there for special or bulk purchases. On such trips, and others made to the neighbouring government offices and Law Courts at Tuasivi, copra could be taken and sold at no extra cost except the freight charge which usually would be more than covered by the higher prices paid.

With the exception of the new coconut plantings of Kauli Long and Tialavea the village coconut plantations had not expanded much after about 1920. Most palms were over fifty years old and with the initially high planting density increased by many self-sown palms the output of the plantation probably had declined in recent years. At the same time population was increasing and with it the consumption of nuts for food. In 1966 nearly thirty per cent of the output of Taga coconut plantations was consumed in the village (Table 23).

Cacao had been planted in Taga at two periods; during the 1930s when it was interplanted with coconuts along the 'eastern stream'[30] and then, after 1945, along the track to Sala'ilua. The earlier planting was no longer productive but the second continued to bear and was being harvested before the hurricane. As with the coconuts, an increasing proportion of a declining output was consumed in the village, and the marketed surplus was falling annually. Altogether about half the copra and cacao produced since 1960 was sold out of the village, mostly at Salelologa.

Most 'āiga sold sun-dried or green copra, as there were only three hot-air dryers in the village. Tialavea bought nuts, undried copra and dried copra, while the Nelson's trading-station bought only dried copra. The labour survey showed that an average of six hours was needed to gather, husk and carry 230 mature coconuts (sufficient to give 100 lbs of copra) down to the village.[31] A further 2·6 hours was needed to remove the kernels and half an hour to tend to the drying. It normally took another half an hour to carry the copra to the store. At £1 16s 0d for 100 pounds of sun-dried first-quality copra the cash returns per hour of labour in production and marketing averaged 3s 8d. Cash returns on copra taken in

---

[30] In 1957 the villagers regarded any cacao harvested from their trees as 'good fortune' (Barrett 1959, p. 210).

[31] The following estimates are based on the average times needed to produce and sell 100 lbs of copra.

relatively small quantities by bus to Salelologa, with only two hours and a one-way fare included as the marketing cost, was about 3s 1d per hour, but if the time and fares were discounted (when on other business, for example), the return was about 3s 9d. On undried copra sold in Taga at the regulation price of 19s 3d per 100 pounds[32] it was only about 2s 1d an hour. Cash returns on coconuts (unhusked) sold in Taga were similar to those in Uafato, about 5s 10d an hour,[33] but this gave the lowest total cash return to the plantations.

### (b) *Bananas and taro*

Bananas were first sold in 1961[34] through the Banana Scheme, and in the following three years production increased rapidly to a peak in 1964 of 8,565 cases, earning the village a cash income of £4,711 or slightly more than copra at its peak in 1950.[35] In 1951 more than this was earned from cacao. The average annual income from cacao between 1948 and 1952 (£2,958) exceeded that from bananas between 1962 and 1965 (£2,677). During 1965 banana production declined as bunchytop spread through the plantations and it is certain that little if any income will be earned from the remnants of the banana plots which might recover from the hurricane. Only £260 was earned from bananas during the period covered by the survey, all of this before the hurricane.

Taro was in its infancy as a cash crop, but many expected it to have a bright future. The pastor, for one, had no doubts about this and he was depending on money earned from taro to finance his new house.[36] It appears that taro was a more profitable crop than bananas at the price paid by the Department of Agriculture in 1966.[37] From the labour survey it was estimated that about 6s an hour could be earned in the production and sale of taro, compared with about 4s for bananas. The export market for taro (New Zealand) was limited, however, and it may never be quantitatively as important.

### 3. *The effect of social and organizational institutions on production*

The social and organizational institutions in Taga, the *fono*, Women's Committee, and *'aumāga*, were similar to those described

[32] See Table 49.
[33] One shilling for eight nuts.
[34] With the exception of bananas shipped to Apia by Tiatia on the Burns Philp launch during the 1950s.
[35] See Appendix Table 5. This may have been exceeded between 1953 and 1960 but the incomplete records for these years, as far as they go, suggest not.
[36] He was later shown to be correct. Much of the money earned by the *'aumāga* taro plots towards the end of 1966 and in 1967 went to pay for his house.
[37] 25s a case containing between 50 and 60 lbs of taro.

for Uafato, but in general they had less influence on the direction and level of demand and production.

Since 1960 there had been no village-level capital works of importance in Taga, but on the other hand there had been a great deal of capital accumulation at the *'āiga* level. This took two main forms: (1) the clearing of forest land along the road and (2) the building of large, in some cases non-traditional, dwellings.[38] The incentive offered by improved marketing facilities for village cash crops, particularly bananas, led to the clearing of forest land close to the road, on which banana production could be increased. Something of a social and political power struggle between two groups of *'āiga* and *matai* in the villages led to attempts by some to increase their prestige and status through the acquisition of new land and the construction of impressive dwellings. These two factors were not unrelated and it appeared that the new economic opportunities offered by the road provided some *'āiga* with both an opportunity and an excuse for open opposition to the authority of the high-status *matai*. A much more intensive study would have to be undertaken in Taga to examine this in any detail but some of the more obvious manifestations were seen during the survey. First there was the fragmentation of several large *'āiga* between 1955 and 1962 giving *matai* status and control over land to a number of relatively young men. This was partly a desire on their part to have an independent source of cash income, but there may have been other, possibly more important, social and political motives. During the survey there appeared to be less sharing of subsistence output between *'āiga* than in the other villages, and commercial transactions between *'āiga* were more frequent. This suggests that social friction in the village led to some decline in the socially regulated non-market exchange system.

During the survey an open break occurred in the Women's Committee; the women from the upper-village withdrew from the old Committee and held their own meetings. There was talk that the upper-village *matai* might withdraw from the *fono*, but this did not happen during the survey.[39] There was, however, some friction in the *fono* over the post-hurricane taro inspections which resulted in the upper-village *matai* inspecting the plantings of their *'āiga* only, and the lower-village *matai* inspecting those of their *'āiga* only. After the hurricane, the upper-village *taulele'a* combined (as an *'aumāga*) to plant taro as a cash crop. Two or three weeks later the

[38] Some of this investment, both in clearing land and building, pre-dated the completion of the road in 1960, but it was clear that anticipation of the road was an important incentive.

[39] The upper-village contained most of the *'āiga* which had split their titles between many holders.

lower-village *taulele'a* followed suit in another location. This sort of fragmentation of authority at the *'āiga* and village level is not uncommon in Samoa:

> Opposition [to authority] may become so fundamental as to result in schismatic segmentation of hitherto integrated elite organizations. This process has apparently been at work throughout Samoan history. . . . Tendencies to factionalism, however, are particularly relevant to an understanding of the modern situation, as such segmentation processes appear to have been accelerating. The security values of alliance and the grim decisions and consolidations of the scene of war which were characteristic of old Samoa are no longer part of the scene where the white man's force keeps peace. Ethnological analysis shows that a number of extended family units [*'āiga*] have been breaking up, with former single titles being split among various family branches, together with lands and honours; the main divisive factor here seems to have been inability to agree on or to force a decision relative to title succession. As an extreme instance, one such title now has approximately a score of holders in different localities. A number of cases have also occurred where there had been a village division on vital issues, and because of pride and strong family feeling the split has tended to persist for years or permanently. For practical purposes the factions thus established form separate villages, with correspondingly lessened political and prestige importance, and also losses in pleasant social rapport and cohesion. (Keesing and Keesing 1956, p. 122)

The effect of this fragmentation of authority on the demand for and production of goods and services was not overtly apparent, except perhaps in the increase in *'āiga* rather than village capital works. When the Women's Committee divided, each part carried on as before and held inspections of pandanus-weaving and household goods in the *'āiga* of its members. The only change here may have been an increase in output resulting from the competition between the two groups. It was apparent before the hurricane that the upper-village women were less enthusiastic about raising money for a new house for the pastor than were those of the lower-village, and the formal division of the committee came, in fact, after disagreement on how the money raised in 1965 for the pastor's house should be used.[40] It is possible that this disagreement extended into the *fono* and that it did delay the raising of money and the actual construction.[41]

Past investment in village capital works had been similar to

[40] Apparently the upper-village women wanted to use the £120 raised in 1965 for the pastor's house to buy flour and rice to supplement the dwindling supplies of subsistence foods.

[41] Discussion of the pastor's house had started after the school was built in 1960, and it was (naturally) encouraged by the pastor. A start was not made on the building until the end of 1967.

that of Uafato. The large church and a small clinic were built in 1952.[42] Local timber was used in parts of these buildings but most timber was shipped from Apia along with the cement, roofing-iron, nails, glass and paint. An Apia builder was employed (in the custom-ary way) and the village provided the unskilled labour force. The church, a 6,500 square feet (130′ × 50′ approx.) building of solid unreinforced concrete construction, with two rows of five concrete pillars supporting the elaborately decorated ceiling and roof, needed well over 1,000 bags of cement, and this, with the other material purchased, had to be transferred from a launch to the shore in whaleboats and canoes. No record had been kept, but it probably cost over £3,000 plus the labour of the village and the traditional valuables and food given to the carpenter.[43]

Much earlier, in 1924 according to one old *matai*, the village built a very large *fale* (about 100 feet long) to house the pastor, and this was still in excellent condition in 1966. Up to 1960 the village school consisted of a number of *fale* in the *malae*. Another earlier capital work had been the construction of a cement and stone wall around a large washing pool at the side of the church.

Between about 1957 and 1960 a great deal of unskilled labour was used on the road. It was organized by the *fono* in much the same way as described earlier for Uafato. During 1960 the village invested labour and cash in a new school building. The pastor thought that about £800 had been collected in the village by subscription to pay for the material and the services of a carpenter. Tialavea was en-gaged as the builder. Again the village provided the unskilled labour and some of the timber from the subsistence sector.

For each of the buildings requiring material and services from the cash sector money was raised in the village partly by subscrip-tion (as in Uafato) but mainly through the production and sale of copra at the village level.

Table 24 gives rough estimates of investment in social and village capital, namely '*āiga* dwellings and household durables, and village and church buildings. It is estimated that about fifty-seven per cent of the investment in these items was of subsistence resources, and forty-three per cent (about £6,521) represents the investment of money in the purchase of market sector material, commodities and services. The cash component was slightly lower than in Uafato (forty-eight per cent) but the total level of this investment per consumption unit was slightly higher. (Taga—£43; Uafato—£40).

---

[42] In 1952 Tiatia also built the first non-traditional dwelling in the village.
[43] Records of the cash cost of the Utuali'i church are given in Chapter Seven, and the example given of Patamea church in the previous chapter applies equally well here also.

Table 24   Taga: Social and Village Capital[a]

|  | Total | Cash component | Subsistence component |
|---|---|---|---|
|  | £ | % | % |
| *'Āiga*: |  |  |  |
| Dwellings | 8,700 | 31 | 69 |
| Furniture | 236 | 50 | 50 |
| Mats etc. | 1,711 | 18 | 82 |
| Utensils & equipment | 683 | 100 | 00 |
| Total | 11,330 | 34 | 66 |
| Village: | 1,781 | 67 | 33 |
| Church: | 2,019 | 74 | 26 |
| Total investment | 15,130 | 43 | 57 |
| Investment per consumption unit[b] | £40 | £19 | £24 |

NOTES:   [a] Estimated costs of the social and village capital existing in 1966

[b] Estimated costs of capital items existing in 1966 divided by the number of consumption units

### INCOME

Estimates of subsistence and cash incomes for Taga over the twelve months December 1965 to November 1966 are given in Table 25.

The imputed value of subsistence income is £12,454 or £34 per consumption unit. In consumption unit terms this was slightly higher than in Uafato (£28·1) but the difference is due mainly to the fortuitously better supply of taro in Taga after the hurricane. There was also a relatively minor difference in the income derived from household durables and this was due mainly to the temporary shortage of pandanus leaves in Uafato. Under more normal circumstances there was not likely to have been a significant difference between Taga and Uafato in their levels of subsistence income.

Cash income in Taga on the other hand was significantly higher than in Uafato. It is estimated to have been £7,210, giving £20 per consumption unit compared to £13·7 in Uafato. This gave Taga a higher level of total income—subsistence plus cash—£54 compared to £45 in Uafato, and a higher monetization factor—thirty-seven per cent as against thirty per cent.

Almost seventy per cent of Taga's cash income was earned through the sale of agricultural products of which copra was by far the most important. Copra provided £3,842 out of the total from agriculture and fishing of £4,946 and the total cash income of £7,210. Remittances from overseas, mainly from New Zealand,

Table 25   Taga: Subsistence and Cash Incomes[a]

| | | Village | | Per consumption unit |
|---|---:|---:|---:|---:|
| | | £ | | £ |
| **SUBSISTENCE** (non-monetary) **INCOME** | | | | |
| Food: | | 11,143 | | 30·6 |
| coconuts[b] | 1,231 | | 3·4 | |
| bananas & breadfruit[c] | 1,380 | | 3·8 | |
| taro and ta'amū[c] | 8,197 | | 22·5 | |
| fish | 149 | | ·4 | |
| pork and chicken[d] | 186 | | ·5 | |
| Buildings: | | 445 | | 1·0 |
| 'āiga | 387 | | ·8 | |
| village | 36 | | ·1 | |
| church | 22 | | ·1 | |
| Household durables: | | 691 | | 1·9 |
| Tools and equipment: | | 175 | | ·5 |
| Total subsistence income | | £12,454 | | £34·0 |
| **CASH INCOME** | | | | |
| Agriculture and fishing: | | 4,946 | | 13·6 |
| bananas | 260 | | ·7 | |
| copra and coconuts | 3,842 | | 10·6 | |
| taro | 589 | | 1·6 | |
| fish | 95 | | ·3 | |
| other | 160 | | ·4 | |
| Wages: | | 571 | | 1·6 |
| Remittances from Apia: | | 575 | | 1·6 |
| Remittances from abroad: | | 898 | | 2·5 |
| Gifts: | | 95 | | ·3 |
| Department of Agriculture prize: | | 125 | | ·4 |
| Total cash income | | £7,210 | | £20·0 |
| **TOTAL INCOME**[e] | | £19,664 | | £54·0 |
| Monetization factor[f] | | 37% | | |

NOTES:   [a] 12 months, December 1965-November 1966

[b] Average per consumption units a week of 6·9 coconuts as food plus 4·1 fed to pigs and chickens; valued at village store buying price of 1s for 8 nuts.

[c] Based on Appendix Table 2 with quantities valued at pre-hurricane market prices in Apia:—taro—6d per lb., ta'amū and breadfruit—4d per lb. and bananas—3d per lb.

[d] A rough estimate of quantity based on observation and valued at 2s per lb. for pork and 2s each for chickens.

[e] Aggregate of imputed value of subsistence income and cash income; intended only for inter-village comparisons.

[f] Proportion of cash income on total income

was an important item giving the village nearly £900. Wages earned in the village and remittances from Apia contributed £1,146 and there was a £125 bonus earned by winning a Department of Agriculture prize for clearing scrub and undergrowth from agricultural lands.

Table 26   Taga: Cash Outlay[a]

| | Village | | Per consumption unit | | Percentage |
|---|---|---|---|---|---|
| | £ | £ | £ | £ | % |
| 'Āiga | | 5,999 | | 16·4 | 92 |
| Food | 2,881 | | 7·9 | | 44 |
| Other commodities | 1,337 | | 3·6 | | 20 |
| Local fares | 1,091 | | 3·0 | | 17 |
| Schooling | 450 | | 1·2 | | 7 |
| Gifts | 240 | | ·7 | | 4 |
| Church and pastor | | 397 | | 1·1 | 6 |
| Village | | 120 | | ·3 | 2 |
| Total | | 6,516 | | 17·8 | 100 |

NOTE:   [a] 12 months, December 1965–November 1966

OUTLAY

Estimates of cash outlay for the twelve months, December 1965 to November 1966, are summarized in Table 26.

1. *Cash expenditure on goods and services*

About £2,881 or £7·9 per consumption unit was spent on food during the twelve-month period; forty-four per cent of the total cash outlay. The most important commodities bought are shown in Table 27. To put these purchases in perspective, average consumption per consumption unit a week was only one pound of sugar, five ounces of herrings, half a pound of flour and rice, and one ounce of corned beef. The consumption of flour and rice was actually slightly higher than this due to the free issue of twenty-seven bags of flour and fifty-two bags of rice by the Hurricane Relief Committee in June. This raised temporarily the average level of consumption to about fourteen ounces a week. The average weekly consumption of subsistence staples was around twenty-three pounds.[44] Rice and flour were fairly standard food items before the hurricane, particularly for schoolchildren. Sugar was used by most

[44] See Appendix Table 2.

Table 27   Taga: Commodity Purchases[a]

|  | Expenditure | | | Main shopping centres | | |
|---|---|---|---|---|---|---|
|  | Village | per con-sumption unit | per-centage | Taga | Salelo-loga | Other |
|  | £ | £ | % | % | % | % |
| Food: |  |  |  |  |  |  |
| sugar | 776 | 2·1 | 18 | 95 | 5 | — |
| flour, rice, bread | 654 | 1·8 | 16 | 58 | 40 | 2 |
| fish[b] | 560 | 1·5 | 13 | 95 | 5 | — |
| meat[c] | 448 | 1·3 | 11 | 77 | 23 | — |
| dripping, salt etc. | 166 | ·5 | 4 | 94 | 4 | 2 |
| tea, coffee, cocoa | 118 | ·3 | 3 | 90 | 5 | 5 |
| dairy products | 88 | ·2 | 2 | 100 | — | — |
| other foods | 71 | ·2 | 2 | 73 | 24 | 3 |
|  | 2,881 | 7·9 | 68 | 83 | 16 | 1 |
| Other: |  |  |  |  |  |  |
| household | 358 | 1·0 | 9 | 67 | 33 | — |
| individual | 263 | ·7 | 6 | 77 | 1 | 22 |
| kerosene, benzene | 260 | ·7 | 6 | 99 | 1 | — |
| soap | 228 | ·6 | 5 | 90 | 6 | 4 |
| tobacco | 228 | ·6 | 5 | 78 | 19 | 3 |
|  | 1,337 | 3·6 | 32 | 81 | 14 | 5 |
| All commodities | 4,218 | 11·5 | 100 | 83 | 15 | 2 |

NOTES:   [a] 12 months, December 1965-November 1966
         [b] 100% tinned fish
         [c] 78% tinned meat

'*āiga* each day—it was the most frequently bought commodity in all villages.

Tinned herrings formed a particularly important item in the Taga diet because there was little fresh fish available. At one shilling and eightpence for a sixteen-ounce tin it was the cheapest source of protein available in the stores. It was also a prestige food (as was virtually anything bought in the stores) and was usually provided at the Sunday feasts and other special meals. Tinned meat, mainly corned beef, was a prestige item, but because of its cost (four shillings and sixpence a pound for the cheapest brand) it was served less frequently than herrings. Fresh meat was not sold in the Taga stores but could be bought at Salelologa. Bread was not available in the Taga stores either but again it could be bought at Salelologa. None of the Taga stores sold pancakes (as did those in Uafato and Poutasi), but in March the lower-village Women's Committee tried to raise money by doing this. The venture was unsuccessful and ceased after about two weeks. Hard sea biscuits were bought for special occasions. When I visited Taga for the first time the *matai* came to the pastor's *fale* (where I was staying) to share an early morning meal and hear what I had to say about the proposed survey in their village. This meal consisted of ten pounds of hard sea biscuits (with jam supplied by me) and hot, very sweet cocoa.[45] Much of the cash expenditure on bakery goods recorded for Taga consisted of biscuits, most of which were taken (by the ten- or fifteen-pound tin) to funerals.

Powdered and evaporated milk were not in general use although they were available in the Taga stores. Purchases of these commodities were recorded only for '*āiga* with a higher than usual level of education or which had frequent contacts with Europeans or with the urban life of Apia.

The commodity group listed as 'dripping, salt etc.' and shown to rank fifth in terms of cash outlay, is a catchall in which are included such items as salt, pepper, curry powder, baking soda and tomato sauce.

Cash expenditure on commodities other than food was about £1,337 or £3·6 per consumption unit for the year—twenty per cent of the total cash outlay. Soap, fuel for lamps, and tobacco were important and regularly bought commodities included here. Household and individual goods are also catchall groups including such items as enamel plates and mugs, cotton material for sheets and clothing, hair oil and combs, bush knives and playing cards, benzene lamps and replacement parts, and so on. Only about nine per cent of cash expenditure was spent on these items.

Most services available in Taga, and the other villages, were in the subsistence sector. These were many and varied and no attempt was made to record or value them. The main purchased services were those of the schools, and the local buses. School fees and related expenses cost the village an estimated £450, or £1·2 per consumption unit, during the twelve-month period (covering the fees etc. for the 1966 school year). Uafato spent almost the same amount per consumption unit. About £1,091, or £3 per consumption unit, was spent on bus and ferry fares and freight, almost double that of Uafato. The same fare (8s return) was paid between Taga and Salelologa, as between Uafato and Apia, and these journeys were made with about the same frequency from each village. The high

---

[45] On a similar occasion in Uafato the meal consisted of village produced pancakes instead of biscuits.

expenditure on fares in Taga is due largely to the high cash cost (£1 10s return) of the less frequently made journeys to Apia.

Sometimes the payment for services had both cash and subsistence components. When the women hired Kauli Long's bus for their New Year *picnic*, they paid him 2s plus one pandanus sleeping-mat each. It was more common, however, to find what were normally subsistence services, particularly those of high status such as house-building and massaging, being paid for in the traditional way with subsistence valuables (*'ietōga*, sleeping-mats etc.) and an additional sum of money. This cash payment was often given 'apologetically' with a casual statement to the effect that 'it is only for fares'. It was of course in recognition of a probable cash cost in giving the service (perhaps only fares), but also, and more importantly, the knowledge that the skilled person would most certainly demand money if it was not forthcoming. An example of this recorded in Taga and Poutasi was payment for the services of a masseuse brought in from another village. The masseuse lived with the Taga *'āiga* for two weeks while treating an old man and when she left she was given ten pandanus sleeping-mats and £5.

The only other services recorded in the cash sector were the use of a billiard table (two were available) and of Tialavea's copra dryer and truck. The billiard tables were seldom used during most of the survey period due to the death of the owner's wife in one case, and the removal of Tialavea's house in the other. Tialavea charged 5s for the use of his dryer (he supplied the wood and labour). On one occasion Tialavea charged a *matai* £3 for carting sand in his truck.

Cash expenditure on services other than schooling fares and freight was very small and for this reason it has not been shown as a separate item in Table 25; where such items of expenditure were recorded, they were included under individual commodity expenditure.

## 2. *Shopping facilities and centres for Taga buyers*

Before 1960 Taga buyers had to do most of their shopping in the Nelson and Burns Philp trading-stations in the village.[46] No doubt travellers to Apia brought back goods which were not stocked in Taga but travel was difficult and Taga people tended to stay at home.[47] The two trading-stations could fill orders for most items likely to be wanted in the village. After the road went through in 1960 shoppers could leave the village by bus on any day of the week, and there was much more shopping in Salelologa and

[46] The trading-stations were stocked with a wide range and variety of goods, and prices generally were no more than 10% higher than those of Apia.

[47] Barrett 1959, pp. 201-5; Fairbairn 1963, pp. 348-9.

Sala'ilua. Journeys to Apia were also more frequent, but because of the costs involved they generally were not made only for shopping. Two new locally owned shops opened in Taga after 1962, both located near the road. One of them had already closed down before the survey started and only the concrete foundations remained.[48] The second store was built by a *matai* after his return from New Zealand in 1964. It was similar in many respects to the small stores in Uafato but the owner had not started to trade in nuts or to buy village copra. His store was conveniently located for families living at the north-western end of the village and along the road; they were his best customers for commodities like sugar, dripping, soap, rice and kerosene.

The Taga stores were adequately stocked with the commodities in common use in the village, and about eighty-three per cent of the purchases recorded for the sample '*āiga* were from them (Table 27). This was unlike the Uafato situation where only a few basic food items were available in the village shops and half the shopping was in Apia. Fifteen per cent of the commodity purchases were made in Salelologa where more special shopping was done. The nearest hospital and post office were at Sala'ilua and some goods were bought there also.

A little more should be said about prices. For many store goods, particularly basic foodstuffs, prices were regulated by a government tribunal at two levels, one for Apia and a slightly higher level for outer-districts. These were maximum prices and a trader could sell below them. The larger Apia companies in general held to the regulation prices in the outer-village stations so that the prices in the Burns Philp station at Taga were virtually the same as those in the Burns Philp stations at Fagaloa Bay, Poutasi and Utuali'i.[49] Significantly lower prices were found, in general, only in the larger independent stores, such as at Salelologa, Sala'ilua, and as will be seen in the next chapter, in Poutasi.

### 3. *The effect of social and organizational institutions on outlay*

The method traditionally used in Taga to raise money for village purposes (the banning of copra production) depended on a strong and unanimous leadership from the *fono* and other groups. By 1960 this leadership and authority was weak. It had become difficult

---

[48] It had been run by a *taule'ale'a* from Taga who died in 1964. His wife found it difficult to continue in the village. She was unable to collect debts owed by Taga '*āiga*, and eventually decided to move back to her own village and '*āiga* and take the store building with her.

[49] Although the price difference between Apia and the outer districts varied from item to item, prices were generally between 5 and 10% higher in the outer districts.

to reach unanimity on questions of village capital works and so fund raising had become less effective. The bans on copra production were still formally imposed but there was much evasion and the full cash proceeds were not passed on from the '*āiga* to the village. Between 1960 and late 1967 apparently only one attempt was made to raise money for a large investment project. This was in 1965 when £120 was collected for the new house for the pastor. The project was then dropped until 1967 when sufficient money was finally collected to start construction in December.

The cash subscriptions raised in the village during the survey were mainly to provide food and drink (tea and cocoa) for *fono*, Women's Committee and '*aumāga* meetings. These totalled about £120, or £0·3 per consumption unit during the twelve-month period—less than half the amount per consumption unit raised in Uafato.

Per consumption unit, less money was raised in Taga also for the pastor and church, £1·1 compared to £1·2 in Uafato.[50] All '*āiga*, however, did contribute to the various church funds and the church was, as in the other villages, an important motivating force for '*āiga* and village participation in the market sector. It is estimated that during the twelve months, December 1965 to November 1966, the pastor and church received about six per cent of the total cash outlay of the village.[51]

In addition, the village provided the pastor and his family with subsistence goods and services. This included housing, food, mats and other handicrafts, and domestic help. As was customary, the Taga women provided a supply of pandanus mats, and in addition bought a quantity of household utensils for the pastor's house.[52]

About £240, or £0·7 per consumption unit, was given by Taga '*āiga* to relatives and others, in and outside the village. In addition, there were frequent gifts of food and other subsistence items between related and neighbouring '*āiga*, and gifts made in other villages of traditional valuables such as '*ietōga* and *siapo*. Gifts of subsistence goods and services were more common than gifts of money.

In summary, the effect of social and organizational institutions on cash outlay in Taga was weaker than in Uafato and Poutasi. In Taga about twelve per cent of the total cash outlay of the village was spent on the church and pastor, gifts and village subscriptions.

---

[50] The £1·1 raised in Taga for the church and pastor was the lowest of the four villages studied.

[51] In Uafato, a smaller village, the pastor and church absorbed 8·8 per cent of the total cash outlay of the village.

[52] The women gave the following items to the pastor in March 1966: 60 floor mats (*papa*), 46 sleeping-mats, 40 food-mats (*laulau*), 30 enamel plates, 36 enamel mugs, 2 spoons, 2 teapots, 1 kerosene lamp, 1 sheet, and 2 bars of laundry soap.

In Uafato it was eighteen per cent and in Poutasi it was seventeen per cent. In Utuali'i, a village in which social and organizational institutions were also weak, the proportion was only ten per cent. The amount per consumption unit in Taga was the lowest of the four villages; £2·1 compared with Uafato—£2·5, Poutasi—£3·6, and Utuali'i—£3·6.

## 4. *Cash savings*

Very few persons in Taga held savings accounts. The pastor and Tialavea, both fairly frequent visitors to Apia, held accounts in the Savings Bank (there was no Savai'i branch) and several other persons, such as the teachers, the '*papalagi*' *matai* and the *matai* who had been a post office employee between 1947 and 1953, held post office savings accounts at Tuasivi, the nearest post office to have such facilities.[53] With such poor facilities it is not surprising that few people had accounts. In December 1965 about £300 were held in various savings accounts held by Taga residents. By July 1966 it had fallen by half. Only in one case had an account increased during the survey period (that of the pastor). There was certainly more cash-in-hand in Taga (per consumption unit) than in Uafato, but few '*āiga* seemed to have more than a few shillings at any one time and most were in debt to the stores. '*Āiga* debts to the stores in fact increased from about £98 in December 1965 to £187 in June 1966.

---

[53] Tuasivi is about five miles north of Salelologa. It is the centre of the government administration for Savai'i Island.

# Chapter 6

# POUTASI

UAFATO and Taga were isolated villages. Their lands bordered on forest rather than the cultivated lands of other villages. They did not have safe harbours for coastal vessels or sheltered lagoons for fishing. At least before 1960 they both had weakly developed linkage with the market sector. Poutasi, the village which was ranked second in terms of linkage, had none of these characteristics. It was one of a group of four closely associated villages at the western end of the Falealili district on the central south coast of Upolu Island. One could walk from Matautu at the eastern end of the group, to 'Ili'ili at the western end, in less than an hour. Alternatively one could paddle a canoe through the quiet lagoon which stretched for a mile out from the shore. Poutasi, at the centre of the group, was chosen for the district hospital (1940), the district (intermediate) school (1958), a police station, and the district office of the Department of Agriculture (1966).

Poutasi was forty-eight miles by road from Apia, about two hours by bus. The road was opened in 1949 and since then a regular daily bus service has linked the village with Apia. Buses leave Poutasi at about 6 a.m. to reach Apia by 8, and they return to Poutasi in the late afternoon. In 1966 the one-way fare was four or five shillings (it varied), the same as the fare between Fagaloa Bay and Apia or Taga and Salelologa.

Falealili was one of the first outer districts to have a trade-store— probably in the 1870s—and although it was not in Poutasi, it was only a ten to fifteen minute walk away. The Falealili lagoon was recognized early as a suitable commercial harbour and it became a regular port-of-call for coastal vessels serving the trade store.[1] In the 1920s two trading-stations of Apia companies (O. F. Nelson & Co., Ltd., and J. B. Foneti) were established in Poutasi itself. In 1959 a large independent trade-store opened and between 1962 and 1965 three small stores were built by Poutasi 'āiga. In 1966 Poutasi had by far the best local marketing facilities of the four villages studied.

[1] For example, see Churchward 1887, p. 38.

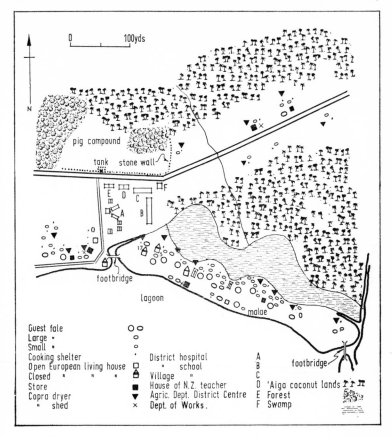

Fig. 7   Poutasi village in 1966

The cleared part of Poutasi's agricultural land extended inland from the village for a distance of about a mile and a half. It was bordered on the west by Saleilua village land, and on the east by land of Vaovai village. To the north was a vast area of forest.

The main part of the village (Figure 8) was on a small 'island', separated from the agricultural lands to the north by a swamp which drained into two streams, one at each end of the village. The 'island', about 1,000 yards long and from 100 to 180 yards wide, had an area of about twenty-two acres. A footbridge at the eastern end led to a similar 'island' on which Vaovai village stood: A footbridge at the western end took one to the 'mainland' part of the village and the road. The 'island' contained the village *malae*,

two churches[2] and the pastors' houses, a trading-station, a small
'*āiga*-owned shop, and the guest and other *fale* and houses of ten
of the sixteen village '*āiga*. Four other '*āiga* had their dwellings
near the minor coast-road to Saleilua where there was also a trading-
station and the large independent trade store. Two '*āiga* and several
families lived near the main road north of the village where there
was another independent (Poutasi-owned) trade store and a small
'*āiga*-owned shop. One *matai* lived in a large two-storey European-
style house near the main road about a mile and a half from the
village; he owned one of the Falealili buses and sold petrol from
this location. The district hospital, the district and village schools,
a European house for the New Zealand headmaster of the district
school, an office of the Department of Agriculture, and a (disused)
depot of the Department of Works, had all been built on a ten-
acre block between the village and the main road.

Water was piped from an inland dam to all houselands, including
those near the main road (1959). This was a modern water supply
system which served the neighbouring villages as well as Poutasi.
In Poutasi each '*āiga* houseland had its own tap and the water
had been connected to the hospital and a number of houses. The
hospital and several houses had septic tanks and water closets.
The large independent store and the New Zealand teachers' house
had their own electricity plants. The hospital was (until the hurricane) in radio communication with Apia.

The village houselands were used extensively as food plots much
as in Uafato. There were the usual coconut palms, breadfruit,
kapok and citrus trees, banana, papaya, pineapple and sugar-cane
plants, and small plots of taro and *ta'amū*. Three or four acres at
the eastern end of the 'island' were planted in the variety of sugar-
cane used for thatches—a project of the Women's Committee. Most
of the *fale* in the village were extremely well thatched and there was
little of the patch-thatching common in Uafato and Taga. Considerable effort was put into keeping the village clean and orderly
and the various buildings in good order, and this was also something
of a contrast to the two villages described earlier. In Uafato and
Taga, for example, the pigs were allowed to forage freely through
the village and near-by agricultural lands despite the fact that
there was a walled pig compound in each. In Poutasi the *fono* (and
government) rule that all pigs should be kept in the pig compound
was strictly enforced.[3]

---

[2] Congregational and Roman Catholic.
[3] The reason this was strictly enforced in Poutasi is of some interest. In 1964
the *fono* did little to enforce this rule and pigs roamed freely in the village and
particularly around the schools. The New Zealand headmaster complained to
the *pulenu'u* about the damage caused to the school playing fields etc., by the pigs

In November 1965 the resident population of Poutasi numbered 436 persons. There were sixteen '*āiga* with a total population of 382 persons, and the remaining fifty-four persons belonged to the families of the pastors, the traders, the hospital and school staff and the policemen. Six New Zealanders lived in Poutasi during the survey—the district school headmaster and his family and two volunteer teachers.

The Poutasi '*āiga* were, in general, considerably larger than those of the other three villages. The average '*āiga* in Poutasi had twenty-four members and the range was from fifty-two to eleven. There had been no title-splitting in Poutasi.

As in the other villages over fifty per cent of the population was under the age of fifteen years. Unfortunately the Congregational Church pastor's annual population reports had not included the village Catholic and other denomination members and were not very helpful as an indication of village population growth. The National Census returns were also unhelpful. The 1951 Census return recorded a total of 287 persons for Poutasi of which only fifty-eight were female—evidently a somewhat unusual situation. There was no evidence, however, to suggest that Poutasi was any different from the other villages studied and its average annual growth rate was probably over three per cent.

PRODUCTIVE RESOURCES

Poutasi was the best endowed of the four villages in terms of its natural resources, and it has invested rather more in producers' capital such as tools and equipment, fencing, and a road into the plantations.

1. *Land*

As in Taga, the land resources were extensive, both the cleared and cultivated area and the reserves of forest land. The land sloped gently inland for about two miles and then rose more steeply to the 4,000-5,000 feet high central mountain ridge of the island about five miles north from the village. Over most of this area soils were moderately fertile, deep and relatively rock-free. While there were no areas of highly fertile soils, such as in Uafato (IV) and the two alluvial strips in Taga, the whole area appeared to be of fairly uniform quality and suitable for all the crops usually grown in the Samoan villages. In 1966 there were approximately 936 acres of cleared land extending in a belt about a mile and a quarter wide

---

but for some weeks nothing was done. Eventually the headmaster borrowed a gun from the *pulenu'u* and shot two of the pigs near the school. After that the *matai* acted and fined the owners of pigs found outside the compound. The motivation was less the loss of the pigs than the loss of village dignity over the incident.

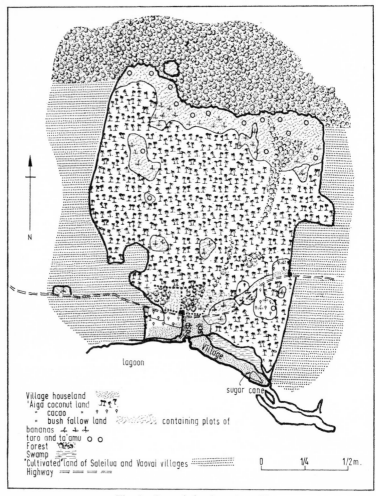

Fig. 8   Poutasi: land use in 1966

for about a mile and a half inland.[4] Beyond the fringe of cultivation were over 2,000 acres of forest yet to be cleared and brought into agricultural use.[5] Rainfall averaged about 180 inches a year, and there was no markedly dry season.

[4] This gave an area per capita of 2·1 acres of cleared land, compared to 1·8 acres in Taga (III) and 1·0 acres in both Uafato (IV) and Utuali'i (I).

[5] Of the other villages, only Taga (III) had large reserves of forest, but it was less fertile and more rocky than that of Poutasi. Uafato (IV) had fewer than 20 acres which could still be cleared of forest and brought into production (and this rather steep), while Utuali'i (I) had no forest reserves at all.

The pattern of land use in Poutasi was similar to that of Uafato. The village area was used for a variety of minor food and other subsistence crops. The coconut area began immediately behind this and extended inland in a fairly unbroken band for about a mile. Then bush fallow cultivation extended to the forest line.[6] This was a typical pattern of land use along the south coast of Upolu and in many other parts of Samoa.

Coconuts took up fifty-six per cent of the total cleared area, and in contrast to the crowded coconut small-holdings of Uafato and Taga, the palms were planted sparsely to an average of between forty and fifty to the acre. Within this area of about 520 acres there were several clearings used for bananas and food crops, and also a few small patches of bush. The coconut small-holdings appeared to have been carefully laid out and planted. Even in the older areas close to the village palms were in rows and spaced with some accuracy. As in Uafato and Taga, there had been little if any replanting of established areas, but again in contrast to these villages there were few self-sown palms and there had been a fairly steady expansion of the coconut area northwards in the last decade.

In 1965 the Department of Agriculture started a project to count all coconut palms on village lands. The Poutasi count was completed before the scheme was abandoned and the results (Appendix Table 3) are of considerable interest. The recent efforts to increase the coconut resources of the village are shown in the large proportion of palms under seven years old and yet to bear—thirty per cent. On the other hand about sixteen per cent were aged and unproductive. Poutasi 'āiga in general had planted new areas rather than replanting the old. The 'āiga of Uafato, Taga and Utuali'i had not done either. Only fifty-four per cent of the palms counted were bearing and many of these were approaching the end of their productive lives.

While most 'āiga had taken part in this recent coconut planting, one 'āiga was responsible for most of it and was in the process of establishing a large single holding—really a small commercial plantation. About half the area was fenced and an access road had been built.[7] Cattle were kept in the fenced areas to keep down undergrowth as was usual on commercial plantations.[8]

In each of the villages studied the *fono* ordered extensive food-crop plantings after the hurricane, but in Poutasi the order also included coconut seedlings—four weekly inspections were held in

[6] See Figure 8.
[7] See Fig. 9 and Table 28. The '*āiga* referred to here is No. 2.
[8] Several other areas of the Poutasi coconut lands were also fenced, and at least three other '*āiga* kept cattle on their small-holdings.

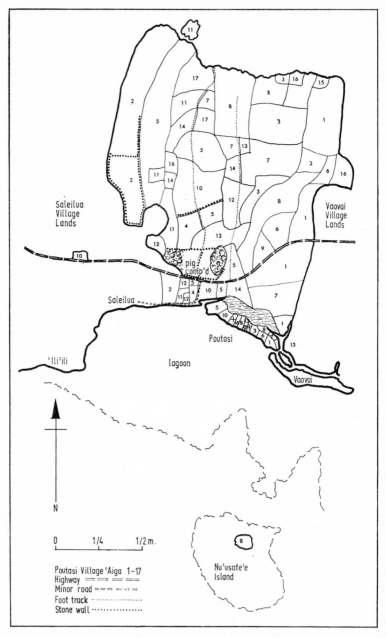

Fig. 9   Poutasi: *matai* land holdings in 1966

Table 28   Poutasi: *Matai* Land Holdings and Land Use in 1966 [a]

| 'Āiga | Number of blocks | House-land | Hospital and school | Coco-nuts | Cacao | Bana-nas | Taro and a'amū | Pig com-pound | Bush fallow | Total area |
|---|---|---|---|---|---|---|---|---|---|---|
| | | acres | acres | acres | acres | acres | acres | acres | acres | acres |
| 1 [b] | 5 | 1·2 | | 75·0 | 4·0 | | 7·3 | | 15·7 | 111 |
| 2 | 2 | | | | | | | | | 110 |
| 3 | 5 | | | | | | | | | 72 |
| 4 | 3 | | | | | | | | | 18 |
| 5 [b] | 8 | 4·0 | | 88·0 | 4·0 | | 5·7 | 13·0 | 25·3 | 137 |
| 6 | 3 | | | | | | | | | 21 |
| 7 [b] | 5 | 0·8 | | 52·0 | 0·5 | | 2·9 | | 18·9 | 75 |
| 8 [b] | 5 | 2·0 | | 75·0 | 0·8 | | 2·2 | | 29·4 | 109 |
| 9 [b] | 3 | 0·4 | | 12·0 | 3·0 | | 3·6 | | 3·9 | 22 |
| 10 [b] | 6 | 3·0 | 10·0 | 38·0 | | 6·0 | 3·1 | 16·0 | 30·9 | 104 |
| 11 [b] | 5 | 2·0 | | 28·0 | 0·8 | | 3·2 | | 1·4 | 35 |
| 12 | 4 | | | | | | | | | 22 |
| 13 [b] | 3 | 0·5 | | 14·0 | | | 3·1 | | 0·9 | 19 |
| 14 | 4 | | | | | | | | | 29 |
| 15 [b] | 2 | 0·6 | | | | | 3·0 | | 0·4 | 4 |
| 16 | 4 | | | | | | | | | 21 |
| 17 (pastor) | 2 | | | | | | | | | 27 |
| | 69 | 29 | 10 | 520 | 30 | 10 | 60 | 29 | 258 | 936 |
| Percentage of total area | | 3·1 | 1·1 | 55·6 | 3·2 | 1·1 | 6·4 | 3·1 | 26·4 | 100·0 |

NOTES:   [a] Estimated roughly from the *matai* land holdings map (Fig. 9) and the land use map (Fig. 8)

[b] Sample *'āiga*

February and March for which each *matai* and *taule'ale'a* had to show where he had planted 300 taro and ten coconuts. The Poutasi leadership demonstrated a much greater interest in cash cropping than was the case in the other villages.[9]

About 618 acres, or about sixty-six per cent of the cleared area was in fixed use either under tree and palm crops or as the village houselands. Most was under coconut palms (520 acres), but there were about thirty acres in cacao, ten acres used for the hospital, schools and other district institutions, twenty-nine acres in the pig-compound, and the village *malae* and houseland covered another twenty-nine acres. Much of the houseland produced subsistence food crops, breadfruit in particular, and three or four acres were planted with sugar-cane of the variety use for thatching. About 318 acres (forty-six per cent of the cleared area) were used to produce crops under the system of bush fallow; in June 1966 about fifty acres were

[9] The Poutasi *fono* forbade the sale of coconuts (as opposed to copra) in the village stores.

in production (bananas—ten acres; taro and *ta'amū*—forty acres).[10]
The usual fallow period allowed on Poutasi lands was about eight
years after eighteen months' use, and on this basis about sixty
acres could have been kept in production at any one time. This
area could have been substantially increased, without reducing the
fallow cycle, by clearing new land from the forest.

Estimates of areas in use under the categories described are
summarized in Table 28. As in the other villages, these estimates
are fairly rough, particularly the areas in production under bush
fallow methods where there were many small scattered plots.

The division of the Poutasi lands between the sixteen *'āiga* is
shown in Table 28 and Figure 9. Compared with Uafato and Taga,
the blocks are much larger and the *'āiga* holdings are much less
fragmented. The 936 acres were divided into sixty-nine blocks
with an average area of 13·6 acres.[11] This was due largely to a
long period of strong leadership in the *fono* from the two high
chiefs of exceptional ability,[12] and partly to favourable natural
resources such as large reserves of good quality land under forest.

The forest was well over a mile from the village, and compared
with Taga where it was very close, the labour costs of extracting
timber were high. But there was a government sawmill a few miles
west from Poutasi and in recent years much of the heavy timber

[10] Only about ten acres of bananas were expected to recover from the hurricane
and these were infected with bunchytop. As in Uafato and Taga new banana
planting had ceased due to the spread of bunchytop before the survey period.
The forty acres under taro and *ta'amū* included the post-hurricane emergency
planting, some of which was intended as a cash crop.

[11] The average block area in Uafato was 2·5 acres; it was 2·9 acres in Taga
and 6·7 acres in Utuali'i.

[12] The holders of the two high chief titles were exceptional men. Tuatagaloa was
a politician of long standing; he served as a district representative from 1940,
became a member of the Legislative Assembly in 1951, served in the Executive
Council 1953-7, and as a Minister from 1957-68. He was 'progressive and extremely able' (Davidson 1967, p. 317). During the 1940s and '50s he had provided
strong and enlightened leadership in Poutasi but during the late 1950s he had
moved permanently to Apia and in recent years he visited Poutasi only occasionally. His children had all been well educated and in 1965 three were government
clerks, two were teachers, one was the assistant librarian in the public library
and one was a policeman. Two other children lived in New Zealand. A son was in
charge of the *'āiga* possessions in Poutasi and he, with his wife and children and a
number of *taulele'a* were included as one of the sample *'āiga*.

Melesia was also a high-ranking *matai* of exceptional ability. He had assumed
the leadership role in the village which had earlier rested with Tuatagaloa.
Melesia was a Samoan judge and his ability and integrity were recognized fully
in 1968 when he was appointed President of the Lands and Titles Court. Like
Tuatagaloa he had both a large nuclear family and a large group of relatives and
others forming his *'āiga*, and he had kept his children at school. In 1966 the oldest
were in wage employment. Unlike Tuatagaloa he had not moved permanently
to Apia although his Court duties kept him away from Poutasi during the week.
In these *matai* were combined important titles, high official status and exceptional
personal qualities of leadership.

used in large *fale* and houses had been bought at the mill and trucked to the village. The newest guest-*fale* in the village had concrete foundations, floor, and posts, and although the costs of extracting timber from the forest was not the main reason for this departure from tradition, the carpenter considered it to be a minor reason.[13] Timber for smaller *fale* and firewood was carried down to the village from the forest wall.

The Faleali'i coastline is sheltered by a broad lagoon and fishing was much less arduous than in Uafato and much more profitable than in Taga. It allowed the women to find various delicacies such as shellfish and sea-urchins. Before the road made it unnecessary the lagoon provided a safe anchorage for coastal launches.

## 2. *Labour*

Village agriculture required few special skills and those with extensive schooling had no particular advantage over those who had attended only the village elementary school. As in Uafato and Taga the men with secondary schooling generally left the village for wage employment in Apia or New Zealand. Only nine of the sixty-one members of the Poutasi *'aumāga* had been to secondary school and several of these were waiting either for a New Zealand visa or a wage job.

But the *'aumāga* did not include twenty young men, all living in Poutasi, who had post-primary schooling. Three of these worked in Apia during the week, two taught in the Poutasi schools, one was a bus driver and another a storekeeper. Seven of the twenty had worked overseas—five in New Zealand, one in Fiji and one in American Samoa. Most of them were waiting for New Zealand visas or were hopeful of getting wage jobs in Apia. In the meantime they lived at home and contributed their labour to the normal village work tasks.

## 3. *Producers' capital*

There was only one significant difference between Poutasi on the one hand, and Uafato and Taga on the other, in the investment in producers' capital. In Uafato there were four copra dryers, three of which were attached to the stores. In Taga there were three dryers and the largest was attached to a store. In Poutasi there were twenty-three dryers and each *'āiga* and each store owned one. This was a fairly recent innovation and although the first was built in 1948, most dated from about 1962, and since then very little sun-dried copra has been produced. The dryers are valued at

[13] This was built by a high chief. It was a particularly imposing piece of conspicuous political display.

£230 altogether. Seventy-five per cent of this represents the cost of purchased components.

Fishing gear and canoes are valued at £247 which is the same value per consumption unit as in Uafato (£0·8), although considerably higher than in Taga (£0·3). Investment in agricultural tools was about the same in Poutasi and Uafato (£0·2 per consumption), slightly below that in Taga (£0·3).[14] Investment in carpentry tools was below that of the other villages, possibly due to greater specialization in house-building within the group of Faleali'i villages. Only two men in Poutasi were recognized builders and one was an old man who no longer carried on his craft.

While several men liked to shoot pigeons and fruit-bats in Uafato and Taga where the forest was close to the village, no one appeared to be interested in this sport in Poutasi, and few 'āiga owned guns. Most 'āiga owned a sewing machine. In general there were no great differences between the villages in the levels of cash and subsistence investment in these categories of producers' equipment, just as there were few differences in the productive tasks they were intended for.

One Poutasi 'āiga owned a bus and another a small truck; a similar investment was found in Taga. Three Poutasi 'āiga had set up stores in the village. Two were similar to those in Uafato but one was much more substantial. Investment in stores and vehicles (or other transport facilities such as the Uafato whaleboats) averaged £4·3 per consumption unit in Poutasi compared to £4·1 in Uafato, and £2·3 in Taga.

Poutasi investment up to 1966 in all these items of producers' capital totalled £2,389, or £7 per consumption unit. Approximately eighty-one per cent represented investment from the monetized sector (Table 29).

There had been a great deal of other investment in Poutasi, particularly from the subsistence sector, which we have not tried to measure. The main road had been completed in 1959 with unpaid Poutasi labour. Labour had also been invested in the various paths through the agricultural lands, in the bridges across the two streams near the village, in cutting down forest cover, in planting tree and palm crops, in the access road to one of the small-holdings, on walls and fences, and in a number of other 'āiga and village assets which were important in the productive life of the village but were difficult to value. Certainly investment in fencing and rock walls, access roads and cleared land was significantly higher

[14] The higher investment in agricultural work tools in Taga was largely due to the need in that village, to sheath the digging stick (*oso*) with purchased metal because of the rocky soils.

Table 29    Poutasi: Producers' Capital[a]

|  | Total | Cash component | Subsistence component |
|---|---|---|---|
|  | £ | % | % |
| Fishing gear and canoes | 247 | 15 | 85 |
| Agricultural tools | 66 | 85 | 15 |
| Copra dryers | 230 | 75 | 25 |
| Carpentry tools | 130 | 86 | 14 |
| Guns | 60 | 100 | — |
| Sewing machines | 260 | 100 | — |
| Motor vehicles | 600 | 100 | — |
| Stores equipment and stocks | 796 | 81 | 19 |
| Total investment[b] | 2,389 | 81 | 19 |
| Investment per consumption unit | £7 | £6 | £1 |

NOTES:   [a] The method by which values have been imputed has been described
on page 50.
[b] An imputed rent for the use of this equipment has been included
as an item of subsistence income (see Table 33). This is based on
the above values and estimates of useful life of the various items.

than in Uafato or Taga. There was also greater investment in
buildings, both at the '*āiga* and village levels.

PRODUCTION

The commodities produced for consumption and sale in Poutasi
were, in general, the same as those produced in Uafato and Taga.
But a somewhat better resource endowment in Poutasi meant that
the effort-costs of production were lower, and the stronger linkage
with the market meant that the cash returns to labour in agricultural production were higher. Poutasi's strong traditional leadership also influenced the level of subsistence and market output.

1. *Subsistence*

(a) *Food*

Poutasi produced the same subsistence foods as Uafato and Taga,
and in much the same ways. But the labour costs of producing a
given quantity of staple subsistence foods such as taro on the
moderately fertile, flat and plentiful Poutasi lands were slightly
lower than in Uafato with its fertile but steep and limited bush-
fallow land. As we saw, the labour costs of production in Taga were
somewhat higher than in Uafato. One basis for estimating these
differences was the labour time needed to clear bush fallow land
and plant 100 taro and *ta'amū*. This took an average of two hours
forty minutes in Poutasi (including the time needed to walk to and

from the plots) as against two hours fifty minutes in Uafato and three hours twenty minutes in Taga.

As with Taga, it was difficult to assess accurately the subsistence food supply in Poutasi because of the hurricane and the decline in banana production due to bunchytop, and because most '*āiga* decided after the hurricane to plant taro for sale as well as consumption. The decline in banana production did not start as early in Poutasi as it did in Taga, and up to the hurricane there was still a good supply of bananas for village consumption, especially undersized bananas which were not acceptable to the Banana Scheme. Towards the end of 1965 some '*āiga* had started to increase their taro and *ta'amū* plantings to substitute for food bananas but this was not on a sufficient scale to compensate for the loss of bananas and breadfruit in the hurricane. The supply of subsistence food staples in the months following the hurricane was in general below that in Uafato and Taga. Post-hurricane planting of taro and *ta'amū* in Poutasi was the most intense of the four villages. Each man averaged 600 plants a month from February to May, compared to 180 a month in Uafato, 330 a month in Taga and 260 in Utuali'i. Many Taga '*āiga* intended to produce a surplus for sale but for most it would have been quite small. In Poutasi all '*āiga* planned for a large surplus and went all out to achieve it.

The Poutasi men put in an average of 9·8 hours a week on subsistence food production during the survey: about 3 hours 50 minutes on taro and *ta'amū*, 3 hours on bananas and breadfruit, half an hour on coconuts,[15] 2 hours' fishing,[16] and about half an hour on miscellaneous tasks such as feeding the pigs and chickens. The women averaged 4 hours a week weeding and harvesting the taro and banana plots and at least an hour harvesting the lagoon. This was less than appeared to be necessary in Uafato and Taga for these various tasks, a difference that was due mainly to the more difficult terrain in these villages. Probably under normal circumstances the Poutasi men would have spent more time fishing than was recorded during the survey—fishing was one activity which suffered as a result of the strenuous efforts made after the hurricane to plant large numbers of taro.

While the estimates of labour costs of food production are very rough it is clear that for a given quantity of food they were lower in Poutasi than in Taga and Uafato. But in each of these villages most of the staple food was produced with a male labour input of less than ten hours a week. The time spent fishing varied consider-

---

[15] 5·8 coconuts per consumption unit per week were used as food and another 1·3 nuts were fed to pigs and chickens.

[16] The average catch recorded during the survey was 1½ lbs. an hour.

ably from week to week, as did the catch per hour; and to some extent the time, particularly the leisure component, depended on the demands on labour made by other activities.

The imputed value of subsistence food supplies for the twelve months from December 1965 to November 1966 is £7,720, or £23·8 per consumption unit. The supply of subsistence staples was somewhat lower than in Taga and Uafato due to a greater reliance on bananas up to the hurricane. In a normal year the differences between these villages were probably very small. The details of the imputed value of the Poutasi subsistence food supply are given in Table 33.

(b) *Housing and household durables*

In Taga the opening of the road was followed by substantial *'āiga* investment in new dwellings and in particular dwellings built of purchased non-traditional material. In Uafato, as yet without road access, there was only one *'āiga* dwelling of a non-traditional type. Since the Poutasi road opened in 1949 several *'āiga* had built open or closed houses and *fale* with concrete foundation-floors and thatch-and-iron roofs. But there was less substitution of non-traditional for traditional dwellings in Poutasi than in Taga; in fact, there was a conscious effort to maintain the traditional Samoan character of this village, particularly in the 'island' section. On the 'island' there were only four non-traditional houses, those of the two high chiefs, Tuafagaloa and Melesia and of the two pastors.[17] In the chiefs' houses, however, the front room consisted of a large thatched *fale* to which had been added timber walls, windows and doors, and, at the back, a closed European house of bedrooms, kitchen and bathroom. On the 'mainland' part of the village several *'āiga* had built houses, both closed and open, in addition to the usual *fale*.

The Poutasi *fale* were generally very well built and maintained, at least compared with those in Uafato and Taga. The larger *fale* were completely rethatched at fairly regular intervals, about once in five or six years. The Women's Committee was a major influence here and was responsible for making the thatches and maintaining a large planting of sugar-cane at the eastern end of the 'island' for the raw material.

The *'āiga* dwellings in Poutasi are valued at £6,884, of which £4,584 (sixty-seven per cent) represented the investment of sub-sistence resources. The subsistence income from the use of these

[17] There were, however, the two churches and two stores in the 'island' section and these were non-traditional buildings.

dwellings over one year is estimated at £284, or £0·9 per consumption unit.

Household non-traditional furniture and bought utensils and equipment were similar to those in Taga and will not be described again here. Several '*āiga*, particularly those of the two high chiefs and the pastors, owned houses which were furnished in full western style, but most '*āiga* had only the usual collection of chests, beds, food-safes and occasionally, tables and chairs. In keeping with the Women's Committee's concern for the tidy appearance of the village and their efforts to maintain uniform thatching, it also maintained the highest standard of pandanus mat weaving observed in the four villages. The Committee held regular 'weaving circles' where it encouraged the production of quality items.

Table 30    Poutasi: Cash Income from Agriculture 1960-5

|                    | 1960 | 1961 | 1962 | 1963 | 1964 | 1965 |
|--------------------|------|------|------|------|------|------|
|                    |      |      | £    |      |      |      |
| Copra[a]           | 3,566 | 2,696 | 3,187 | 4,627 | 5,634 | 7,347 |
| Bananas[b]         | 2,893[d] | 5,349 | 5,562 | 2,516[d] | 6,318 | 2,619 |
| Cacao[c]           | 41 | 83 | 353[e] | 91 | 29 | 51 |
| Total              | 6,500 | 8,128 | 9,102 | 7,234 | 11,981 | 10,017 |

NOTES:   [a] Value of copra purchased by the Nelson, Lee Chang and Ioane stores in Poutasi. These figures include copra brought from neighbouring villages and exclude the copra sold by Poutasi '*āiga* out of the village and to one small trading-station in Poutasi.

[b] Records of the Banana Scheme

[c] Value of cacao bought by the Lee Chang store. The other Poutasi stores did not buy cacao during this period but part of the total output could have been sold in Apia.

[d] The low income from bananas in 1960 was due to damage caused by a severe storm. I am able to offer no explanation for the similar low figure for 1963.

[e] 1962 was the peak cacao production year for Western Samoa (marketed output). This is also seen for Taga in Table 23. I am unable to offer any reason for this sudden increase (quantity and price).

## 2. *Market*

Copra, bananas and cacao are the main cash crops in Poutasi. Copra was produced in the 1870s, and probably even earlier. Cacao dates from after the Second World War, and bananas were marketed after the road opened in 1949. Over the six years 1960-5 the village earned an average yearly cash income of £4,510 from copra, £4,210 from bananas and £110 from cacao.[18] As in Taga,

[18] See Table 30.

there was a very small internal village market for village output such as fish, Samoan tobacco and milk. The Poutasi Women's Committee sold thatches at a nominal cash charge in the village, and at a commercial rate of £1 10s per 100 thatches on orders from other villages.[19]

Since the earliest contact with the market sector, probably in the 1870s, copra has been sold in the Falealili district. Poutasi producers never had the physical difficulties and high labour costs of marketing which had characterized Taga before the 1920s and Uafato up to the present time. During the 1920s the marketing situation in Poutasi was made even easier. Two trading-stations were opened in the village itself. From the 1870s to 1949 there was a coastal shipping service between the district and Apia. After 1949 Apia was only a two-hour bus journey away, and buses left the district each day. Road-transport made it possible for independent traders to establish stores in Poutasi. In 1959 a large trade-store was built by a Chinese trader, Lee Chang; in 1953 a Poutasi *taule'ale'a* returned from New Zealand and set up a smaller but still fairly well-stocked store; and in 1964-5 another *taule'ale'a* and a *matai* each built a small shop.

Lee Chang attracted a large share of the copra output of Poutasi and considerable quantities from the neighbouring villages by offering a very wide range of goods for sale at prices similar to those in Apia, by allowing liberal credit, and by supplying on credit building material used in the house being built for the Congregational pastor.[20] When Ioane, a Poutasi *taule'ale'a*,[21] began business in March 1963, he made further inroads into the copra purchases of the old trading-stations and to some extent also into Lee Chang's business.[22] The competition between Ioane and Lee Chang for copra led them to offer a slightly higher price than was paid by the trading-stations, which observed the Copra Board regulations. Ioane did not allow much credit or have the attraction of a large variety of goods for sale, but he bought all the copra from his own *'āiga*, much of that from his friends and related *'āiga*, and because of the location of his store on the main road, he bought a good deal of copra from Poutasi and Vaovai *'āiga* living near by or

---

[19] During 1965 the Women's Committee raised money to build a maternity ward for the district hospital partly through the sale of thatches in villages near Apia. They earned about £200 in this way during the year.

[20] Lee Chang allowed the village £2,800 credit for the pastor's house in 1959. The debt was paid off by the end of 1962. This debt was repaid by a copra subscription levied on each *matai* and *taule'ale'a* (of the Congregational Church) who was required to supply Lee Chang with 100 lbs. of copra each week.

[21] Ioane had trained as a teacher, emigrated to New Zealand and then returned to Poutasi to invest his New Zealand savings in a store.

[22] See Table 31.

with dryers near the road. But not all Poutasi copra was sold in
the village. Two large producers sold much of theirs directly in
Apia and most '*āiga* occasionally took copra to Apia by bus when
making the journey for other reasons.

Table 31    Copra Sold to Three Poutasi Trade-Stores 1960-6

|           | 1960 | 1961 | 1962 | 1963 | 1964 | 1965 | 1966 |
|-----------|------|------|------|------|------|------|------|
|           |      |      |      | (1,000 lbs) | | | |
| Lee Chang | 176  | 143  | 200  | 183  | 181  | 218  | n.a. |
| O. F. Nelson | 13 | 32   | 17   | 12   | 3    | 11   | n.a. |
| Ioane     |      |      |      | 87   | 119  | 155  | 98   |
|           | 189  | 175  | 217  | 282  | 303  | 384  | n.a. |

SOURCE: Records of the stores

The sale of coconuts (rather than copra) was prohibited by the
Poutasi *fono*, but a few *taulele'a* did sell nuts in Vaovai village,
and to Ioane and the other small Poutasi store near the main road
at the usual price of eight mature nuts for one shilling. But compared to Uafato and Taga the trade in nuts was very small.

The labour costs of producing copra were lower in Poutasi
than in Uafato and Taga. The variable was the time taken to
gather the nuts and carry them to the dryer—the other costs,
such as the time taken to remove the kernel and dry the copra,
were similar in all villages. The Poutasi coconut small-holdings
were all within a quarter of an hour's walk from the main road,
and about half an hour from the village, that is, somewhat closer
to the point of processing than in Uafato and Taga. Most of the
Poutasi coconut small-holdings were sparsely planted and were
kept relatively free from bush and dense undergrowth so that the
nuts were more easily found. It took an average of 8·4 hours to
produce 100 pounds of copra in Poutasi compared to about 9·1
hours in both Uafato and Taga.[23] This difference did not appear
to affect the quantities of copra produced in the three villages,
and it had less influence on the net cash return per hour of labour
in the production of copra than other factors such as marketing
costs.

After 1950 bananas rivalled copra as the main source of cash
income from agriculture. After about 1960 Poutasi growers waged

[23] Based on data obtained from the labour survey. Although it did not show in
the labour survey, it was clear that more labour was applied to keeping the coconut
lands clear of undergrowth in Poutasi than in Taga and Uafato and this was
an additional cost of production. Several '*āiga* had fenced some of their coconut
small-holdings and kept cattle to keep the weeds and undergrowth down.

a continuous war against the inroads of bunchytop disease and, by 1965, the battle appeared lost and most growers ceased to replant. In January 1965 forty-six Poutasi growers sold bananas through the Banana Scheme and by January 1966 only eleven of these were still operating. Production declined through 1965 as follows:

| | | | |
|---|---|---|---|
| 1965 | Jan. | 908 | cases exported |
| | Feb. | 667 | |
| | Mar. | 557 | |
| | Apr. | 483 | |
| | May | 411 | |
| | June | 299 | |
| | July | 367 | |
| | Aug. | 250 | |
| | Sept. | 190 | |
| | Oct. | 313 | |
| | Nov. | 92 | |
| | Dec. | 225 | |
| 1966 | Jan. | 236 | |

In 1964 an average of 958 cases a month were sold. As in Taga, few growers expected to be able to market bananas when the existing banana plots recovered from the damage caused by the hurricane. This was one reason for the considerable post-hurricane planting of taro, as growers expected to sell taro towards the end of 1966.

Cacao was only a minor cash crop. In the first two months of the survey some cacao was harvested but most of it was consumed in the village. The hurricane destroyed the maturing crop which would have been sold in the following months.

### 3. *The effect of social and organizational institutions on production*

The institutions of *fono*, Women's Committee and *'aumāga* were particularly strong in Poutasi and their influence on the level and composition of output, both for subsistence use and cash-earning, were direct and considerable.

The *fono* forbade the sale of coconuts in the village, partly to reduce the incidence of coconut stealing, and partly to maximize cash incomes from the coconut small-holdings. After the hurricane, the *fono* instructed each *matai* and *taule'ale'a* to plant a certain number of coconut seedlings in addition to taro and *ta'amū*. This had been the practice before the hurricane also. The Poutasi *fono*, unlike those in Uafato and Taga, took measures to increase the cash income of the village.

The *fono* also influenced the division of land between *'āiga*. In

1964, for example, a section of the forest line was carefully divided between the six *matai*. They were each given a frontage of 200 feet and the right to clear back towards the mountains. There had been much more co-operation between the *matai* in the division of lands than was evident in Uafato and Taga, and this had resulted in larger blocks.

The Poutasi *matai* had co-operated closely with the district agricultural officer in matters of food crop planting (after the hurricane)[24] and in bunchytop control.

> Planters' Committees are very helpful in controlling this disease (bunchy-top) especially in the Falealili district where the committee (*fono*) were very strict and any planter who had Bunchytop was fined heavily by the committee. (Dept of Agric. Forests and Fisheries, Annual Report for 1963, p. 11)

Being on the main south-coast road within two hours of Apia, and in the 'progressive' Falealili district, Poutasi received more assistance from the district agricultural officer than Uafato and Taga.[25]

After the hurricane, the *fono* maintained a high level of taro planting in the village, and its inspections, assisted by the district agricultural officer, were thorough and regular. For the last two weeks in February and in March and April, weekly planting quotas of 300 taro or *ta'amū* plus ten coconuts for each *matai* and *taule'ale'a* were set and weekly inspections were held.[26] In addition to inspections of food and coconut planting, weeding and other land clearing was also supervised by the *fono*.

Since 1964 the Poutasi *fono* has strictly enforced its ruling that village pigs be kept in the pig compound. During the survey two '*āiga* were fined after their pigs were found to have strayed.[27] The *fono* also banned horses in the village because, it said, they would damage the crops.

Immediately after the hurricane, the *fono*, Women's Committee

---

[24] A District Agricultural Officer was stationed permanently in Poutasi in 1966.

[25] My first visit to Poutasi, before it had been selected as a sample village, was with the Livestock Officer on a normal part of his work in which he collected a bull from Lotofaga village and trucked it to Poutasi where it was lent to a Poutais *matai*. Visits by agricultural officers to Uafato were very infrequent and to Taga were less frequent than the weekly visits to Poutasi and neighbouring villages. This is another direct effect of easier linkage with the advanced sector.

[26] Compare this with Uafato where only three inspections (fortnightly) were held—50 taro per *matai* and 100 taro per *taule'ale'a*; Taga where there were seven inspections between February and June ranging from 200 to 500 taro per *matai* and *taule'ale'a*; and Utuali'i with only three inspections—two fortnightly inspections of 200 taro or *ta'amū* per *taule'ale'a* and one inspection at the end of April (after six weeks) of 1,000 per *taule'ale'a*.

[27] See footnote 3, pp. 126-7.

and *'aumāga* set about restoring the village grounds and *fale*. The Women's Committee met each day for a week and made thatches. The *'aumāga* repaired damaged *fale* and removed fallen trees and other debris. By the time I reached the village, a week after the hurricane, there was little sign of damage (which had been considerable) except for several *fale* which were considered beyond repair. The *matai* and several *taulele'a* restored the water supply which had been blocked by erosion and fallen trees. In the weeks that followed, the *matai* and *'aumāga* helped repair the district school, which had been severely damaged by the high winds, and cleared fallen trees from the hospital grounds. This rapid organized reconstruction was not found in the other three villages where each *'āiga* was left to its own devices, and village level needs, such as clearing the Uafato-Samamea path and the Taga road, were neglected for some weeks.

But Poutasi had a special reason for rapid reconstruction. Two weeks after the hurricane, the village Congregational *'āiga* hosted a meeting of south-coast pastors, deacons and their families. For about a month before the hurricane the Women's Committee had been preparing for this by weaving floor and sleeping-mats. Each woman made ten pandanus sleeping-mats and twenty floor mats for this occasion.

The Committee normally held a 'weaving circle' each Tuesday and Thursday. The women assembled at about 7 a.m., and worked fairly continuously until about 5 p.m., taking their meal together. Mats were prepared for village purposes,[28] and for individual *'āiga* needs. In February 1966 the Congregational pastor was supplied with the following: 120 floor mats (*papa*), twenty-six special floor sleeping-mats (*tapito*), forty-two large sleeping-mats (*tu'ulaufala*), and 100 food-mats (*laulau*).[29] Mats were also presented to the Catholic catechist.

Through the village organizations Poutasi invested a great deal of subsistence and cash resources in village capital works, some of which, for example, the schools and water supply, were joint projects with neighbouring villages. In 1951 the first elementary school was built (in Poutasi) for the four villages. The cash cost of about

---

[28] Poutasi was regarded in government circles in Apia as a good village to show European visitors. These were usually presented with gifts of mats etc., by the village. The hospital and district school were visited in much the same way and this also often involved the village in some formal function including a presentation of mats.

[29] Similar gifts given to the pastors of the other villages were as follows:

| | | | | | | |
|---|---|---|---|---|---|---|
| Uafato | — 50 floor-mats, | 32 sleeping-mats, | 50 food-mats | | | |
| Taga | — 60 | ,, | 46 | ,, | 40 | ,, |
| Utuali'i | — 40 | ,, | 40 | ,, | 20 | ,, |

£1,800 was shared equally by the four villages and each contributed unskilled labour. The Poutasi share of the money was raised
in five weeks by subscriptions yielding nearly £100 a week. In 1958
three new classrooms were added to the existing building at a cost
to each of the four villages of about £300. These rooms were used
by the district school which started in that year. By 1961 the district
school had outgrown this accommodation and a new building
(four classrooms) was constructed at a cost of about £1,000, for
the elementary school, leaving the whole of the original building
for the district school. The four villages shared the one elementary
school until 1964 when a second one was built in Vaovai. In the
same year each of the four villages provided a small house for the
district school teachers in Poutasi. The total cash contribution to
the development of the schools and teachers' houses from Poutasi
'āiga between 1958 and 1966 appeared to have been about £1,200.[30]

The Poutasi hospital was a district facility. It was used by the
neighbouring villages and built by the government. In 1965 the
Poutasi Women's Committee enhanced its social prestige in the
district by financing a modern maternity ward. Money was collected
by selling thatches and by subscription (altogether about £600).
The building was formally opened with a large feast attended by
the Women's Committees of the district, the Minister of Health
and other officials just before my first visit to the village. During
the survey period the Poutasi 'aumāga built a large *fale* in the hospital grounds to house the families attending hospital patients.
Poutasi village provided the doctor, the hospital staff and the
teachers with their subsistence food needs.  But while Poutasi
gained a great deal of status from having these district facilities and
from adding to them from time to time, there was a cost both in
cash and subsistence resources. The result was to increase the level
of demand for cash and subsistence resources in two ways: first,
by requiring substantial investment over relatively short periods,
such as when the various buildings were being constructed, and
second, by requiring relatively small but continuous outlay, mainly
of subsistence resources, in the supply of foodstuffs and general
maintenance of hospital and school grounds. After the hurricane
one of the tasks of the 'aumāga was to plant a large plot of taro near
the hospital for the use of the doctor and his family and the 'aumāga
undertook to keep this weeded and in continuous production.

Investment in church buildings in Poutasi was higher than in

[30] The Poutasi pastor and many of the 'āiga bore an extra cost associated with
the schools. Fifty children attending the schools from the neighbouring villages
stayed with Poutasi 'āiga during the week days and they, of course, had to be fed.
This service was regarded as an 'āiga social responsibility which might be recipro-
cated in another form in the future; there was no cash or other charge.

the other villages studied, mainly because two denominations—the Congregational and Roman Catholic groups—were represented. There were two church buildings, both of them fairly old, and two houses for the pastor and catechist, both very new. The Catholic '*āiga* built a large open-house for their catechist in 1958 at a cash cost of about £700. This demonstration of status was followed immediately by the construction of a very large house for the Congregational pastor at a cash cost of over £3,500. In both cases unskilled labour was contributed by the '*āiga* concerned. The cash debts incurred for both houses were fully paid up by the end of 1964.

Two other examples of community capital works in Poutasi were the wooden footbridges, one at each end of the village. That at the western end was built in 1964 by the Poutasi '*aumāga* and the other was a co-operative effort by Poutasi and Vaovai. The story behind the new bridge at the western end of the village is similar to that behind the enforcement of the rule to keep pigs in the compound. The New Zealand headmaster of the district school complained to the *pulenu'u* that the children had to cross a dangerously dilapidated bridge. In fact, everyone had to use it to get to the main stores, the bus, the hospital and the agricultural lands. For several weeks, and after several complaints, nothing was done. The headmaster eventually threatened to close the school if a new bridge was not built. After some time the '*aumāga* was ordered to build the bridge in time for a scheduled visit to the village by the Minister of Education (a Poutasi *matai*) and his Director. The motivation which finally moved the *matai* to action was less the safety of the children, than the social prestige which would be derived from displaying this new facility to the important visitors. This sort of social motivation was also behind the quick cleaning up of the village after the hurricane.

In Table 32 estimates of cash and subsistence investment in social and village capital are given. About fifty-three per cent had been in cash, and the rest had been in village labour and other subsistence resources. The total investment was £65 per consumption unit, compared with only £43 in Taga and £40 in Uafato. The monetary proportion was also higher in Poutasi—fifty-three per cent, compared to forty-three per cent in Taga and forty-eight per cent in Uafato. In Poutasi, as in the other villages, I was not able to value other important investments, such as the construction of the road and the footbridge and water supply, which had large subsistence components. It is clear, however, that contributions to these items (apart from the road) were somewhat higher in Poutasi than in Taga and Uafato.

It is apparent that the strong social and organizational institutions in Poutasi had raised the level of demand for subsistence and market goods and services to a considerably higher level than in Taga and Uafato. This affected not only the large capital projects, such as the pastors' houses and guest-*fale*, but also consumer durables and consumption goods, such as pandanus mats and subsistence and purchased foods.

Table 32    Poutasi: Social and Village Capital[a]

|  | Total | Cash component | Subsistence component |
|---|---|---|---|
|  | % | % | % |
| '*Āiga* |  |  |  |
| Dwellings | 6,884 | 33 | 67 |
| Furniture | 329 | 60 | 40 |
| Mats etc. | 1,647 | 12 | 88 |
| Utensils & equipment | 527 | 100 | — |
| Total | 9,387 | 34 | 66 |
| Village | 4,670 | 70 | 30 |
| Church | 6,134 | 70 | 30 |
| Total investment | 20,191 | 53 | 47 |
| Investment per consumption unit[b] | £65 | £35 | £30 |

NOTES:    [a] Estimated costs of the social and village capital existing in 1966. Buildings provided by the government, such as the hospital, are not included. Other items for which values were not estimated, such as the two footbridges, are not included.

[b] Estimated costs of capital items existing in 1966 divided by the number of consumption units.

INCOME

Total income in Poutasi for the twelve-month period, to 30 November 1966 is estimated at £17,311, or £54·3 per consumption unit. This is derived from an imputed value of subsistence (non-monetary) income £8,733, or £27·9 per consumption unit[31] and cash income of £8,578, or £26·4 per consumption unit. The monetized proportion of total income is therefore fifty per cent ('monetization factor').[32]

Fifty-five per cent of the cash income was earned from the sale

[31] The imputed value of subsistence income is below the estimates for Uafato (£31·1 per consumption unit) and Taga (£34 per consumption unit) largely because of a lower supply of staple foods in Poutasi after the hurricane. In a normal year this component of subsistence income was probably very close to that of Taga and Uafato.

[32] Compared with a 'monetization factor' in Uafato of 31% and in Taga of 37%.

of village agricultural products, mainly copra. Cash income from copra was higher in Poutasi than in Taga and Uafato, both in total and per consumption unit, due to a larger output and somewhat higher prices.

Wages were a more important source of income in Poutasi than in Uafato and Taga. In Poutasi they contributed £8·1 per consumption unit compared to £1·6 in Taga and £2·2 in Uafato. Wages contributed thirty per cent of the total cash income of Poutasi. Two teachers, a nurse, a 'housegirl', a bus driver and a Department of Agriculture employee held jobs locally, and several other persons had casual wage jobs. A judge and two employees of the Department of Agriculture commuted weekly to Apia. The wages of these persons and of the *pulenu'u* totalled £2,628 for the twelve-month period.[33]

Details of subsistence and cash income for the village are summarized in Table 33.

OUTLAY

Estimates of cash outlay for the twelve months, December 1965 to November 1966 are shown in Table 34.

1. *Cash expenditure on goods and services*

Forty-six per cent of all cash expenditure during the twelve-month period was on food. This amounted to about £3,294, or £10·2 per consumption unit, of which over eighty per cent was spent on flour, rice, bread, sugar, fish and meat. The only important difference between Poutasi and Taga is that bakery products were available in Poutasi and not in Taga. Apia-baked bread was delivered to the Lee Chang store five days a week and in addition Lee Chang made 'pancakes' for sale. There was also a slightly higher expenditure on flour and rice in Poutasi which could be expected to result from the poorer supply of staple subsistence foods after the hurricane. The quantities of food purchased, however, were still very small in relation to the supply of subsistence foods. Flour and rice were issued to the village by the Hurricane Relief Committee in June (thirty-five bags of rice and eighteen bags of flour) and this increased the average consumption of flour and rice from one pound to 1·3 pounds per consumption unit per week.

[33] The only wages included in this estimate were those earned by members of the sixteen Poutasi *'āiga* when those members resided in Poutasi. Residence was accepted if the wage-earner lived in Apia during the week but returned to Poutasi at weekends. This definition was used also for Uafato where there was one such wage-earner. There were no examples of this in Taga as this village was too far from Apia and the journey was too expensive for such weekly commuting to be possible.

Table 33    Poutasi: Subsistence and Cash Incomes[a]

|  | Village | | Per consumption unit | |
|---|---|---|---|---|
|  | £ | | £ | |
| SUBSISTENCE (non-monetary) INCOME |  | | | |
| Food: |  | 7,720 | | 23·8 |
| coconuts[b] | 585 | | 1·8 | |
| bananas and breadfruit[c] | 1,490 | | 4·6 | |
| taro and ta'amū | 5,161 | | 15·9 | |
| fish | 319 | | 1·0 | |
| pork and chicken[d] | 165 | | ·5 | |
| Buildings: |  | 480 | | 1·5 |
| 'āiga | 284 | | ·9 | |
| village | 102 | | ·3 | |
| church | 94 | | ·3 | |
| Household durables: |  | 473 | | 2·0 |
| Tools and equipment: |  | 60 | | ·6 |
| Total subsistence income | | £8,733 | | £27·9 |
| CASH INCOME |  | | | |
| Agriculture and fishing: |  | 4,743 | | 14·6 |
| bananas | 208 | | ·6 | |
| copra and coconuts | 4,472 | | 13·8 | |
| fish | 38 | | ·1 | |
| other | 25 | | ·1 | |
| Wages |  | 2,628 | | 8·1 |
| Remittances from Apia |  | 63 | | ·2 |
| Remittances from abroad |  | 1,144 | | 2·9 |
| Total cash income | | £8,578 | | £25·8 |
| TOTAL INCOME[e] | | £17,311 | | £54·3 |
| Monetization factor[f] | | 50% | | |

NOTES:    [a] 12 months, December 1965-November 1966

[b] Average per consumption unit a week of 5·8 coconuts as food plus 4·5 fed to pigs and chickens. Coconuts are valued at 1s for 8 nuts, the price received at stores in neighbouring villages.

[c] Based on Appendix Table 2 with quantities valued at pre-hurricane market prices in Apia:—taro—6d per lb., ta'amū and breadfruit—4d per lb. and bananas—3d per lb.

[d] A rough estimate of quantity based on observation and valued at 2s per lb. for pork and 2s each for chickens.

[e] Aggregate of imputed value of subsistence income and cash income; intended only for inter-village comparisons.

[f] Proportion of cash income on total income

Table 34   Poutasi: Cash Outlay[a]

|  | Village | | Per consumption unit | | Percentage |
|---|---|---|---|---|---|
|  | £ | £ | £ | £ |  |
| 'Āiga |  | 6,418 |  | 19·9 | 90 |
| Food | 3,294 |  | 10·2 |  | 46 |
| Other commodities | 1,483 |  | 4·6 |  | 21 |
| Local fares | 749 |  | 2·3 |  | 11 |
| Gifts | 490 |  | 1·5 |  | 7 |
| Schooling | 242 |  | ·8 |  | 3 |
| New Zealand fares | 160 |  | ·5 |  | 2 |
| Church and pastor |  | 504 |  | 1·6 | 7 |
| Village |  | 189 |  | ·6 | 3 |
| Total |  | 7,111 |  | 22·1 | 100 |

NOTE:    [a] 12 months, December 1965-November 1966

Cash expenditure on commodities other than food is estimated at £1,486, or £4·6 per consumption unit, almost £1 more per consumption unit than in Taga. This was partly the result of an order by the Women's Committee that each Congregational 'āiga buy certain household items in preparation for the church meeting held in Poutasi two weeks after the hurricane. Poutasi people were also generally better and more expensively dressed than their 'country cousins' in Taga and Uafato and they had more occasions for wearing their 'best' clothes. Visits to Apia were frequent and so were social occasions in the village, such as visits by distinguished persons. In this way the social and political prominence of the village had the effect of raising the level of demand for purchased goods as well as subsistence products.

As in the other villages the main services purchased were those of the buses and schools. The average expenditure on bus fares was £2·3 per consumption unit which represented the cash cost of six return fares to Apia.

Poutasi 'āiga spent less money on school fees than the other three villages, because in 1966 few children attended mission or government secondary schools. The position may have been quite different earlier. With the district (intermediate) school in Poutasi, however, there was less need to send children to mission schools for the first three years of the post-elementary education. Fees were charged by the district school but they were considerably lower than those of most mission schools. Despite the lower cash expenditure on school fees, more post-elementary school children remained at school in Poutasi than in either Uafato or Taga. School fees were, however, only part of the total costs of school education and the other costs, such as the investment in school buildings, and teacher housing, and the food provided regularly for the school staffs, were considerably higher in Poutasi.

Table 35    Poutasi: Commodity Purchases[a]

|  | Expenditure | | | Main shopping centres | |
|---|---|---|---|---|---|
|  | Village £ | Per consumption unit £ | Percentage | Poutasi % | Apia % |
| Food: | | | | | |
| flour, rice, bread | 1,014 | 3·2 | 21 | 81 | 19 |
| sugar | 823 | 2·5 | 17 | 96 | 4 |
| fish[b] | 566 | 1·7 | 12 | 73 | 27 |
| meat[c] | 421 | 1·3 | 9 | 82 | 18 |
| dripping, salt etc. | 162 | ·5 | 3 | 98 | 2 |
| tea, coffee, cocoa | 137 | ·4 | 3 | 85 | 15 |
| dairy products | 85 | ·3 | 2 | 100 | — |
| other foods | 86 | ·3 | 2 | 70 | 30 |
|  | 3,294 | 10·2 | 69 | 85 | 15 |
| Other: | | | | | |
| household | 535 | 1·7 | 11 | 85 | 15 |
| tobacco | 316 | 1·0 | 7 | 100 | — |
| individual | 232 | ·7 | 5 | 91 | 9 |
| kerosene, benzene | 208 | ·6 | 4 | 87 | 13 |
| soap | 192 | ·6 | 4 | 96 | 4 |
|  | 1,483 | 4·6 | 31 | 91 | 9 |
| All commodities | 4,777 | 14·8 | 100 | 87 | 13 |

NOTES:    [a] 12 months, December 1965-November 1966
          [b] 100% tinned fish
          [c] 74% tinned meat

There was a slightly wider variety of services in the market sector in Poutasi: a weekly cinema show, for example.

## 2. *Shopping facilities and centres for Poutasi buyers*

Since the opening of Lee Chang's store in 1959 Poutasi has had very good local shopping facilities. The range of goods in this store far exceeded that available in the older trading-stations. Lee Chang's prices were often lower than those of the trading-stations. He declared that he aimed to sell at Apia prices and for many

Table 36  Money Owed by the Sample *'Āiga* to Three Poutasi Stores, May 1966

| *'āiga* | Lee Chang | Nelson's | Ioane |
|---|---|---|---|
|  |  | £ |  |
| 1 (c) | 60 | 9 | 8 |
| 5 | 56 | 12 |  |
| 7 | 9 |  |  |
| 8 | 40 | 4 |  |
| 9 (b) |  | 1 | 7 |
| 10 (a) | 38 | 21 |  |
| 11 | 11 | 1 |  |
| 13 | 14 | 2 |  |
| 15 | 12 | 2 |  |
| Women's Committee | 52 | 5 |  |
| *matai* | 12 | 3 |  |
| *'aumāga* | 55 |  |  |
| Totals (d) | 359 | 60 | 15 |

NOTES:  (a) *Taule'ale'a* head of this *'āiga* is married to a daughter of Lee Chang.
  (b) Ioane's *'āiga*
  (c) *'Āiga* of Ioane's wife
  (d) The totals are the debts only of the sample *'āiga* and the three village organizations shown.

commodities this was found to be so. Consequently there was much less need to go to Apia for special purchases and during the survey eighty-seven per cent of the purchases made by the sample *'āiga* were made in Poutasi.[34] Lee Chang offered the additional advantage, which was not available in Apia, of quite liberal credit.[35] Compared with Uafato and Taga, however, it was still cheaper to go to Apia from Poutasi and to take advantage of the wider range of goods and services offered there. Both in terms of the local shopping facilities and the cash and labour cost of shopping in Apia, Poutasi *'āiga* were better off than those in Uafato and Taga.

3. *The effect of social and organizational institutions on outlay*

Quite clearly the decisions by the *fono* and Women's Committee to involve the village in substantial investment in village and church capital works has had a considerable influence on the direction of the outlay of cash and subsistence resources in Poutasi. During the survey period there was no activity of this kind, nor to my knowledge were there any plans for future investment in village capital works. But from time to time during the survey relatively small cash subscriptions were raised in the village for a variety of purposes, such

[34] See Table 35.
[35] See Table 36.

as to provide purchased food for *fono* and Committee meetings, to
buy equipment for the Poutasi rugby teams, and to pay a fee of
£1 per tap to the district water-supply committee for maintenance
work in the dam and pipeline. It is estimated that over the twelve-
month period £189, or £0·6 per consumption unit, was collected
in the village for these various purposes. At the same time there
was also a considerable outlay of subsistence resources—food and
labour—for the maintenance of the hospital and school and their
staffs.

Over the twelve-month period £504, or £1·6 per consumption
unit, was raised for the churches and their pastors. In 1966 the
Poutasi Congregational pastor received a cash income of £193
which, even with the loss of village cash income due to the hurricane,
was slightly more than he received in 1965 (£179), and considerably more than was received in 1966 by the pastors of Taga (about
£100) and Uafato (£87). The Poutasi pastor was also considerably
better housed than were his counterparts in Taga and Uafato, and
he received a larger supply of pandanus mats.

During the survey there appeared to be more 'social' events
involving individual Poutasi *'āiga* (both in Poutasi and in other
villages) than in Taga and Uafato. There were, for example, two
funerals in the village, one title dedication in which a Poutasi
storekeeper, Ioane, received a title from his mother's *'āiga* in another
village, and two weddings in other villages involving related *'āiga*
in Poutasi. The Poutasi rugby team may also be mentioned in this
context; it played host to teams from other south-coast villages
each Saturday throughout the rugby season, and it played two
matches in Apia. These events usually required the participating
*'āiga* or individuals to contribute money, bought and subsistence
foods and time, and sometimes also to contribute traditional valuables such as *'ietōga*. As an example, a fairly detailed record was
obtained of the cash and commodity contributions at the funeral
in May of Ioane's mother, the wife of a Poutasi *matai*. On that
occasion the *'āiga* (mainly Ioane) provided purchased foods for
the Poutasi *matai* and their wives, and visiting relatives from other
villages, costing about £20, and a large quantity of subsistence
foods. The other Poutasi *'āiga* gave formal gifts of purchased foods,
costing altogether about £50, and £5 12s in cash. The visiting
relatives provided yet more food which cost them about £26, and
fourteen *'ietōga* which, with some of the food (such as tins of biscuits
and fish) were formally distributed among the attending *matai* of
rank. Most of the cost (cash and subsistence) of the funeral was born
by the *'āiga* responsible and its relatives. The unrelated *matai* of
Poutasi in general returned from the funeral with gifts which more

than compensated for the contribution they made to the supply of food.

Another example of the redistribution of cash and subsistence resources through '*āiga* social events was found in the wedding of a relative of two Poutasi '*āiga*. The wedding took place in another village. Together the two Poutasi *matai* contributed £30, a five-tiered cake bought in Apia for £6, and two large pigs. They returned from the wedding with twelve '*ietōga*, ten pandanus sleeping-mats and a wedding dress.[36]

In calculating the cash outlay on gifts in Table 34 gifts of bought food and other commodities were converted into cash values (purchase prices) so that, say, ten one-shilling loaves of bread taken to a funeral does not appear as a food purchase but as 10s in the gift category.[37] It is estimated that cash and purchased goods were given by the Poutasi '*āiga* during the twelve-month period to the value of £490, or £1·5 per consumption unit. This was considerably more than was given by the Taga and Uafato '*āiga* (£0·7 and £0·5 per consumption unit respectively). It was also a great deal more than was recorded as gifts received in Poutasi (£0·2 per consumption unit). But while this exchange may well get out of balance in the short run it would probably achieve a more even balance over a longer period than that covered by the survey.

Because the village and '*āiga* level social institutions and organizations were much stronger in Poutasi than in Taga and Uafato, they played a much more important role in determining the level of village income (subsistence and cash), and the distribution or the use made of that income.

### 4. Cash savings

As in the other villages, data on cash savings were difficult to obtain. Most people with wage and salary jobs in Apia, and the village storekeepers, had bank or post office savings accounts but the actual savings were not known. The nearest bank and post office savings account facilities were in Apia. '*Āiga* indebtedness to the Poutasi stores as indicated in Table 36 was fairly high, particularly in relation to Taga and Uafato. In May 1966 an average of £1·9 per consumption unit (in the sample '*āiga*) was owed to the

---

[36] Generally the bride is provided with several wedding dresses by different relatives and these are distributed among the important and appropriate guests.

[37] This method was used also for the other villages. It was, however, less important in Uafato and Taga than in Poutasi and Utuali'i. In the same way gifts of purchased food etc. received in another village and brought home have also been valued at approximate purchase prices and included in the gifts received category.

Poutasi stores. Local store debts averaged only £0·4 in Taga and
£0·3 in Uafato per consumption unit. In addition, in Poutasi
the village groups—*matai*, Women's Committee and *'aumāga*
owed altogether £119 to the Poutasi stores (£0·4 per consumption
unit averaged over the whole village). The debt of the sample
*'āiga* in Poutasi increased over the survey period from about £253
in December 1965 to about £315 in May 1966.

In general the Poutasi survey data show that over the twelve-
month period to 30 November 1966, cash income exceeded expenditure by £1,464, or £4·5 per consumption unit. While this cannot
be assumed to indicate the actual level of cash savings over the
period it does suggest that it was probably considerably higher than
in Taga and Uafato.

# Chapter 7

# UTUALI'I

BECAUSE of its location near Apia and in the 'plantation belt' of Western Samoa, Utuali'i has a long history of strong linkage with the market sector.

There are thirty villages strung along the twenty-three miles of north-west Upolu coastline from Apia to the Mulifanua inter-island ferry wharf and the Faleolo airfield. Utuali'i is one of these. Along large stretches of this coastline it is often difficult to find where one village ends and the next begins. The main features of north-west Upolu have been summarized as follows:

> The region which is markedly distinctive in essence as well as in degree is North-western Upolu where the combination of large coconut, cacao and rubber estates, small leasehold plantations, cattle stations and village gardens provides great variety in agricultural economy and organization. The presence of the commercial and administrative centre of Apia, the overseas port, the airstrip and the seaplane base make this region the focus of almost all economic activity within the territory. A much wider range of employment opportunities is available than in any other region. Furthermore, North-western Upolu is distinctive in terms of its population, for here are the largest villages, the greatest densities of population, and the highest proportions of Europeans and part-Samoans. (Fox and Cumberland 1962, p. 291)

Utuali'i has had close contact with European missionaries since 1845 when the London Missionary Society established its headquarters and a seminary for the training of Samoan pastors at Malua on Utuali'i land. It was only about ten miles by sea from the harbour at Apia which started to develop as the commercial centre for the islands in the 1850s.[1] During the second half of the nineteenth century extensive areas of the broad plain to the west of Apia were acquired by European planters for coconut plantations. In 1895 the Malua compound and the land lying inland from it (about 375 acres) was given to the London Missionary Society by the Utuali'i high chief and this became the freehold property of

[1] The sea journey from Utuali'i to Apia could be made almost entirely within the broad lagoon which sheltered the entire north-west coast.

the church. At about this time another forty acres of Utuali'i land
was sold to a European planter for a coconut plantation,[2] and an
area of houseland was leased to a *matai* from another part of Samoa.
With the growth of Apia and Malua, and the expansion of commercial plantations in the area, there was a parallel development
of commercial facilities such as trade-stores, and transport facilities,
such as coastal shipping and roads.

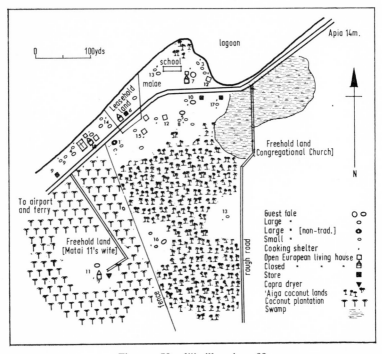

Fig. 10    Utuali'i village in 1966

By 1910 the coastal road west from Apia had been built to a
point well beyond Utuali'i, and there was a network of secondary
roads running inland from various points to the commercial
plantations. In 1925 the main London Missionary Society Secondary
School was transferred from the village of Leaulumoega to the

---

[2] In 1966 this plantation was owned by a part-Samoan female descendant of
the original planter who was married to a *matai* of the neighbouring village of
Tufulele. The plantation was still run on close to commerical lines—*'āiga* labour
was supplemented by hired labour, an old but very large dryer was used, and the
copra output, about 25 tons a year, was sold directly to an Apia exporter who
took delivery at the plantation. The copra output of this small plantation was
about 95% of the total copra output of the whole village during the survey period.
This *'āiga* was included as part of the Utuali'i sample.

Malua compound only ten minutes walk from Utuali'i village. During the Second World War the coastal road between Apia and Utuali'i was sealed and there were regular bus services along the north-west coast. From this time it was possible to commute daily to wage jobs in and near Apia, and to get to Apia for shopping and other purposes in about half an hour. In 1966 the bus fare into Apia was only sixpence on several buses and one shilling on others. All the south-coast buses from as far as the Falealili district (Poutasi) passed through Utuali'i on the way to and from Apia each day, and there were many buses which ran shuttle services all day along the north-west coast.

The main coastal road, the busiest in Western Samoa, ran through the Utuali'i *malae* (see Figure 10). There was little to distinguish Utuali'i village from many other villages along this coast but it was quite different from Poutasi, Taga and Uafato. Most of the houses and larger *fale* faced the road from either side; and there were more non-traditional than traditional dwellings. As in the other villages the church was an imposing building and it was flanked by a large European house occupied by the pastor (similar to the one in Poutasi), a large open-house used as a meeting hall, and several *fale* used as service buildings. Across the road from the church were the ordered rows of palms of the small commercial plantation. At the other end of the village stood the new elementary school (1958), two trading-stations (Burns Philp and O. F. Nelson) and a large European-style house of the high chief (1963). There were several other European-style houses in the village, and two old store buildings used as dwellings. Ten *taule'ale'a* families lived on inland blocks, some as far as two miles from the village. Two secondary roads led inland from the village; one marked the boundary between Utuali'i and Malua land, and the other served much the same purpose between Utuali'i and the neighbouring village of Tufulele. Utuali'i and Tufulele were closely related villages which, in the past, had apparently formed a single village. Utuali'i lands were all under the control (*pule*) of a single *matai* title, as were the *matai* titles of the village.[3]

[3] All the traditional titles of the village were controlled by the high chief Mata'u and the holders owed him allegiance and service (*tautua*). This control over the village titles was demonstrated in 1967 when no less than eleven Utuali'i men were given titles by Mata'u who had decided to stand as a candidate for the Legislative Assembly in which election only *matai* could vote. There were four other *matai* resident in Utuali'i who were not related to Mata'u, and did not pay him *tautua*. One (plantation) held a Tufulele title, two held titles from other villages but were married to Utuali'i women, and another held the lease for a houseland block in the village but was otherwise not connected to Utuali'i. Mata'u had allowed all these *matai* (related and unrelated) to use blocks of Utuali'i agricultural land for subsistence and cash crops, and to harvest coconuts from an area near the village which was under his direct control.

Utuali'i was predominantly a Congregational church village and this was a second point of departure with Tufulele which was largely Catholic and Methodist. The Congregational church and pastor in Utuali'i served the Congregational '*āiga* of Tufulele. The two villages, however, shared one *pulenu'u* (a Utuali'i *matai* during the survey, but it had earlier been a Tufulele *matai*) and one elementary school (in Utuali'i). The forest inland from the two villages had been open for Utuali'i or Tufulele '*āiga* to clear and claim, but as Tufulele was a much larger village its clearings extended much farther than those of Utuali'i. Since about 1955 there was no forest area which could still be cleared by Utuali'i '*āiga*. Utuali'i was therefore the only village of the four studied which had no forest reserves at the time of the survey.

With a population of 261 in November 1965 Utuali'i was the smallest of the four villages studied. There were seventeen '*āiga* but because five titles were unfilled there were only twelve *matai*. The largest '*āiga* had twenty-eight members but these were divided between six family groups of which only that of the *matai* lived permanently in the village—the other family groups lived on agricultural blocks inland from the village. This was a Mormon '*āiga*— the only non-Congregational '*āiga* in the village. The average '*āiga* in Utuali'i consisted of sixteen persons as in Uafato.

Two '*āiga* did not belong traditionally to Utuali'i but had become permanent residents because the *matai* had wage jobs in the area and had settled in their wives' village.

It is difficult to build up a precise picture of population changes in recent years. The Congregational pastor's annual population figures combine the two villages (Tufulele and Utuali'i) as did the 1951 Census. It is apparent, however, that for the two villages combined, the average annual growth rate between 1950 and 1965 was about four per cent, that is, somewhat higher than in the other three villages. It is also apparent that the growth rate in the first half of this period was considerably higher than in the second half. Part of Utuali'i growth resulted from people from outer-villages settling there after obtaining wage jobs in or near Apia.

PRODUCTIVE RESOURCES

1. *Land*

There were only about 266 acres of Utuali'i land including the forty-acre freehold plantation. The area was flat and the soils were moderately fertile under natural conditions. The average annual rainfall was between 100 and 200 inches but most of this fell between November and April and there was a marked dry season between

May and October.[4] The coconut was, of course, the oldest commercial crop and as in most of Western Samoa the main period of
expansion of this crop had been between 1890 and 1920. This
applied to the small plantation as well as to the village small-
holdings and it was clear that virtually no new planting or replanting
had taken place between about 1920 and 1958. In 1958 one *matai*
started to interplant coconuts in an area of cacao trees (planted
about eight years earlier) and by 1965 this small-holding of about
two acres had started to bear. During the 1950s about seventeen
acres were planted in cacao, in small scattered plots, and this provided a fairly important source of cash income for three *'āiga*.[5]
Altogether, about ninety-two acres were under tree crops (cacao
and coconuts)—thirty-five per cent of the total area. The village
itself, including houselands, school, stores and church, and the road,
occupied about thirty-nine acres and, with the area under tree
crops, made up half the total area. The rest of the land, a narrow
strip about a quarter of a mile wide, from about three-quarters of a
mile to two miles from the coast, was used mainly for subsistence
food crops, and in recent years, a variety of European vegetables
(mainly beans, tomatoes and cucumbers).[6]

No forest remained available to Utuali'i *'āiga* as the whole area
had been brought into use at least by the mid-1950s. Although the
practice was still to shift plots after one or two crops of taro, the
area in which this could be done was narrowly defined. Some
years appeared to have been overcropped in the past ten years or
so and production was maintained only with much effort in weeding.
A number of *taule'ale'a* families had built *fale* on inland blocks and
lived there more or less permanently, partly so that they could give
more time (particularly the women and children) to weeding.

The division of land between the seventeen *'āiga* is shown in
Table 37 and Figure 12. Most *'āiga* had at least two blocks—houseland in the village and an inland block. Apart from the small
plantation, only two *matai* had substantial holdings, but a large
part of the coconut land of the high chief, Mata'u, was used by the
whole village as a 'communal' source of coconuts for food. During
the survey a number of *'āiga* produced no cash crops at all and their
inland blocks were mainly under bush fallow with a few small
scattered plots of taro and *ta'amū*. The blocks on which the *taule'ale'a*
families lived were used both for food and cash crops (vegetables
and cacao). They were kept in production by continuous weeding

---

[4] The average monthly rainfall for January was about twenty inches while for
July it was only about five inches.
[5] Due to the hurricane, no cacao was harvested in Utuali'i during my survey
after January.
[6] See Figure 11 and Table 37.

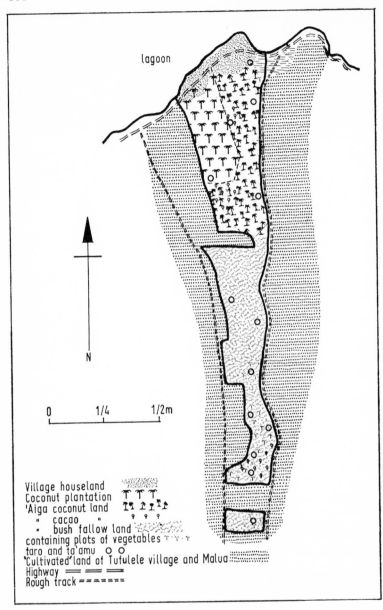

Fig. 11   Utuali'i: land use in 1966

and the fallow period allowed between crops was relatively short. With the post-hurricane emergency food planting these blocks were almost completely brought into production, while other inland blocks remained almost completely in fallow.

## 2. *Labour*

Eleven men held full-time wage jobs and others were employed for short periods as casual labourers in Apia or on the near-by plantations. Several women had casual labouring jobs on the plantations (including that in Utuali'i). Full-time wage employment was more common in Utuali'i than in the other three villages surveyed; there were two teachers, two clerks, two bus drivers, one truck

Table 37 Utuali'i: *Matai* Land Holdings and Land Use in 1966[a]

| 'Āiga | Number of blocks | House-land | Schools, stores and church | Coco-nuts | Cacao | Coco-nuts and cacao | Taro, ta'amū, bananas and vege-tables | Bush fallow | Total area |
|---|---|---|---|---|---|---|---|---|---|
| | | acres | acres | acres | acres | acres | acres | acres | acres |
| 1[b] | 5 | 3·5 | | 5·5 | 5·0 | 4·0 | 2·8 | 12·7 | 33·5 |
| 2 | 1 | | | | | | | | 2·0 |
| 3 | 2 | | | | | | | | 17·0 |
| 4 | 1 | | | | | | | | 1·4 |
| 5[b] | 2 | 2·0 | | | | 5·0 | 0·6 | 4·4 | 12·0 |
| 6 | 2 | | | | | | | | 11·3 |
| 7[b] | 4 | 0·8 | 5·5 | 22·0[c] | | | 0·7 | 11·6 | 40·6 |
| 8 | 3 | | | | | | | | 17·6 |
| 9 | 2 | | | | | | | | 11·2 |
| 10[b] | 2 | 2·1 | 1·0 | | | | 1·3 | 4·9 | 9·3 |
| 11[b] | 3 | 1·0[d] | | 39·0[d] | | | 1·4 | 20·6 | 62·0 |
| 12 | 2 | | | | | | | | 12·5 |
| 13[b] | 2 | 0·3 | | | | | 0·5 | 2·0 | 2·8 |
| 14 | 2 | | | | | | | | 8·5 |
| 15 | 2 | | | | | | | | 10·5 |
| 16[b] | 1 | 0·2 | | | | 1·2 | 0·5 | 0·1 | 2·0 |
| 17[b] | 2 | 2·0 | | 3·0 | | | 0·3 | 0·7 | 6·0 |
| Pastor | 2 | | | | | | | | 6·0 |
| | 40 | 30·5 | 8·5 | 75·0 | 7·0 | 10·2 | 18·4 | 116·0 | 265·6 |
| Percentage of total area | | 11·5 | 3·2 | 28·2 | 2·6 | 3·9 | 6·9 | 43·7 | |

NOTES: [a] Estimated roughly from the Land Holdings Map (Fig. 12) and Land Use Map (Fig. 11)

[b] Sample *'āiga*

[c] Area of coconut land open to whole village for subsistence food purposes

[d] Freehold coconut plantation

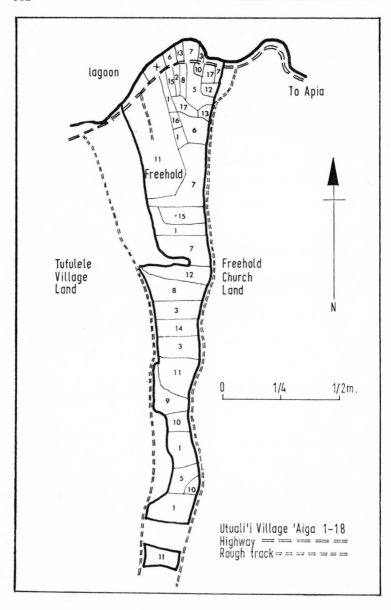

Fig. 12   Utuali'i: *matai* land holdings in 1966

driver, one airport worker, one policeman and two shop assistants. Due to the hurricane, the opportunities for part-time wage employment after January was much reduced, particularly on the cacao plantations, and this source of cash income was of negligible importance during most of the survey period. In the other three villages, particularly Uafato and Taga, it was fairly uncommon to find a *taule'ale'a* or *matai* who had, in the past, held a wage job. In Utuali'i it was uncommon to find someone who had not. During the survey period wage employment was an important source of cash income in Utuali'i, but apparently in previous years it had been even more important. With the availability of labouring jobs in the area, school education was a less important prerequisite for wage employment than in the other villages. However, several Utuali'i *'āiga* had invested fairly heavily in the education of their children and as a result had been able to abandon the land as a source of cash income. Most Utuali'i people who held wage jobs in Apia continued to live in the village and use the cheap and convenient bus service along the north-west coast of Upolu to commute to work daily. The *'āiga* concerned were able, therefore, to draw on a larger proportion of the wage-earnings of their members than was possible in the other villages whose wage-earners generally had to live in Apia or some village near Apia such as Utuali'i.[7]

During the survey there was no shortage of labour for subsistence food and cash cropping. The labour supply in most *'āiga*, however, was differently organized from that in the other villages. Most *taulele'a* were allowed a great deal of freedom to live apart from their *matai*, to grow their own food crops (and some for their *matai*) as they pleased, and to earn and control money from cash cropping or wages. No large *'āiga* in Utuali'i worked as a single production unit as they did in the other villages. One result of this weakening of the *'āiga* productive unit, and the accompanying decline in the organizing role of some *matai*, was that the level of subsistence food production declined well below that observed in the other villages.

### 3. *Producers' capital*

Generally speaking there had been less investment per consumption unit in producers' capital in Utuali'i than in the other three villages. On the negative side there had been no investment

---

[7] There were, in fact, several *taulele'a* living in Utuali'i who had come originally from other villages so that they could work on the near-by plantations. Their cash earnings contributed more to their Utuali'i *'āiga* than to their home-village *'āiga*.

in stores or in copra dryers except for one dryer on the plantation, built in the 1930s. Other items, however, such as fishing gear and canoes, agricultural and carpentry tools and sewing machines, were owned in much the same variety and quantity. Total stocks of producers' capital in Utuali'i is valued at about £600, of which seventy-seven per cent had been cash investment (Table 38). Total investment per consumption unit was £3, compared to £8 in Poutasi, £5 in Taga and £7 in Uafato.

As in the other villages, the items in Table 38 are only part of the actual investment in producers' capital. Many years ago, Utuali'i labour had constructed the main road and two minor roads. The main investment, however, was in the plantation, which was well fenced and had its own access road. There had been investment of subsistence and cash resources in the school building, the church, the pastor's house, the church hall and an open-house used by the Women's Committee. These items will be discussed later.

PRODUCTION

Ten years earlier the commodities produced for consumption and sale in Utuali'i were probably the same as those produced in the other three villages surveyed. At that time copra, bananas and cacao beans were the main cash crops and taro, *ta'amū*, breadfruit and bananas were the main subsistence food staples. But the last bananas were produced for sale in Utuali'i in the mid-1950s and

Table 38   Utuali'i: Producers' Capital[a]

|  | Total | Cash component | Subsistence component |
|---|---|---|---|
|  | £ | % | % |
| Fishing gear & canoes | 124 | 16 | 84 |
| Agricultural tools | 41 | 95 | 5 |
| Copra dryer | 100 | 75 | 25 |
| Carpentry tools | 115 | 91 | 9 |
| Guns | 20 | 100 | — |
| Sewing machines | 180 | 100 | — |
| Copra scales | 20 | 100 | — |
| Total investment[b] | 600 | 77 | 23 |
| Investment per consumption unit | £3 | £2 | £1 |

NOTES:   [a] The method by which values have been imputed has been described on page 50.

[b] An imputed rent for the use of this equipment has been included as an item of subsistence income (see Table 42). This is based on the above values and estimates of the useful life of the various items.

by 1965 virtually no bananas were grown even for food. With the growth of a local-products market in Apia over the past ten years or so, a number of Utuali'i '*āiga* became regular suppliers of certain European vegetables, mainly tomatoes, beans and cucumbers.[8] The Apia local-products market not only provided a commercial outlet for Utuali'i agricultural products and fish, but it also became a dependable source of village staple foods and reduced the dependence of Utuali'i '*āiga* on their own production of these foods for consumption purposes.

## 1. *Subsistence*

### (a) *Food*

Utuali'i was the only village of the four studied which had cheap and convenient access to a market supply of subsistence foods. In the Apia local-products market taro, *ta'amū*, bananas, coconuts, breadfruit, taro leaves, fresh and cooked fish and other village foods were available every weekday. In addition to this regular supply the Banana Scheme frequently sold cases of bananas rejected for export. This assured supply of staple foods was an important factor in the decline of subsistence food production in Utuali'i. Before the hurricane, only about seventy per cent of the taro, *ta'amū*, breadfruit and bananas consumed in Utuali'i was produced in the village and many '*āiga* regularly bought bananas and taro in Apia to supplement their own subsistence supplies.[9]

There were other complementary factors which contributed to the decline in subsistence food production in Utuali'i. First, the labour costs of taro, *ta'amū* and banana production were somewhat higher than in the other three villages. Between 1948 and 1955 bananas were produced in Utuali'i for export, and this period saw the clearing of all remaining forest available to Utuali'i producers. By about 1955 banana production could be maintained only by reducing the fallow period. This in turn called for greater efforts to weed producing plots and to clear abandoned land for replanting. The response of the Utuali'i growers to this increased production cost was to abandon bananas as a cash crop altogether. At about that time the cacao seedlings planted after the war came into production and provided an alternate source of cash income, and some '*āiga* were also starting to supply coconuts, fish and European

[8] In July 1966 I made a fairly detailed survey of the Apia local-products market which showed that the main suppliers of tomatoes, beans and cucumbers came from Utuali'i and several neighbouring villages. See my essay, 'Produce marketing in a Polynesian society, Apia, Western Samoa', in H. C. Brookfield 1968.

[9] Consumption of flour, rice and bread were also higher in Utuali'i before the hurricane than in the other villages studied.

vegetables in the Apia market. During the survey period growers still had to put more effort into weeding food plots than in the other villages. Several *taulele'a* who lived on the inland blocks said that they planted only as much land as they could keep weeded and this was why they did not increase staple food production or their output of European vegetables. These men, however, worked fewer hours per week on their land than did the *taulele'a* in the other three villages. It took an average of 210 minutes to clear a plot and plant one hundred taro and/or *ta'amū*. The same task in Taga took an average of 200 minutes, but this included about forty minutes' walking time between the plot and the village—a minor component in Utuali'i. In Poutasi and Uafato it took only 160 and 170 minutes respectively. The Utuali'i *taulele'a* were quite aware that the returns to their labour in the production of taro and *ta'amū* (and presumably bananas also) were lower than in most outer-villages, as they had all spent time with related *'āiga* in other districts.

These higher labour costs did not apply to the production of breadfruit or fish. In a normal year, breadfruit accounted for nearly forty per cent of the subsistence staples produced in Utuali'i and, as in the other villages, the labour costs of this food were very small.[10] The broad lagoon provided productive fishing grounds, as in Poutasi, and during the survey the men spent an average of two and a half hours a week fishing. An average catch of five pounds of fish per hour was recorded over the five weeks of the Utuali'i survey and this was considerably higher than in the other villages. Also a larger proportion of the fish was sold, mainly in the Apia market.

Utuali'i men worked an average of about ten hours a week to produce subsistence foods, about the same as in Poutasi. But while this effort supplied about thirty pounds weight of staple foods per consumption unit per week in Poutasi, it produced only twenty pounds in Utuali'i. In addition, the Utuali'i women averaged about ten hours a week helping their menfolk, particularly in weeding and this was much higher than in the other villages.

Another factor which possibly contributed to the lower level of subsistence food output in Utuali'i was the fact that, before the hurricane, many Utuali'i men and women took casual wage jobs in near-by plantations, where they were paid partly in cash and partly in 'rations'. At least during these periods of employment, those involved were less dependent on village food supplies. After the hurricane this supply of food was no longer available, because the plantations, particularly the cacao plantations, cut back on the employment of casual labour.

[10] See Appendix Table 2.

There was another contributing factor, the importance of which could not be ascertained. The Malua College and school maintained quite extensive food plots on land close to the Utuali'i inland blocks. A large proportion of the output of these plots was regularly stolen and it was strongly suspected that some Utuali'i *taulele'a* were at least partly responsible. There was also a large stand of breadfruit trees close to the secondary road between Malua and Utuali'i land, about half a mile inland from the college, and this also was known to contribute to the supply of food in some Utuali'i *'āiga*. Further, it was known that the extensive Malua coconut resources were regularly harvested by Utuali'i people who used the nuts both as subsistence foods and to sell in Apia. It need hardly be mentioned that this source of food in Utuali'i had a particularly low labour cost and it was almost as dependable as the supply in the Apia local-products market.

The imputed value of subsistence food supplies for the twelve months from December 1965 to November 1966 is £2,312, or £11·8 per consumption unit. This was considerably lower than the other villages and it was clear that the difference represented a normal situation where, in Utuali'i, subsistence supplies of staple foods were supplemented by supplies purchased in the market sector. Estimates of the values of subsistence foods produced during the twelve-month period are shown in Table 42.

(b) *Housing and household durables*

Table 39 shows the estimated floor areas of dwellings in each of the four villages. Two interesting points emerge from this; first, the villages rank in terms of floor area per consumption unit, from the largest to the smallest area, as follows—Utuali'i, Taga, Poutasi and Uafato; and second, they rank in the same order according to the proportion of total floor area in houses and *fale* built of non-traditional material, such as concrete floors and iron roofs.[11] The two factors are of course related in that the replacement of a round or oval *fale* with a rectangular open-house almost always increased the floor area, and in general the houses and *fale* built with non-traditional materials were larger than traditional *fale*.

In Utuali'i about forty-nine per cent of the floor area of the *'āiga* dwellings was concrete, compared to twenty-eight per cent in Poutasi, twenty-one per cent in Taga, and four per cent in Uafato. If village-owned dwellings such as the pastors' houses are included, the differences between the villages are more marked still—Utuali'i—fifty-six per cent, Poutasi—thirty-nine per cent,

[11] These calculations include dwellings such as those of the pastors, teachers and nurses, owned by the village.

Taga—twenty per cent and Uafato—four per cent. In Taga there was a considerable increase in the number of non-traditional dwellings when the road gave easier access to store supplies of cement and roofing iron. Much the same had occurred in Poutasi after 1949. It has yet to happen in Uafato. Utuali'i had relatively easy access to supplies of non-traditional building material even

Table 39    Proportion of Traditional to Non-traditional Dwellings in 1966

| Type of dwelling | Utuali'i (I) | | Poutasi (II) | | Taga (III) | | Uafato (IV) | |
|---|---|---|---|---|---|---|---|---|
| | No. of dwellings | Approx. floor area per consumption unit (sq. ft) | No. of dwellings | Approx. floor area per consumption unit (sq. ft) | No. of dwellings | Approx. floor area per consumption unit (sq. ft) | No. of dwellings | Approx. floor area per consumption unit (sq. ft) |
| Traditional | | | | | | | | |
| guest-*fale* | 6 | 10·7 | 15 | 16·2 | 13 | 12·9 | 10 | 17·5 |
| large *fale* | 9 | 10·1 | 12 | 8·5 | 20 | 12·1 | 11 | 12·1 |
| small *fale* | 28 | 15·7 | 42 | 14·2 | 68 | 20·5 | 33 | 18·2 |
| | | 36·5 | | 38·9 | | 45·5 | | 47·8 |
| Non-traditional | | | | | | | | |
| oval house | 1 | 1·8 | 1 | 1·1 | 4 | 3·8 | | |
| open-house | 6 | 11·2 | 3 | 3·4 | 5 | 4·8 | 1 | 1·8 |
| closed European house | 5 | 33·2 | 6 | 20·0 | 1 | 2·7 | | |
| | | 46·2 | | 24·5 | | 11·3 | | 1·8 |
| Total dwelling area[a] | | 82·7 | | 63·4 | | 56·8 | | 49·6 |
| Proportion of non-traditional on total dwelling area[b] | | 56% | | 39% | | 20% | | 4% |

earlier than Poutasi and, in addition, had been unable to extract large timber from its own forests since the mid-1950s. Most of the large posts, and the sugar-cane thatches used in the three guest-*fale* and two non-traditional *fale* built in Utuali'i since 1956, had been bought from timber mills and stores.

The carpenters employed in Utuali'i also added more to the cash costs of building than they did in the other villages by demanding a larger proportion of their payment in money rather than traditional valuables. This was probably welcomed by most Utuali'i *matai* because they found it hard to acquire traditional valuables.

The estimated cash and subsistence costs of five Utuali'i dwellings, their guest-*fale* and two other large *fale* built largely with purchased material are shown in Table 40.

The '*āiga* dwellings in Utuali'i are valued at £6,079, of which

Table 40   Estimated Cash and Subsistence Costs of Three Guest-*fale* and Two Non-traditional *Fale* in Utuali'i

| '*Āiga* | 7[a] | 5[a] | 10[a] | 13[b] | 1[c] |
|---|---|---|---|---|---|
| Year built | 1956 | 1957 | 1965 | 1965 | 1965 |
| Cash payments: (£) | | | | | |
|   material | 2 | 3 | 12 | 80 | 95 |
|   carpenter | 55 | 35 | 60 | | 40 |
| Subsistence payments to carpenter: (Nos) | | | | | |
|   '*ietōga* | 52 | 8 | 12 | | 17 |
|   *siapo* | 20 | 10 | 5 | | 6 |
|   sleeping-mats | 50 | 30 | 50 | | 30 |
| Unskilled '*āiga* labour: (hrs) | 1300 | 1300 | 1060 | 650 | 1300 |
| Total cost: (£) | | | | | |
|   Cash | 57 | 38 | 72 | 80 | 135 |
|   Imputed value of subsistence payments[e] | 316 | 73 | 112 | | 117 |
|   Imputed value of unskilled labour[d] | 100 | 100 | 80 | 50 | 100 |
| Total | 473 | 211 | 264 | 130 | 352 |

NOTES:   [a] Traditional guest-*fale*: main structural timbers brought from the south coast of Upolu.

[b] Small oval-open house built by the *matai* himself (who was a skilled carpenter), entirely of materials purchased in Apia.

[c] Large oval *fale* with cement foundation-floor and iron roof. Most materials were purchased in Apia.

[d] Unskilled '*āiga* labour (rough estimate) valued at 1s 6d an hour

[e] Imputed values: '*ietōga*—£5; *siapo* (tapa cloth)—6s; sleeping-mats—£1

£3,019 represented the investment of subsistence resources.[12] The subsistence income derived from the use of these dwellings during the twelve-month period, December 1965 to November 1966, is estimated at £215, or £1·1 per consumption unit.

Household non-traditional furniture and bought utensils and equipment were similar to those described for Poutasi and Taga. Ownership of non-traditional furniture, such as tables and chairs, however, was more widespread and the production of traditional furniture, such as the various mats, was below that of Poutasi and Taga. The Utuali'i Women's Committee did not hold 'weaving circles' or encourage in any way the production of pandanus mats, and other traditional goods.

### 2. *Market*

Of the main Samoan village cash crops—copra, bananas and cacao beans—only copra was produced in any quantity in Utuali'i, and most of this came from the small plantation. Bananas were an important cash crop before 1955, but since then sales have been negligible. Cacao trees were planted after the war and harvested up to the hurricane. During the twelve months from December 1965 to November 1966 copra and cacao beans earned £1,263, or £6·4 per consumption unit, most of it from copra, and most of the copra from the plantation. This was forty per cent of the total village cash income from agriculture. The main agricultural commodities sold by the rest of the village were coconuts, fruit, sugar-cane, and European vegetables. These earned a total cash income during the twelve-month period of £1,535, or £7·8 per consumption unit, that is, about fifty per cent of the total village cash income from agriculture. Fish was a fairly important source of cash income for several *'āiga*.

The two stores built in Utuali'i in the 1920s originally had been trading-stations, and until buses gave cheap access to Apia, most Utuali'i copra was sold to them. Since the war, however, the quantities of copra produced in the village (with the exception of the plantation, which marketed its output directly in Apia) has declined and the trading-stations in the village have become retail stores. The available records show that the last copra bought by the O. F. Nelson station was in 1961 and the Burns Philp station had stopped buying copra several years earlier.

Apparently there was a substitution of coconuts (sold in the Apia local-products market) for copra (sold in or near the village).

---

[12] The proportion of total investment in dwellings from the monetized sector was higher in Utuali'i (50%) than in Poutasi (33%), Taga (31%) and Uafato (10%).

Cash returns from coconuts sold husked in Apia were quite high. For most of the survey period eight large mature nuts or ten to twelve smaller immature nuts sold for two shillings or double the outer-village store price. The nuts were sold in Apia for food and not for making copra. Utuali'i *'āiga* earned more money by selling nuts than they would have from copra. But the labour costs of marketing coconuts were often high—considerably higher than the production and marketing costs of copra. Generally the older children were sent into Apia to sell coconuts (bus fare one to two shillings return, but rarely any freight charge) and it took anything from one to five hours to sell the usual quantities taken in. In addition, an hour was spent on the bus and an hour or more was needed to gather and husk the nuts. The cash return to labour from the sale of coconuts in Apia varied correspondingly, and as many villages tried this, it tended to fall as the weeks passed after the hurricane.[13] By March the sale of Utuali'i coconuts threatened to reduce the supply available for subsistence food needs and the *fono* forbade the sale of nuts for two months.

There was always a ready market in Apia for fresh fish and several individuals in Utuali'i had 'specialized' in this cash-earning activity. As with coconuts, the job of taking the fish into Apia and selling it was often given to the older children. Marketing costs were rarely as high for fish which was a scarce commodity in Apia, but both involved an hour in the bus (half an hour each way) and one or two shillings in fares. One *'āiga* sold fish regularly, sending small bundles into Apia almost every day and earning between five and ten shillings a day. The *matai* usually spent four or five hours a day out on the lagoon, and he supplied the food needs of his own *'āiga* and often some to distribute in the village as gifts, and to sell.[14]

The sale of fruit in the Apia local-products market gave some *'āiga* a small cash income. Mango, lime and orange trees had been planted in the village in the past and a part of the crop was sold. Several *'āiga* grew a few pineapples and stands of sugar-cane and occasionally marketed some of the output. Apart perhaps from the

[13] After the hurricane copra and coconuts were vitually the only cash crops left for several months and the supply of nuts offered for sale in Apia increased considerably. The cash returns to labour in the Apia sale of Utuali'i coconuts varied from 9d to 1s 9d an hour.

[14] This particular *matai* enjoyed his fishing immensely and by distributing part of his daily catch among his neighbours and one of the storekeepers he received in return a fairly regular supply of staple foods, bread, tinned meat and tobacco. His cash income came from the sale of coconuts and fish. He and his *'āiga* planted very little taro or *ta'amū* between September 1965 and May 1966. He appeared to have no social ambition but was content to live in a very small *fale* and spend most of his time out on the lagoon.

pineapples, there was no attempt to expand this source of cash income and the attitude was simply 'well, we can sell limes in Apia so why not?'

The production of vegetables for sale was the main source of cash income for several *'āiga*. Most of the vegetables were raised by seven or eight *taulele'a* who lived on inland blocks, although most *'āiga* and family groups produced small quantities, particularly cucumbers, near their living *fale*. The beans, tomatoes and cucumbers were grown specifically for sale and only a small proportion was consumed in the village. The Apia local-products market was the main outlet but small quantities were sometimes hawked around Malua.

European vegetables were interplanted with the subsistence staples—taro and *ta'amū*. The production costs (mainly weeding) were low since much of the weeding would have been necessary for the taro alone. Apart from weeding, and staking up beans and tomatoes, the vegetables needed little other attention. But if production costs were low, marketing costs were fairly high. Each Wednesday and Friday evening the beans, tomatoes and cucumbers were harvested and tied into bundles (beans) or packed in brown paper bags (tomatoes). In the market the next day, the produce would be sold by these units for relatively fixed sums rather than by weight. Nothing in the market was weighed. Beans, for example, were sold by the sixpenny or shilling bundle, tomatoes by the one or two shilling bag, cucumber and the various fruits by the heap. When preparing these selling units the evening before, the producers took into account the sizes ruling on the last market day, and possibly a predication of the following day's weather as this affected the number of sellers and buyers who would arrive. Once in the market the sellers could observe the sizes of the bundles of other sellers, and could adjust theirs to suit the demand and supply situation on the day. If necessary they changed their prices by increasing or reducing the size of their bundles. The money prices— sixpence, one shilling or two shillings per bundle—did not vary, either during the day, or from day to day. Sellers who desired to spend only a short time in the market sold out quickly by displaying larger bundles; those prepared to sit around all morning, or even all day, displayed smaller bundles. The sellers attempted to sell out completely by the end of the period they wanted to spend in the market, and this was usually achieved. Because of this variety of factors it is very difficult to calculate the actual cash returns to labour in the production and sale of vegetables, particularly as there was the added complication of the hurricane which destroyed most of the vegetable crops in Utuali'i. It was about two months before production started to improve again and about six months before it was back to pre-hurricane levels.

### 3. *The effect of social and organizational institutions on production*

The traditional social institutions of *fono*, Women's Committee and *'aumāga* had much less influence on the level and direction of productive activity than in the other three villages. None of these bodies met regularly and although they had the same formal roles and responsibilities as in the other villages they did not appear to exercise the same control over village and *'āiga* affairs. For example, the *fono*, through the *pulenu'u*, instituted a taro-planting programme on the village *taulele'a*, but this did not start until March and then the quota was very light—100 taro plus 100 *ta'amū* per *taule'ale'a*. In April each *taule'ale'a* was instructed to plant 1,000 taro and/or *ta'amū*, but in May the quota was back to the March level. Inspections by the *matai* were not thorough and I did not hear of any fines being levied, although several men failed to carry out the instructions. In fact most *'āiga* did plant a great deal of taro and *ta'amū* on their own initiative and most exceeded the quota requirements. The point here is that the *fono* took only a small and limited part in organizing this aspect of subsistence food production, and it did not succeed in forcing even its own minimum quotas in some *'āiga*. The *fono* also appeared ineffective in preventing Utuali'i *taulele'a* from stealing staple foods and coconuts from Malua lands, despite complaints from church officials at Malua and a general understanding in the village of what was going on and who was responsible.

The Utuali'i Women's Committee was inactive. It did not meet regularly and, at least during the survey, it did not impose mat-weaving quotas or special purchases of household goods or inspect dwellings. The *'aumāga* was fairly inactive, too. There were only two occasions when it operated during the survey; once to clear weeds from the road between Malua and Utuali'i, and once to build a cricket pitch in the *malae*.

But while the traditional social institutions were relatively weak the church was particularly strong. The pastor was a well-educated and progressive leader, with boundless energy, and with great influence in the village and high standing in the Congregational Church in Samoa. It was largely through his encouragement that the village school was built in 1957-8 and was subsequently managed in a businesslike manner. His wife was instrumental in establishing a Utuali'i-Tufulele-Malua School Mothers' Association of about sixty women, the purpose of which was to raise money for the school and to assist financially any pupil of the school able to get a place in Samoa College, the main secondary school in Apia. This organization was started in November 1965 and during the survey its main concern was to build up its funds.

By far the largest village capital investment was in church buildings. These were a church (1947), a European house (1950), a bell tower and bell (1953), an open-house meeting hall (1965) and a *fale* (1965). The pastor was appointed to Utuali'i in 1942 and in keeping with his general businesslike approach to church and village affairs, had kept a fairly detailed diary-record of all these activities. It was something of a unique document and it told the story of Utuali'i investment in church buildings as follows:

> The Utuali'i congregation agreed after a meeting on September 1st, 1937 to build a church, and to engage the services of Chief Maualaivao Neru from Malie village, a deacon, as head carpenter. The church was to be in gothic style and measure 84 feet by 40 feet. The corner-stone was laid on December 15th, 1937, and on January 3rd, 1938, the wall and roof were completed. The carpenter then returned to his village while the congregation paid for the material bought on credit (£402) and used to complete this stage of the church. The first money we received for the church came from the choir (£30) and the women (£70). We raised additional money to repay the debt to Morris Hedstrom store in four ways: (1) by working as labourers in cacao plantations for three shillings a day, (2) by fishing and selling fish for one shilling for 15-20 fish of 8-9 inches long, (3) by growing and selling bananas at 10s. a case, and (4) by cutting copra and selling it at 1s. 9d. per 100 pounds.[15]
>
> In 1942 the Marines landed in our country and there was a station of about twenty marines in Utuali'i. From the marines we collected £154 by building several Samoan *fale* for them.[16] In February 1945, we decided to hold a '*tusigaigoa*', a special day when our relatives could come and write their names to pledge whatever money they pleased, while we provided them with food for the day. On February 9th, 1945, the day arranged, we collected £444 from our relatives from all over Samoa. On May 20th, 1946 the carpenter returned with his men and the work started again. We completed the church on the 8th, February 1947 and the dedication took place on the 20th.
>
> On the day of the dedication the relatives came again from all over Samoa with gifts of money to help pay the debts of the church. They were provided with food by their families in Utuali'i. At that time there were 14 families—7 *matai*, 21 *taulele'a* and the women and children, making up

---

[15] The pastor said that he obtained this information from his predecessor in 1942.

[16] The pastor was proud of his technique of raising money from the marines. The marines asked the village to build the *fale* and this was done. When they then offered to pay and for a price, the village, in the Samoan fashion, said that they did this free for their guests and that if the marines were happy with their treatment in Utuali'i they could give what money they pleased. They gave, of course, far more than was necessary for the work done.

a congregation of 125. The money came to us in these ways: (1) the 14 families of the congregation collected £884 from their relatives, (2) the choirs invited to the first service gave £269, (3) other invited groups gave £87, (4) invited individuals gave £54, and (5) £33 was raised at a dance the night before the dedication. This gave a total of £1,327.

We gave the following to the carpenter and his men:

(1) 130 sleeping-mats
(2) 13 'soft sleeping-mats' (*falalaui'e*)
(3) 103 small pieces of tapa cloth (*siapo*)
(4) 13 big pieces of tapa cloth (*pupuni*)
(5) 100 bottles of Samoan oil (coconut oil scented with *moso'oi*)
(6) 32 *'ietōga*
(7) £1,327 in cash.

Because the carpenter was quite satisfied with the way he had been treated, he accepted everything except the money which he divided in this way:

(1) £5 for the Leuluomoegafou school (Malua) boys who came and helped us serve the guests at the dedication,
(2) £10 for the old pastor who was here before,
(3) £10 for a set of glasses for Holy Communion,
(4) £20 for the congregation to have a feast after the great work was done,
(5) £60 for our pastor who hadn't had any money since the work started six months before,
(6) £809 to pay the debts of the church, and
(7) in the words of the carpenter, 'what is left is our money which I will share with my men' (£413).

The *matai*, *taulele'a* and women of the congregation worked free and provided food for the carpenter and his men each day.

Three years after the church was finished the congregation thought about building a house for the pastor. This time they decided to have Siolo Ulvao, a *matai* of the congregation, to be the builder. In July, 1950 the foundations were dug for a building to measure 60 feet by 30 feet. In February we held a Thanksgiving Service and there we collected £87. That was the first money and we began the work. I gave that money to O. F. Nelson Company where we bought all the materials for the house with the arrangement that we pay the balance when the celebration was over. The work finished in September 1950.

On 3rd February 1951 we held a big feast to celebrate the new house, and there we received gifts of £389 from the people we invited to attend. When the building was finished we were in debt for £799 to O. F. Nelson Company as the whole building cost £886. We paid the £379 at once, and the balance of the debt was divided into three parts, the responsibility of the *matai*, the women, and the *taulele'a*. We raised the money to pay this debt in the same way we paid for the church—copra, bananas, fishing, and working in the cacao plantations. The carpenter did not like to be paid for his work but we gave him £10, 50 sleeping mats, 1 *falalau'ie* and 2 *'ietōga*. Again the congregation did the labouring work and provided the food for the carpenter each day.

In August 1965 we had £100 from our Sunday offering in the bank and decided to build a hall measuring 46 feet by 23 feet. We obtained a bank loan of £150 and with the £250 we bought timber and cement. The roofing iron was provided by the *matai* and *taulele'a* of the congregation—each *matai* gave three 8 feet lengths and each *taule'ale'a* gave two. The women bought the paint. We built the house in two weeks and paid the loan in five months at £30 per month.

The builder was Pualele Mao [who also built the school], the son of Maualaivao Neru who had built the church. He didn't want to receive any payment for his work saying that it was to help in the work of God in the village. Nevertheless the congregation gave him a gift of £11, 20 sleeping-mats and two *'ietōga*. The congregation provided food and labour as before.

Table 41    Utuali'i: Social and Village Capital[a]

|  | Total | Cash component | Subsistence component |
|---|---|---|---|
|  | £ | % | % |
| *'Āiga* |  |  |  |
| Dwellings | 6,079 | 50 | 50 |
| Furniture | 233 | 60 | 40 |
| Mats etc. | 539 | 12 | 88 |
| Utensils & equipment | 285 | 100 | — |
| Total | 7,136 | 49 | 51 |
| Village | 1,540 | 71 | 29 |
| Church | 3,447 | 70 | 30 |
| Total investment | 12,123 | 58 | 42 |
| Investment per consumption unit[b] | 40 | 15 | 25 |

NOTES:    [a] Estimated costs of the social and village capital existing in 1966
          [b] Estimated costs of capital items existing in 1966 divided by the number of consumption units in 1966

In Table 41 estimates are given of cash and subsistence investment in social and village capital. About fifty-eight per cent of the total investment had been in cash and the rest had been in village labour and other subsistence resources. The total investment averaged £64 per consumption unit, which was similar to that in Poutasi. The proportion of cash in total costs was also similar in Utuali'i and Poutasi.

There had been other investment, particularly of subsistence resources, which have not been valued or shown in Table 41. In particular there was the secondary road along the boundary between

Table 42   Utuali'i: Subsistence and Cash Incomes[a]

| | Village | | Per consumption unit | |
|---|---|---|---|---|
| SUBSISTENCE (non-monetary) INCOME | £ | | £ | |
| Food: | | 2,312 | | 11·8 |
| coconuts[b] | 298 | | 1·5 | |
| bananas.& breadfruit[c][d] | 477 | | 2·4 | |
| taro and *ta'amū*[c] | 1,200 | | 6·2 | |
| fish | 239 | | 1·2 | |
| pork and chicken[e] | 98 | | ·5 | |
| Buildings: | | 300 | | 1·6 |
| '*āiga* | 215 | | 1·1 | |
| village | 31 | | ·2 | |
| church | 54 | | ·3 | |
| Household durables: | | 285 | | 1·5 |
| Tools and equipment: | | 86 | | ·4 |
| Total subsistence income | | £2,983 | | £15·3 |
| CASH INCOME | | | | |
| Agriculture and fishing: | | 3,037 | | 15·8 |
| copra | 1,235 | | 6·3 | |
| coconuts | 540 | | 2·8 | |
| fruit & vegetables | 995 | | 5·1 | |
| cacao | 28 | | ·1 | |
| fish | 228 | | 1·4 | |
| other | 11 | | ·1 | |
| Wages: | | 2,073 | | 10·6 |
| Remittances from abroad: | | 1,838 | | 9·4 |
| Gifts: | | 31 | | ·2 |
| Total cash income | | £6,979 | | £36·0 |
| TOTAL INCOME[f] | | £9,962 | | £51·3 |
| Monetization factor[g] | | 70% | | |

NOTES:
[a] 12 months, December 1965-November 1966

[b] Average use per consumption unit a week of: 4·4 coconuts as food plus 0·4 fed to pigs and chickens. Coconuts are valued at 1s for 8 nuts as in the other three villages, although Utuali'i sellers actually earned a higher price for units sold in Apia.

[c] Based on Appendix Table 2 with quantities valued at pre-hurricane market prices in Apia: taro—6d per lb., *ta'amū* and breadfruit—4d per lb. and bananas—3d per lb.

[d] Mainly breadfruit harvested before and immediately after the hurricane.

[e] A rough estimate of quantity based on observation and valued at 2s per lb. for pork and 2s each for chickens.

[f] Aggregate of imputed value of subsistence income and cash income; intended only for inter-village comparisons.

[g] Proportion of cash income in total income

Utuali'i and Malua lands, and a modern water supply system.[17] There had also been substantial investment of cash and subsistence resources in the plantation although much of this, the fencing, copra dryer and house, had been before the war. The main road through Utuali'i was probably built with village labour (early in the century) but it had been sealed during the war by the government. Utuali'i had benefited by its proximity to Apia and its location between Apia and the airfield and inter-island ferry service in that some of the capital etc. had been made by the government. In some respects Utuali'i was on the fringe of the Apia urban area.

### INCOME

The total income in Utuali'i for the twelve-month period to 30 November 1966 is estimated to have been £9,962, or £51 per consumption unit (Table 42). The imputed value of subsistence (non-monetary) income is £2,983, or £15·2 per consumption unit, to which has been added the estimated cash income of £6,979, or £35·8 per consumption unit. The monetized proportion of total income is therefore seventy per cent.

The value of the subsistence component of total income in Utuali'i (£15·2 per consumption unit) was well below the estimates for the other three villages: Poutasi—£27·9; Taga—£34; and Uafato—£31·2. Without the hurricane the levels of subsistence incomes in Poutasi, Taga and Uafato would have been fairly

Table 43　Utuali'i: Cash Outlay[(a)]

| | Village | | Per consumption unit | | Percentage |
|---|---|---|---|---|---|
| | £ | £ 6,298 | £ | £ 32·1 | % 94 |
| 'Āiga | | | | | |
| Food[(a)] | 3,649 | | 18·7 | | 54 |
| Other commodities[(a)] | 1,213 | | 6·1 | | 18 |
| Local fares | 645 | | 3·3 | | 10 |
| Gifts | 294 | | 1·5 | | 4 |
| Schooling | 257 | | 1·3 | | 4 |
| New Zealand fares | 240 | | 1·2 | | 4 |
| Church and pastor | | 357 | | 1·8 | 5 |
| Village | | 47 | | ·2 | 1 |
| Total | | 6,702 | | 34·1 | 100 |

NOTE: [(a)] 12 months, December 1965-November 1966

[17] The Utuali'i water supply system was an extension of the Apia system and had been installed shortly after the war by the Department of Works. Utuali'i unpaid labour had been used.

similar. But the considerably lower level in Utuali'i, while it was also affected by the hurricane, was clearly a normal feature of that village which went back many years before the survey and indicated a permanent change in the relationship between subsistence and cash income.

Table 44   Utuali'i: Commodity Purchases[a]

|  | Expenditure | | | Main shopping centres | |
|---|---|---|---|---|---|
|  | Village | Per consumption unit | Percentage | Utuali'i | Apia |
|  | £ | £ | % | % | % |
| **Food:** |  |  |  |  |  |
| flour, rice, bread | 1,268 | 6·5 | 26 | 35 | 65 |
| meat[b] | 623 | 3·2 | 13 | 41 | 59 |
| taro, bananas etc. | 582 | 3·0 | 12 | — | 100 |
| fish[c] | 404 | 2·0 | 8 | 24 | 76 |
| sugar | 394 | 2·0 | 8 | 59 | 41 |
| dripping, salt etc. | 175 | ·9 | 4 | 57 | 43 |
| dairy products | 76 | ·4 |  | 44 | 56 |
| tea, coffee, cocoa | 69 | ·4 | 4 | 42 | 58 |
| other foods | 58 | ·3 |  | 25 | 75 |
|  | 3,649 | 18·7 | 75 | 33 | 67 |
| **Other:** |  |  |  |  |  |
| individual | 365 | 1·9 | 8 | 20 | 80 |
| household | 342 | 1·7 | 7 | 9 | 91 |
| tobacco | 242 | 1·2 | 5 | 68 | 32 |
| kerosene, benzene | 126 | ·6 |  | 55 | 45 |
| soap | 110 | ·6 | 5 | 46 | 54 |
| handicrafts | 28 | ·1 |  |  | 100 |
|  | 1,213 | 6·1 | 25 | 32 | 68 |
| All commodities | 4,862 | 24·8 | 100 | 33 | 67 |

NOTES:   [a] 12 months, December 1965-November 1966
         [b] 60% tinned meat
         [c] 100% tinned foods

Only forty-four per cent of the village cash income was earned from the sale of agricultural products and fish. Thirty per cent came from wages, and the rest was received as remittances from abroad. Most 'āiga received money from wages and remittances during the survey and several relied on this as their sole source of cash income. Both in amount per consumption unit, and as a proportion of total village cash income, wages and remittances were higher than in the other three villages. One result of the hurricane, felt more strongly in Utuali'i than in the other villages, was the decline in wage employment, particularly casual wage employment, in the cacao plantations.

OUTLAY

Estimates of cash outlay for the twelve months December 1965 to November 1966 are summarized in Table 43.

*1. Cash expenditure on goods and services*

Of the four villages, the highest cash expenditure on food was recorded for Utuali'i. It amounted to £18·7 per consumption unit over the twelve-month period or fifty-four per cent of the total cash outlay. Staple foods, such as flour, rice, bread, taro and bananas, accounted for half the food expenditure (Table 44) and although part of this was a result of the hurricane-caused shortage of sub-sistence foods, a relatively high expenditure on staples was a normal feature of the Utuali'i economy. This was the only village of the four which had easy and cheap access to market supplies of Samoan foods and even after the hurricane, when these commodities were dear relative to flour and rice, some '*āiga* continued to buy them in the Apia local-products market. Bread and other bakery products were available each weekday both in Utuali'i and Apia, and ex-penditure on this food category was much higher than in Poutasi, the only other village studied where bread could be bought. Expenditure on flour and rice was double that of Poutasi. In addi-tion free issues of flour and rice came from two sources—the Hurri-cane Relief Committee and the Mormon church[18]—and the quan-tity received per consumption unit was the highest of the four villages. Over the survey period the consumption of bought foods in Utuali'i per consumption unit per week averaged about two pounds of flour and rice, two pounds of Samoan staples, eight ounces of tinned herrings, one pound of sugar and two ounces of tinned meat.

Other (non-food) commodity purchases accounted for eighteen per cent of all cash outlay (£6·1 per consumption unit) and twenty-five per cent of all commodity expenditure. Tobacco was

[18] During the survey period the village received 3 bags of flour, 6 bags of rice, 6 boxes of tinned salmon and 12 boxes of tinned milk (June) from the Hurricane Relief Committee, and there was another issue of flour and rice in July which was not recorded. The Mormon '*āiga* received 150 lbs of flour, 200 lbs of rice and 120 lbs of sugar from the Mormon church and some of this was distributed through the village.

the most important single item in this category and the average expenditure on tobacco was much higher than that recorded for the other three villages. Expenditure on other personal items, and on services such as entertainment, was also substantially above that recorded in the other villages.

Although the bus fare to Apia from Utuali'i was much lower than from the other three villages, the constant coming and going between Utuali'i and Apia meant that in fact more was spent on fares per consumption unit than in the other villages.

Cash expenditure on education during the survey period was higher in Utuali'i than in the other villages. The facilities available locally for elementary and intermediate schooling were similar to those in Poutasi.[19] More Utuali'i *'āiga* sent the children who were eligible to these schools.[20] In 1966 one *taule'ale'a* completed his teacher training and received his first appointment, and another completed his final year at the Agricultural College and migrated to New Zealand; there were four Utuali'i boys at the Agricultural College, three boys and three girls at the main government secondary school in Apia, and the eldest son of the pastor entered Malua Theological College. It was apparent from the number of Utuali'i people with skilled jobs—teachers, nurses, clerks and so on—and the number who emigrated to New Zealand, that proximity to Apia had raised the level of general education in Utuali'i well above that in the other villages. Most Utuali'i *'āiga* had supported at least one child through secondary school, but in the other villages studied only a few had done this.

The services other than transport and education, which Utuali'i people could purchase locally, were far more varied than in the other villages, since Utuali'i had ready access to all services available in Apia.

## 2. *Shopping facilities and centres for Utuali'i buyers*

Utuali'i shoppers obviously had the best facilities of the four villages studied because the Apia stores and market were so easily accessible to them. In the village itself there were two reasonably well stocked shops where most of the items in daily consumption were purchased. But in Apia there was a full range of goods and services which was not equalled anywhere else in Samoa. Not only was the range of goods and services wide but the prices were lower than in the outer villages. The only disadvantage of shopping in

[19] The district (intermediate) school was about half an hour's walk from Utuali'i.

[20] All children attended the village elementary school but only a proportion were admitted to the district intermediate school.

Apia as against village stores was that credit was not generally given. Of the sample '*āiga* only two were in debt to Apia stores. The plantation-owning *matai* had bought building material on credit from the trading company to which he sold his copra, and this debt was systematically reduced each time he sent in a truck-load of copra.[21] Another *matai* was allowed a small account by a small Apia store in which he worked. The two stores in the village allowed credit to most *matai* and to some individual *taulele'a*; Except for four *matai* who had assured incomes from wages and remittances, however, the amounts were small. Total indebtedness to the local stores did not change over the survey period.

The two local stores, which had roles similar to suburban corner shops, absorbed about thirty-three per cent of the village cash expenditure on food and other commodities. The rest of the shopping was done in Apia (Table 44).

### 3. *The effect of social and organizational institutions on outlay*

During the survey the traditional social organizations in Utuali'i had little effect on the outlay of cash or subsistence resources and this appeared to have been so for many years. Cash subscriptions were raised by the '*aumāga* to buy cement for a cricket pitch and by the School Mothers' Association, but generally the amounts were small and there were few occasions when subscriptions were made. An average of £0·2 per consumption unit was raised during the twelve-month period by the *fono*, Women's Committee and '*aumāga*, the lowest of the four villages. The only major building financed by the village through the *fono* was the school (1957-8).

The church, however, had absorbed a large proportion of the village cash earnings for many years. Over the twelve-month period under review £357, or £1·8 per consumption unit, was given to the pastor and the various church funds. In per consumption unit terms this was the highest of the four villages. In addition to a cash income in 1966 of about £190, the pastor was also provided with elaborate housing and with subsistence food and mats.

About the same level of cash outlay on gifts was recorded for Utuali'i as for Poutasi, £1·5 per consumption unit. This included cash expenditure on food and other commodities taken to funerals and so on as gifts. As in Poutasi, the receipts of gifts—cash and the value of bought commodities—appeared to have been quite small. There can be little doubt that *matai* and '*āiga* which are known to have reasonable high cash incomes, such as the plantation-owning *matai* in Utuali'i, are made the butt of continuous requests for

[21] In December he owed about £450 to this company and by May the debt had been reduced to £264.

'assistance' and these requests are very difficult to refuse. This *matai* was sincerely worried about his inability to save money and he just didn't understand where his money went. During the survey he asked me to show him how to keep financial records so that he could keep track of his income and outlay and he thereafter kept these records with diligence.

## 4. *Cash savings*

With the need to buy more food than usual after the hurricane, with the prices of taro and bananas in the local-products market rising to over twice their pre-hurricane levels, and with cash income from vegetables and wages cut considerably in many '*āiga*, it was clearly not possible for most Utuali'i '*āiga* to increase their savings during the survey period. In many savings declined. Most *matai* and many others had bank or post office savings accounts and several '*āiga* maintained balances of between £50 and £60 each. Only in two of the sample '*āiga* were there no savings accounts and these were the two '*āiga* which earned virtually no money from wages, and relied mainly on sales in the Apia local-products market for their cash income. In all four villages it was generally only the '*āiga* which included wage-earners or shopkeepers which had savings accounts and significant cash savings, and in Utuali'i most '*āiga* were in this position.

The survey data on cash income and outlay indicates that over the twelve months income exceeded outlay by £1·9 per consumption unit. This is, of course, only a balancing item between two independently made estimates, and the other evidence suggests that it could be quite high as an indication of savings.

PART III:

# THE PROCESS OF ECONOMIC CHANGE

Chapter 8

# FROM PRIMITIVE AFFLUENCE
# TO ECONOMIC
# DEVELOPMENT?

THE village Samoans on the whole reacted to the incentives offered by the market sector in a predictable and measurable way: the greater the incentive, the higher were their cash earnings. They were willing to take on new cash crops as these became available, and to earn money from other sources such as wage employment when opportunities were presented. All *'āiga* had invested labour in establishing sources of cash income in their villages, such as their coconut, cacao and banana small-holdings. Some had attempted to increase their cash incomes further by investing labour and money in such capital items as a cropa dryer, a whaleboat, truck or bus, or a village store. For the same reason, most had invested money in their children's schooling, and some also in sending individuals to New Zealand.

Even in the case of Utuali'i and Poutasi, however, villages with strong links with the market sector, the average level of cash income was unexceptional. Before the disturbing influences of bunchytop and the hurricane annual cash income per head was less than £35, only about U.S.$60.

There are a number of apparent contradictions on Samoan economic life—low cash incomes but unexploited resources, a recognized responsibility for future generations but a concentration on short term returns, little economic development but a looming population problem and a considerable development potential, long-term social and political goals but short-term economic goals. These are examined further in the final section of this chapter.

The formal objectives of the study, to test empirically the propositions underlying Fisk's model of the transition from pure subsistence to the production of a market surplus in an economy of primitive affluence are examined in the first three sections.

PRIMITIVE AFFLUENCE

*Proposition* 1   Subsistence production in a situation of primitive affluence is limited by demand for the goods and services the subsistence unit can produce rather than by any shortage of factors of production, and therefore *per capita* subsistence output tends to be maintained at a constant level.

As Samoan villages have been participating in the market sector for many decades it was not possible to observe a pure subsistence unit (page 5 above). Nevertheless, each of the villages studied retains a substantial subsistence component in its total income, and with Uafato (IV) where this was about seventy per cent, we are still reasonably close to Fisk's ideal unit. In examining the possible validity of Proposition 1 therefore, we will treat Uafato as the main case study, but at the same time we can see also how well it describes the subsistence sectors of the other villages. It is clear enough from the previous four chapters that total output is still well below potential. It could be raised considerably, and sustained at the higher level probably indefinitely, without any undue pressure on the factors of production, without major changes in technology, and within the present social and economic organization of the village and its component '*āiga*. Each village has gone through periods in the past when it did reach a much higher level of output; for example, during the construction of its church. But generally it did not sustain this higher level for longer than it needed to complete its particular investment project. That it was able to do this is evidence in favour of Proposition 1. Why it failed to maintain the higher level over a long period is a problem that is examined in section four.

1. *Land*

It is fair to say that in Uafato (IV) crops such as coconuts and bananas planted to provide a cash income have affected the production of subsistence food crops. During the first two decades of this century when coconut palms were being regularly and extensively planted they took over the major areas which at that time were used for taro, *ta'amū*, bananas and other subsistence food crops. The expansion of banana planting after 1954 had something of the same effect although new land was cleared also. By 1960 most taro was grown on small steep plots on the valley sides, sometimes in fairly inaccessible areas. Labour costs of taro production have increased steadily over the past sixty years or so with the increasing difficulty of clearing forest and scrub from the steep slopes and weeding the plots, and also with the widening distances between the plots and the village. On the other hand, these are probably the most fertile areas for taro production available to the growers, in fact, the most fertile in Western Samoa. The plots are generally abandoned when the growers consider it easier to clear a new area than to control (by cutting) the weeds on the old. Many of the steeper and less accessible plots are abandoned after only two or three years. Those closer to the village are usually kept in production for a much longer period as they can be given more regular weeding, particularly by the women. If more effort could be put into weeding, the total area under taro at any one time could be greatly increased. In addition there are still areas under primary forest which can be cleared for taro or banana production.

Table 45   The Availability of Land for Bush Fallow Cultivation in 1966

|  | Utuali'i (I) | Poutasi (II) | Taga (III) | Uafato (IV) |
|---|---|---|---|---|
| Cleared area not under long term tree crops (acres) | 134 | 318 | 416 | 105 |
| Reserves of forest land | nil | large | large | small |
| Usual fallow period (years) | 6 | 8 | 6 | 5 |
| Cleared area which potentially could be maintained in production (acres) [a] | 40 | 60 | 90 | 63 |
| Area in production in May 1966 (acres) [b] | 18 | 50 | 60 | 33 |

NOTES:   [a] Assuming plots were kept in continuous use for the following periods before being abandoned to bush fallow: Utuali'i, Poutasi and Taga—18 months; Uafato—36 months. The cleared area could have been greatly enlarged in Poutasi and Taga, and slightly enlarged in Uafato by cutting down the forest.

[b] Includes the areas planted in taro and ta'amū up to the end of May 1966 and rough estimates of the remnants of the banana plots which could be productive after recovery from hurricane damage.

It would take much less effort to increase breadfruit production in Uafato. There was ample room in and near the village for additional trees.

Similarly, land is not the limiting factor on pandanus production. Once the women had been organized they set to work and planted about two hundred seedlings after the hurricane. They could have planted far more if they had wanted larger supplies of this raw material. As it was their efforts were expected to provide enough pandanus for village subsistence use and for the tablemats and baskets they sold in Apia.

Clearly land is not yet a limiting factor on village output. Both subsistence food and cash crops could be expanded either by clearing forest or by using land already cleared more intensively (Table 45).

In Taga (III) coconuts and subsistence staples are grown in completely different locations and it is unlikely that the expansion of the coconut area early in the century had absorbed land being used for taro and bananas. Similarly the expansion in banana planting after 1960 took place mainly along the new road, in a rocky forest area which had not been used for subsistence food crops earlier. Taga 'āiga preferred to plant their subsistence foods in the alluvial soils of the northern stream area which, even with the post-hurricane taro planting, was not fully used. The 'āiga which established permanent dwellings on rocky land along the road proved that subsistence food crops could be grown satisfactorily in this area, although the soil was less fertile. Several thousand acres of this poorer land is still under forest. There is no shortage of cultivable land in Taga.

Poutasi (II) is also well endowed with land. Its subsistence food plots were pushed inland as coconut plantings were increased, and most of the bananas produced for sale were grown amongst the plots of taro near the forest line, but there is still a large area of good land under forest which can be cleared for cultivation.

The land situation in Utuali'i (I) is not as good as in Uafato, Taga and Poutasi. There is no longer a reserve still under forest. But while several inland blocks were fairly intensively cultivated for taro, ta'amū and European vegetables, at a relatively high labour cost for weeding, most are hardly used at all and certainly could produce additional supplies of subsistence food. The coconut area behind the village is in a very poor state. An organized effort to clear secondary bush growth and to replant could double the coconut output.

## 2. Labour

To raise the subsistence output from the present levels requires not only additional land in production but also additional labour. A labour survey carried out during the second, third and fourth visits to the villages suggests strongly that it was available. Even during that period when extra efforts were being made to plant taro, the Uafato men put in an average working week of twenty-six hours, including time given to subsistence and cash production and fono and other group meetings (Table 46). The longest average working week was recorded for Poutasi where the men put in thirty-three hours; the lowest was in Utuali'i where the men worked an average of only sixteen hours. These figures are broadly supported by the results of two earlier surveys of village labour use in Western Samoa shown in Table 47. Even after padding out the figures to include reasonable allowances for the hundred and one

Table 46    The Average Number of Hours Spent a Week per Adult Male
in the Main Productive Activities[a]
March-June 1966

|  | Utuali'i (I) | Poutasi (II) | Taga (III) | Uafato (IV) |
|---|---|---|---|---|
| Subsistence activities |  |  |  |  |
| Food production: |  |  |  |  |
| taro and *ta'amū* | 11·1 | 13·2 | 13·7 | 8·8 |
| gathering coconuts | 0·2 | 1·2 | 0·2 | 0·3 |
| fishing | 1·1 | 2·4 | 2·0 | 7·5 |
| Other *'āiga* subsistence tasks | 0·8 | 0·1 | 1·5 | 0·4 |
|  | 13·2 | 16·9 | 17·4 | 17·0 |
| Village level subsistence tasks | 0·5 | 8·1 | 3·2 | 7·4 |
|  | 13·7 | 25·0 | 20·6 | 24·4 |
| Cash earning activities | 2·2 | 8·1 | 4·7 | 1·9 |
|  | 15·9 | 33·1 | 25·3 | 26·3 |

NOTE:    [a] The labour survey covered all tasks observed to be of particular
importance in maintaining the material well-being of the villagers.
The estimates include not only the actual times taken to complete
various tasks such as weeding or planting, but also the time taken
to reach the place of work and to return again to the village. It
should be pointed out that there was more than usual taro-planting
activity during the period surveyed and no activity at all associated
with banana production.

Table 47    Comparisons of Labour Surveys 1950, 1961 and 1966

|  | Hours per week per adult male | | |
|---|---|---|---|
|  | 1950[a] | 1961[b] | 1966[c] |
| Routine agricultural tasks mainly associated with subsistence food crops | 11 | 12 | 12 |
| Fishing | 6 | 3 | 3 |
| Copra production and other cash-earning activities (excluding wage labour) | 8 | 7 | 5 |
| Other subsistence tasks | n.a. | 2 | 5 |
|  | 25 | 24 | 25 |

NOTES:    [a] Part of an agricultural census carried out by officers of the New
Zealand Department of Agriculture in 1950 and summarized by
Bryan H. Farrell in his chapter 'The Village and its Agriculture' in
Fox and Cumberland 1962, pp. 196-7. These figures do not include
(apparently) the time spent in walking to and from the place of work.
   [b] Ian Fairbairn, 'More on the Labor Potential—Some Evidence from
Western Samoa', *Economic Development and Cultural Change*, vol. 16,
no. 1, Oct. 1967, pp. 97-105. These figures are averages for two
villages surveyed—Taga and Poutasi.
   [c] Averages of the four villages surveyed from Table 46

small tasks associated with village economic and necessary social life which were not adequately recorded in these surveys, and recognizing that much of the work was extremely hard physical labour, it is clear that the village Samoans did not, in general, work as many hours a week as it might be expected they could. The Western Samoan Economic Development Plan stated: 'there is little question that there is under-employment in village agriculture in the sense that much less than an average of forty hours a week is spent by the average Samoan in working on village plantations during the year' (W.S.E.D.P. 1966-70, p. 13).

Subsistence production is not limited by a shortage of land and labour.

### 3. Capital

The main agricultural implements are the *oso* and the bush knife. The *oso* can be found easily in the forest, and most '*āiga* earn enough money to buy as many knives as they need. Fishing gear is equally simple and the hooks, lines and other bought items are cheap. There is no reason at all for any shortage of these production aids.

### 4. Demand

Subsistence output is maintained at a level well below that which full exploitation of the available factors of production could make possible. It is not limited by resources being used in alternative cash-earning activities, and each village has a long way to go before it makes undue demands on leisure or can overcrop its land. There must, therefore, be a limited demand for subsistence goods and services. As each village produces the same few commodities at about the same labour costs, and each individual has the resources to produce as much as he wants, there must come a point where he is completely satisfied and prefers leisure to further unnecessary work. As Fisk proposes, the result is probably the maintenance of a fairly uniform level of output.

But this can not be tested in a pure subsistence situation in Western Samoa since demand for subsistence goods and services has long been affected by the market sector which has raised the level of demand for goods and services. Uafato and Taga villages, however, still maintain very similar levels of subsistence food production per head in the absence of any major substitution in favour of market goods, and in Poutasi where there is more substitution, subsistence output has declined only slightly. At the other end of the scale Utuali'i purchases a good deal of its staple food and subsistence production has declined considerably.

The substitution of market for subsistence goods is, of course, a characteristic of the post-contact period. But there is evidence that in the pre-contact period the average level of demand for village-produced goods and services per head may not have been uniform between '*āiga* and villages or constant over time, as Fisk proposes. He is referring to the individual demand for goods and services which gives a normal socially accepted level of living. But in the Samoan village, with its highly complex social and political structure, the total demand for subsistence goods and services was very likely to have exceeded the aggregate demand from individuals. The level of demand, and productive activity, was raised by a need for various community facilities and for social and political prestige, status and power. These motives for additional subsistence output varied between '*āiga* and villages, and over time. The extent to which they affected the level of output depended usually on the strength of the village leaders and institutions.

We have examples from the current Samoan situation. Where an individual may not need a road, a school, a latrine, or a piped water supply, the village community may. Where an individual may not want to tax his energy by building a large impressive dwelling, his *matai* probably does. Where the individual, and even the *matai*, might prefer to supply labour and finance for a simple church, the *fono* probably wants to compete with those of neighbouring villages by building an impressively large church which could accommodate two or three times the normal congregation.

Community and prestige demand takes two forms. First, there is a constant demand for village output—additional to that of individuals—a sort of running cost. Certain community tasks are performed fairly regularly such as maintaining paths and bathing pools, supplying the pastor and his family with staple foods, pandanus mats and domestic help, cleaning and maintaining the *malae*, the church and other significant buildings, and occasionally adding to the stock of village capital by completing small projects like a community latrine, a footbridge and a piped water supply. Second, there are occasional projects of major proportions such as the construction of a road, the building of a church, a European-style house for the pastor, or a school, and at the '*āiga* level, the construction of a traditional guest-*fale* or non-traditional dwelling. The only large-scale project observed during the survey was the work on the Uafato road, although in both Uafato and Taga a start was made to raise money for new pastors' houses.

In the long run the small villages like Uafato and Utuali'i probably place greater demands per head on their subsistence resources for community and prestige needs than do larger villages like Taga and Poutasi. Because these villages are at different stages in the process of building up their stocks of village capital it is rather difficult to quantify this, but Uafato (IV) had invested a great deal more per consumption unit in its church buildings than had Taga (III)—£12 6s as against £5 7s, and Utuali'i (I) had invested slightly more than Poutasi (II)—£18 3s as against £17. The pastors in all four villages were fairly equally provided with food and other subsistence goods and this represented a greater contribution per consumption unit in Uafato and Utuali'i than in Taga and Poutasi.

At any particular time the main factor which determines the level of community and social demand is the strength, unity and influence of the village leaders and institutions. In two of the four villages—Utuali'i and Taga—the traditional institutions of *fono* and women's committee were weak at the time of the survey. Many of the Utuali'i *matai* were too involved with politics and other matters beyond the village boundaries to give their full attention to the village itself. In Taga there was a political split between two groups of '*āiga*, and although the *fono* had not formally divided, this had happened in the women's committee, and to some extent also in the '*aumāga*. Neither village had started any major capital works for several years, the last being the construction of the schools. But in Utuali'i strong leadership came from the pastor, and it was in the church buildings that Utuali'i had invested heaviest. In Taga strong leadership was expressed in some cases at the '*āiga* level with the result that much recent investment in that village had been in '*āiga* dwellings. In neither village did the women's committee appear to enforce minimum quotas on members for the production of pandanus mats and other subsistence household goods. In neither village did the *fono* have much influence on the '*āiga* in post-hurricane food crop planting, although in most cases the '*āiga* themselves made substantially increased efforts.

In Uafato and Poutasi the *fono* and women's committee were strong and well organized, and there was a great deal more community productive activity than in Taga and Utuali'i. In Uafato the *fono* organized and supervised the road work, the pipeline construction and post-hurricane food crop planting. The women's committee managed the replanting of the pandanus groves and the manufacture of mats. In Poutasi the *fono* organized the post-hurricane cleaning-up and reconstruction, repair work on the school and hospital, clearing bush and weeding in the coconut areas, the formal division of land between certain '*āiga*, post-hurricane coconut and food planting, and a number of other activities. The women's committee managed the production of mats, maintained its pandanus and sugar-cane plots, provided various services to the school and hospital, and ran a small business manufacturing sugar-cane thatch. It might be mentioned also that the Poutasi *fono* and women's committee had earlier decided to preserve the traditional appearance of the 'island' part of the village and had not permitted the construction of obviously non-traditional dwellings there. This had undoubtedly prevented some *'āiga* from investing in concrete and iron open-houses and explains partly why there had not been in Poutasi the sort of post-road-building boom seen in Taga.

Although these illustrations are taken from the present they probably vary only in detail from the pre-contact past. Such influences on demand made it unlikely that there was a uniform or constant level of subsistence output between *'āiga* and villages (subsistence units). It seems equally unlikely that the passage of time would have smoothed out the variations completely. Possibly the variation between villages in strength of leadership and level of output during the period of first contact with missionaries and traders gave some villages an early advantage over others in their dealings with the embryonic market sector. More recently this could explain why Poutasi rather than its two more populous neighbours developed as the district centre.

MARKET INCENTIVE

*Proposition* 2   The degree of participation in the market sector by the subsistence unit will vary with the strength of the incentive factor, which in turn will depend largely on the development of effective linkage with the market sector.

The spadework for testing this proposition in the Samoan context was to rank the four villages in terms of (1) an assessment of the strength of linkage between each village and the market sector, and (2) a measure of the extent of market participation. The first ranking is assumed to approximate one based on a complete measure of the incentive factor in the Fisk model. The second will in fact consist of two rankings based on (a) the level of cash income per consumption unit, and (b) the monetization factor, or the proportion of money income in total income. Proposition 2 will be considered to have accurately predicted economic behaviour if the villages are found clearly to fall in the same order in the two rankings.

1. *Market linkage*

The original selection of the four villages was based on a rough assessment of strength of linkage and the Roman numerals which have been used in the text to identify the villages indicate this rank order. During the course of the survey this early ranking was confirmed by additional data, and although the facts have been presented in the previous four chapters they are summarized below in three categories: (a) the time factor in the development of linkage, (b) the effort cost of earning a cash income and (c) the facilities for using money. With minor exceptions the four villages fall in the same rank order in each category.

### (a) Development of linkage

Two factors are considered here: communications facilities between the village and Apia, and the market for village produce.

Utuali'i (I) village is clearly the best placed of the four in terms of ease and cheapness of travel to Apia. Apia is only thirteen miles away and even before buses started to ply the route the journey was an easy one by foot, horseback or canoe. Closeness to the London Missionary Society's headquarters at Malua and to various commercial plantations in the area ensured Utuali'i the best communications facilities available in Western Samoa from the earliest days of contact with the market sector. The road was sealed during the war but it was constructed much earlier. Two trading stations were opened in Utuali'i during the 1920s but one of the earliest trade stores was only five miles away. Utuali'i was able to produce bananas for export well before Poutasi, and at least since the war it has been able to produce fruit and vegetables for sale in Apia.

Poutasi (II) was no farther from Apia than Uafato (IV) but it had a vastly different history of market contact. Like Utuali'i one of the earliest outer-district trade stores was built in the next village and was serviced by sea. Two Apia-based trading-stations opened in the village during the 1920s and brought with them a much improved launch service. In 1949 the Apia-Poutasi road was completed. Thereafter a daily bus service operated between Poutasi and Apia, bananas were sold in quantity through the Banana Scheme whose trucks could now reach the village, and a number of new stores were opened in the village. With the construction of a hospital in Poutasi the village started to develop as a district centre.

Taga (III) was one of the most isolated villages in Western Samoa before its road was completed in 1960. During the 1920s, however, two Apia-based trading-stations were opened in the village and a launch called at least once a month. In terms of linkage with the market sector this gave Taga an early advantage over Uafato which had probably been in the better position earlier. Taga's big advantage over Uafato came in 1960 with the road to Salailua to the west and the inter-island ferry terminal at Salelologa to the east. This opened up new market outlets for village produce, including bananas sold through the Banana Scheme, and gave Taga people easier and more dependable transport to Apia.

Uafato (IV) had the worst communications with Apia and the outside simply because it could not be reached by road. Being a small village it had not attracted a trading-station to its shores and therefore did not even have the monthly visit from a launch which after about 1930 had eased Taga's isolation. The Banana Scheme provided a special launch service after 1959 but by then the Fagaloa Bay road was almost finished and this was more important as a general improvement in communications. Facilities for selling Uafato produce were very poor. Only two 'āiga owned whaleboats and in combination with their stores this gave them almost a monopoly over the marketing of copra. Marketing costs for all produce except bananas were very high, for both the store-owning and other 'āiga.

While the rank order is clear enough from this description one more piece of evidence is given in Table 48: the cash and time costs of travel from the village to Apia, and in the case of Taga from that village to Salelologa.

Table 48   Travel Costs in 1966

|  | Bus fare | Travel time | Cash plus imputed value[d] of travel time |
|---|---|---|---|
|  | s d | hrs | s d |
| Village to Apia |  |  |  |
| Utuali'i    (I) | 6d – 1.0 | $\frac{1}{2}$ | 1.3 – 1.9 |
| Poutasi   (II) | 4.0 – 5.0 | 2 | 7.0 – 8.0 |
| Taga     (III) | 14.0 – 15.0[b] | 7–8 | 25.6 – 27.0 |
| Uafato   (IV) | 4.0 – 5.0 | 4–5[a] | 11.0 – 11.6 |
| Taga (III) to Salelologa[c] | 4.0 – 5.0 | 2 | 7.0 – 8.0 |

NOTES:   [a] Includes one to two hours walking or rowing time between Uafato and the nearest bus.

[b] Includes a nine-shilling fare on the inter-island ferry.

[c] Taga people more frequently travelled to Salelologa for special shopping and government business than to Apia.

[d] Travel time is valued at 1s 6d an hour.

(b) Costs of earning money

Three factors are briefly considered here: the labour costs of cash cropping, marketing costs and prices, and the opportunities for earning money outside village agriculture.

Generally the labour costs of producing copra, bananas or cacao

Table 49    The Villages Ranked by Cash Returns to Labour in the
Production and Sale of Copra [a]

|  |  | Cash costs | | Labour costs | | Cash returns | |
|---|---|---|---|---|---|---|---|
|  | Where sold | Price re-ceived [b] | fares & freight [c] | produc-tion | market-ing [d] | per 100 lbs copra | per hr labour |
|  |  | s d | s d | hrs | hrs | s d | s d |
| Utuali'i (I) | Apia | 44.0 | 0.6 | 8 | $\frac{1}{2}$ | 43.6 | 5.1 |
| Poutasi (II) | Poutasi | 38.0 | nil | 8 | $\frac{1}{2}$ | 38.0 | 4.6 |
|  | Apia | 44.0 | 4.0 | 8 | 2 | 40.0 | 4.0 |
| Taga (III) | Taga | 36.0 | nil | 9 | $\frac{1}{2}$ | 36.0 | 3.8 |
|  | Salelologa | 38.0 | 4.0 | 9 | 2 | 34.0 | 3.1 |
| Uafato (IV) | Falefā | 38.0 | 2.0 | 9 · | 6 | 36.0 | 2.5 |
|  | Apia | 44.0 | 4.0 | 9 | 7 | 40.0 | 2.5 |

NOTES:    [a] Calculations based on average costs and returns per 100 lbs copra
[b] Price for 100 lbs 'hot air dried No. 1' copra
[c] Based on the average cost per 100 lbs when copra was taken in relatively small lots (200-300 lbs) by bus. Only one-way fares are included
as it is assumed that the return fare could be charged to other business
transacted in Apia, Salelologa or Falefā.
[d] Does not include the time spent in Apia waiting for the bus to return
to the village.

beans for sale, the labour skills required, and the methods of production used, were fairly similar in the four villages. The natural
resource base varied, of course, but often a disadvantage in one
respect was compensated for by an advantage in another. For
example, Uafato lands were steep and less extensive than those of
Taga, but at the same time they were generally more fertile and
could be kept in production for a longer period. Taga lands were
more widely dispersed and farther from the village than those of
the other villages, but they were relatively close to the road. Coconuts were more easily collected from the Poutasi lands, but this
was the result of more labour applied to clearing undergrowth.

Copra was the only cash crop produced in all villages during the
greater part of the survey and the main evidence of production
costs for comparative purposes is therefore restricted to this (Table
49). Labour time was the only cost of harvesting, and labour and
depreciation of dryers were the only costs of processing. Processing
costs were the same in all villages. Harvesting costs varied more
widely between different small-holdings in a village than on
average between villages. It took an average of 1·9 hours in Poutasi
(II) to gather 100 coconuts and carry them to the village, and

slightly longer in the other villages; two hours in Utuali'i (I) and about 2·3 hours in both Taga (III) and Uafato (IV). These differences are slight compared with those found in other factors such as the costs of marketing.

The costs of producing other crops such as bananas, taro and European vegetables were probably about the same in Uafato, Taga and Poutasi, but were somewhat higher in Utuali'i which was unable to draw on reserves of fresh land. Increasing production costs, mainly weeding, apparently decided Utuali'i 'āiga to give up bananas as a cash crop a decade earlier, although there were other factors also behind this decision such as a developing market for European vegetables and an expansion in cacao bean production.

Although there were differences in production costs the evidence is not strong enough, and probably the differences are not marked enough, to rank the villages on this factor.

Marketing costs and prices are closely related factors which provide a more solid basis for ranking the villages in terms of rewards for labour in cash cropping. Copra again provides the main evidence and this is shown in Table 49. Banana prices were uniform between villages and as the Banana Scheme arranged to take delivery in the villages or along the roads close to the banana plots marketing costs were also similar, although possibly slightly higher in Uafato where the cases of bananas had to be taken by whaleboat and canoe out to the launch.

The regulation prices for copra gave a substantial margin to those producers who took their copra to Apia for sale. This margin was earned by the independent traders in outer-district villages and the small freehold plantation at Utuali'i. Village producers themselves, when they could take their copra to Apia, probably received a slightly smaller margin. All Utuali'i producers, most in Uafato and a few in Poutasi did this. A number of independent traders paid slightly higher than the regulation outer-district prices as a way of attracting business. Most of the Apia-based trading-stations kept to the regulation prices. Thus, Uafato copra sold in Falefā, Poutasi copra sold to Lee Chang and Ioane, and Taga copra sold in Salelologa, earned slightly more a bag than that sold in the village trading-stations, although less than copra sold in Apia.

Utuali'i producers had the lowest copra-marketing costs, and at the same time received the highest possible prices. The bulk cf the Utuali'i output, that from the freehold plantation, was trucked into Apia by the buying company at a small charge per load. Smaller producers took their copra to Apia by bus and paid only a sixpenny fare and one shilling a bag freight.

Poutasi producers sold most of their output in the village, to Lee Chang and Ioane, at a small labour cost incurred in carrying the copra to the stores. They usually received slightly better than the regulation prices. One Poutasi *matai* owned a truck and generally sold his copra, and sometimes that of relatives and friends, in Apia. Occasionally individuals travelling by bus to Apia on business or for social purposes took small quantities of copra to sell whilst there.

Taga producers sold most of their copra in the village trading-stations receiving the regulation prices but incurring only a small labour cost in carrying the copra to the station. Kauli Long took his copra to Salelologa in his bus at little cost since this was his normal daily bus route. Other *'āiga* occasionally took small amounts to Salelologa by bus, or with Kauli Long, and there they received a small margin over the regulation price. In general marketing costs were very similar to those in Poutasi: village against village, and Salelologa against Apia, and the transport facilities available for the out-of-village marketing were also very similar. Poutasi's main advantage, and one which gave its producers a higher cash return than earned by Taga producers, was the higher price received in each comparable market.

Uafato producers were unable to sell copra in the village. Their nearest market was in the trading-stations at Fagaloa Bay. After the considerable effort of getting their copra there by whaleboat or canoe they were paid only the regulation price. Their alternative was to take the copra on to Falefā or Apia by bus, and for a number of reasons described in Chapter 4, they opted mainly for Apia. The costs of getting their copra to Apia, mainly the labour of the first stage to Fagaloa Bay, resulted in their earning by far the lowest cash returns to labour in copra production and sale of the four villages studied. It was little wonder that most Uafato *'āiga* preferred to sell unhusked coconuts to the two store-whaleboat-owning *'āiga* and let them shoulder the high marketing costs.

The net result in terms of cash returns to labour in the copra business shown in Table 49 gives a clear basis for ranking the villages and confirms the original rank order. The same order is found again when we consider the opportunities available to individuals in each village to earn wages or a salary. People could, and did, commute daily to jobs in or near Apia from Utuali'i. This was possible from Poutasi and Uafato also but the bus journey took much longer and cost much more and most Apia job-holders from these two villages preferred to live in Apia. Some returned to the village at weekends but most visited their homes less frequently. Both cost of travel and distance precluded Taga people from commuting, and also from returning regularly to the village at week-ends. Only in Utuali'i could a large proportion of the wage-earnings of its Apia job-holders be included in the estimates of village cash income. A few individuals earned wages for jobs held in or near their own village. Utuali'i, of course, could include Apia and its environs in this category, but of the other villages Poutasi was clearly the best placed with jobs available in its hospital, school, and Department of Agriculture Office and near-by coconut nursery. Taga was next with jobs in its school and occasional labouring jobs on the blocks of Kauli Long and Tialavea. The only wage job available in Uafato was that of district nurse; no Uafato people qualified for the teaching positions in the village.

The village rank order is again clear: Utuali'i (I), Poutasi (II), Taga (III) and Uafato (IV).

(c) *Shopping facilities*

Utuali'i (I) had Apia as its main shopping centre. Its shoppers behaved rather like suburban dwellers, making special and occasionally bulk purchases in the city stores, but dealing when more convenient with the local shops. About thirty-three per cent of the purchases of the sample *'āiga* were made in the village and the rest in Apia. In Poutasi (II) there was much less dependence on Apia for special purchases and about eighty-seven per cent of all shopping was done in the village. There were fairly frequent trips to Apia when advantage could be taken of the slightly lower prices, the much greater variety, and the possibilities of bulk purchases. Poutasi shoppers behaved somewhat like those living in a provincial town. Taga (III) shoppers were much more limited in their choice of goods and services, as a journey to Apia was costly. Eighty-one per cent of all purchases recorded for the sample *'āiga* had been made in Taga and the rest mainly in Salelologa where there was a slightly better choice. Taga shoppers behaved like those of a small country town, occasionally shopping in the provincial centre and only rarely going to the city. Uafato (IV) was more like a farm community keeping its own bulk stores of staple foods in its larder and dependent for all other purchases on the provincial centre or city. About half the purchases recorded for the Uafato sample *'āiga* (excluding as far as possible the replacement of store stock) were made from the village stores, and the rest were made mainly in Apia.

Retail prices varied in a predictable way, lowest in Apia, slightly higher in Poutasi and Salelologa, still higher in Taga, and generally at a Western Samoa maximum in Uafato. The range and variety of goods varied predictably in the opposite direction, greatest in

Apia and very limited in Uafato. There was, however, one advantage of shopping in the village which often outweighed considerations of price and variety: generally only the local stores sold on credit. Shopping outside the village also had a cash cost in bus fares. They were lowest for Utuali'i shoppers, about the same for Poutasi and Uafato shoppers going to Apia and Taga shoppers going to Salelologa. But they were very high for Taga people going to Apia, as well as taking many hours and requiring an overnight stop in Apia. Uafato people had the added inconvenience of the walk between the village and Fagaloa Bay.

All these factors point to a clear ranking of the villages in the order Utuali'i (I), Poutasi (II), Taga (III) and Uafato (IV).

It is assumed that this ranking based on certain important linkage factors indicates that which would be found if we could measure the incentive factor, and it gives us one side of the picture presented in Proposition 2. The proposition predicted that we would find the same village order expressed in the extent of market participation in each village.

Table 50   Incomes[a]

|  | Utuali'i (I) | Poutasi (II) | Taga (III) | Uafato (IV) |
|---|---|---|---|---|
|  | ($\pounds$ per consumption unit) | | | |
| SUBSISTENCE (non-monetary) INCOME | | | | |
| Food | 11·8 | 23·8 | 30·6 | 28·6 |
| Buildings | 1·6 | 1·5 | 1·0 | 1·0 |
| Household durables | 1·5 | 2·0 | 1·9 | 1·2 |
| Tools and equipment | ·4 | ·6 | ·5 | ·5 |
| Total: | 15·3 | 27·9 | 34·0 | 31·3 |
| CASH INCOME | | | | |
| Agriculture and fishing | 15·8 | 14·6 | 13·6 | 7·5 |
| Handicrafts | | | | 2·1 |
| Wages | 10·6 | 8·1 | 1·6 | 2·2 |
| Remittances from Apia | | ·2 | 1·6 | ·8 |
| Remittances from abroad | 9·4 | 2·9 | 2·5 | 1·0 |
| Gifts | ·2 | | ·3 | ·1 |
| Other | | | ·4 | |
| Total: | 36·0 | 25·8 | 20·0 | 13·7 |
| TOTAL INCOME | 51·3 | 54·3 | 54·0 | 45·0 |
| Monetization factor | 70% | 50% | 37% | 30% |

NOTE:   [a] 12 months, December 1965-November 1966

## 2. *Ranking participation*

The evidence for ranking the villages on the basis of market participation is easy to present although it took most of the survey time to establish. It is given in Table 50. A rough adjustment to these estimates to account for some of the distortions due to the hurricane is given in Table 51 but these do not alter the rank order of the villages. The test results are shown in Table 52 and are as predicted in Proposition 2.

MARKET PARTICIPATION

*Proposition* 3 Participation in the market sector may be expected, initially, to be supplementary to subsistence production, and therefore to represent additional income and consumption rather than mere substitution.

The evidence from Uafato, Taga and Poutasi villages appears to support this proposition fairly well. The levels of subsistence income were similar, and total income varied almost directly with the level of cash income. But these villages are no longer in the 'initial' stage of contact with the market sector specified in the proposition, and in each there was a certain amount of substitution of market sector

Table 51 Income Adjusted for Hurricane and Bunchytop Losses
12 months

|  | Utuali'i (I) | Poutasi (II) | Taga (III) | Uafato (IV) |
|---|---|---|---|---|
|  | ($£$ per consumption unit) | | | |
| Subsistence income[a] | 24 | 36 | 40 | 39 |
| Cash income[b] | 46 | 40 | 27 | 21 |
| Total income | 70 | 76 | 67 | 60 |
|  | per cent | | | |
| Monetization factor[c] | 66 | 53 | 40 | 35 |

NOTES: [a] The imputed value of staple foods only—bananas, breadfruit, taro and *ta'amū*—have been adjusted. Other subsistence income estimates are taken from the survey data as shown in Table 50. The staple foods have been adjusted on the basis of the observed supply in December 1965 and January 1966 as shown in Appendix Table 2.

[b] The survey estimates shown in Table 50 have been adjusted in two ways: cash income from bananas is taken as the average over the period 1959-65 for Poutasi and Uafato, and over the period 1961-5 for Taga, as shown in Appendix Table 5. Cash income from fruit and vegetables in Utuali'i is taken as double that recorded during the survey period.

[c] Proportion of monetized income on total income

Table 52   Proposition 2 Test Results

| Village order based on strength of market linkage | Cash income per consumption unit (year) | Monetization factor |
|---|---|---|
| | £ | % |
| (I)   Utuali'i | 36 | 70 |
| (II)   Poutasi | 26 | 50 |
| (III)   Taga | 20 | 37 |
| (IV)   Uafato | 14 | 30 |

goods and services for those of the subsistence sector. Furthermore, the extent of substitution in each village was closely related to the strength of its linkage with the market sector. Uafato had the weakest linkage and the least substitution. Poutasi had the strongest linkage and the most substitution. While Uafato and Taga maintained very similar levels of staple food production and did not consume normally very much flour, rice and bread which were reasonable substitutes, Poutasi appeared to have reached a stage where the use of purchased staples had led to a small decline in demand for, and therefore production of, taro and bananas.

In Uafato there was only one dwelling which had been built largely with purchased material. The situation was very much the same in Taga before 1960, but the opening of the road heralded a minor building boom and many dwellings were built with purchased material. Poutasi had a similar experience when its road was opened, although it was modified by a strong *fono* which attempted to preserve the traditional character of the island section by forbidding the construction there of non-traditional dwellings. Only the two high chiefs had built European-style dwellings near the *malae* and each skilfully and expensively incorporated a large *fale* at the front. Many of these non-traditional dwellings in the villages, including the one in Uafato, replaced *fale* built of local material. In the same way the pastor's houses in Poutasi, which were exempted from the *fono*'s general ruling, replaced large *fale*, and the school in each village replaced the *fale* which had been used earlier.

Utuali'i village had gone a great deal farther in substituting purchased for subsistence goods and services. Non-traditional dwellings were more common. Some Utuali'i residents even dispensed with the services of their friends in favour of regular visits to Apia barbers. But it was in the extent of staple food substitution that Utuali'i departed most from the general pattern found in the other three villages. The use of flour, rice and bread was far more common than in Poutasi. They were given regularly not only to schoolchildren but also to those who commuted daily to wage jobs in Apia, and to the fruit and vegetable sellers when they went to market. In addition, Utuali'i was the only village with easy and cheap access to the Apia local-products market where village staples like taro, *ta'amū* and bananas could be bought and where supplies were assured. With this dependable source of traditional staples there was probably not as much pressure on Utuali'i '*āiga* to maintain full production in the village as there was on the '*āiga* in the other villages which had no alternative sources of regular supplies. Another important factor in Utuali'i was that it had virtually given up the production of bananas during the 1950s rather than permanently apply additional labour effort to weeding banana plots. Thereafter Utuali'i '*āiga* bought most of their food bananas in Apia, either in the market or from the Department of Agriculture which sold export rejects. Finally, many Utuali'i people took casual labouring jobs in near-by coconut and cacao plantations where they were usually supplied with meals. To the extent that this had become a normal feature of the Utuali'i food front there would have been a natural decline in the demand for food from other sources including the village plots. The availability of alternative supplies in the market sector, coupled with the some-what higher labour costs of subsistence food production in Utuali'i and the greater opportunities for earning money from the village probably explains in large part the decline in demand for subsistence food in this village and the relatively low level of output.

In another way also Utuali'i appears to have departed from the general pattern. Although cash income per consumption unit was considerably higher during the survey its total income was below that of Poutasi and Taga. The rough adjustments to agricultural cash incomes affected by the hurricane raises it above Taga but not Poutasi. But it is possible that another source of cash income was seriously affected by the hurricane—that from labouring jobs on the plantations, and under normal conditions this could have raised total income close to or even higher than that in Poutasi. Utuali'i was certainly one of the villages referred to by Stace:

> There can be little doubt that there is a large reserve of under-employed people in Samoa, particularly in Upolu. This is clearly indicated in the fact that New Zealand Reparation Estates, for example, regularly builds up its labour forces from 1,600 to 4,000 employees during the months of the year when the village people, too, are busy with their cocoa harvesting and all commercial plantations are actively seeking labour. Even under these seasonal pressures most employers experience little difficulty in securing the additional workers required (1956, p. 39).

The fact remains, however, that subsistence food production in Utuali'i had declined much more than in Poutasi and this indicates that many Utuali'i people found that they could maintain the level of living they wanted by depending more on the market sector and less on the subsistence sector. They appeared to have a great deal more leisure, owned more market sector goods, and consumed as much food and were as well housed as the people in the outer villages. When they could get it they preferred wage jobs to work in village agriculture. The work was probably harder, the pay was no higher per hour, but there was added prestige and independence from the *matai*.

A QUESTION OF ECONOMIC DEVELOPMENT

All the evidence presented so far points in one direction: Samoans are generally content with the life they lead. They have little interest in the outside world which intrudes on them in the form of the market sector. They likewise have little evident concern for the future, little interest in productive investment, little willingness to 'develop'.

The four villages varied considerably in the strength of linkage with the market sector. Total income per head in a normal year in Uafato where linkage was extremely weak was about £40 (Table 51). In Utuali'i with its long history of easy access to Apia it was only about £10 higher, and in Poutasi with its strong links with the market sector and abundant natural resources it was only £60. The average cash income per head in Utuali'i and Poutasi was less than £35. Very few villages in Western Samoa earned more, but most, like Taga and Uafato, earned considerably less. All four had the resources available with which they could have increased their cash earnings and therefore total income. But in Utuali'i the men averaged only three hours a week in cash cropping; and the Poutasi men, who worked as hard as any villagers in Samoa, averaged only eight hours a week. These figures point to a decided lack of interest in earning money through village agriculture, and yet there were very few other opportunities.

It is the same story when we consider the use of natural resources and cash-earning assets. Early in the century the Samoans were forced by the German administration to expand their coconut plantings. By 1920 most of the present coconut lands were established, and these have been the mainstay of village cash incomes ever since. But since then the Samoans have not expanded the coconut holdings to any significant extent, or even maintained them. A majority of palms is now approaching retirement age, a significant proportion has already indeed retired, yet there has been little replanting. In many coconut areas the jungle is returning. The village copra industry is no longer stagnant; it is in decline. Other tree crops, like cacao and coffee, have been taken up in a small way in most villages and in a larger way in a few, but as with coconuts they have been neglected. For whatever reason an initial effort was put into planting tree crops; it is rarely extended to regular weeding and other maintenance work or into a long-term programme of expansion.

Production methods, too, have hardly changed. They are about the same as when John Williams landed in 1830. The *oso* and the knife—the knife is new—are the main implements used; simple bush fallow methods produce the main food crops and bananas; and the tree crops are merely harvested. Few villagers have adopted commercial plantation methods on their coconut and cacao small-holdings, although most know about them. Poutasi coconut lands had been carefully planted in rows with good spacing but this was not so in the other villages studied, including Utuali'i which is next to a commercial plantation. A few Poutasi and Taga *matai* had fenced their coconut areas and kept cattle and horses to control undergrowth, and were taking the first steps towards a modern agriculture. Other *matai* showed no interest in following suit and no one in Utuali'i and Uafato had taken these first steps. No *'āiga* in the four villages had ever used fertilizer, although several Uafato *matai* claimed that chemical fertilizers had caused bunchytop.

Most villagers regard pests and diseases such as rhinoceros beetle and bunchytop fatalistically. The Department of Agriculture has preached the evils of the rhinoceros beetle for decades, but village methods, and until recently those of many plantations, '. . . have favoured the beetle much more than the palm. Even now, beetle breeding is more actively pursued in Western Samoa than copra production' (Pieris 1965, p. 6). During 1965 the Department of Agriculture publicized widely by radio a simple method of bunchy-top control—to spray infected plants with a mixture of kerosene and water and cut them down and burn them. Most growers cut out their infected plants, but few really understood the importance of spraying and destroying them. The response was so poor that the Department employed teams to inspect village banana plots and to destroy infected plants. While many Samoans simply did not understand how the bunchytop virus spread, although they were told frequently on the radio to which they listened avidly, they did know perfectly well how to control rhinoceros beetle and could see the damage it was doing to their palms. But in general they responded to both in the same way: they stopped planting.

P

Most people living in commercial societies want to own and accumulate commodities which they need in their daily lives, or simply like. If they want a particular article they generally try to buy it; if they want to dispose of one they already own, they generally try to sell it. They work within the market system whether the transaction is with friends, relatives or strangers. Samoans in general do not act in this way. Their exchange system has developed differently; goods and services are transferred on request as gifts or assistance, and carry with them an obligation on the part of the receiver to reciprocate at some time in the future. Gift-giving adds to social prestige because it is a way of obligating others—a source of goods and services reserved for the future, a guarantee against future hardship.

Under this system people are less likely to want or be able to accumulate material wealth—especially money. They have little incentive to work harder or produce more than the next person if they can have a particular item simply by openly admiring it and thereby encouraging the owner to display his generosity by giving it. They are unlikely to work hard to acquire a particularly desirable item if they may eventually have to give it away. The process is well illustrated by the tale of a colourful shirt I admired in Poutasi. It was worn to the village by a visiting Apia youth who presumably bought it in a store. When he went back to Apia it remained with his Poutasi friend. In the course of the next few months I saw it being worn by four other Poutasi men, each of whom had obtained it from his friend or relative simply by expressing his admiration, or if this did not work, by asking for it. Another example concerns the redistribution of a stock of carpentry tools. When I first visited Poutasi I met an elderly *matai* who was a respected craftsman builder. He owned an impressive collection of tools but, he said, he had completed his last big job and wanted to spend his time making and repairing canoes. Seven months later his tool collection was depleted—scattered between men in his own '*āiga*, Poutasi and Vaovai villages. The tools had been borrowed and he did not expect them to be returned. He was finished with them; others had use for them. The system developed to suit a subsistence situation of resource affluence, but it has not changed to meet the new conditions of a commercial world—another example of the Samoans' reluctance to change a socio-economic system with which they are satisfied.

The system by which the Samoans control their main productive asset, land, is another vestige of the pre-contact past. Since it was codified by the German administration it has been preserved with the utmost tenacity by the *matai*. In 1966 the legislature, which is composed entirely of *matai*, rejected a plan to permit *matai* to lease land under their control to other *matai*. Suggestions that *taulele'a* be allowed to lease land, even from their own *matai*, were not considered. No Samoan has any security of tenure over land controlled by his *matai* in trust for the *'āiga*. It is accumulated by clearing forest and, consequently, holdings often bear no relation to the willingness and ability of the controlling *'āiga* to make use of it. Even *matai* often see little value in developing land when they have no guarantee that their sons, or their sons-in-law, will succeed them to the title. A number of writers on the Samoan economy (Stace, Pieris) see the *matai* land control system as the main blockage to economic development but to me it seems to be just one more illustration of the Samoans' general satisfaction with things as they are. They could change the system if they wanted to.

The overriding ambition of Samoan youth is to become *matai*: to enjoy the prestige and status of the *élite* in Samoan society. The more ambitious might aspire to a high-ranking title which would give them additional political influence and authority. As a second preference many would want to become pastors, which in most churches in Samoa excludes them from holding *matai* rank but nevertheless carries very high status. Others might want to migrate to New Zealand which again gives certain prestige and often a title as well. Most *taulele'a* do not have to have any special ability to join the ranks of the *matai*, and most realize their ambition in time if they serve their *matai* and *'āiga* with reasonable diligence. Often the process can be speeded up by doing well at school and getting a wage job, or by working in New Zealand, remitting money home regularly, and eventually returning to invest savings in an *'āiga* store, bus or European-style dwelling. Few Samoans have been able to do this by putting extra effort into village agriculture. Samoans do not attain *matai* status by rebelling against the system however unfair it might seem to them as *taulele'a*. But few want to rebel since any change of the system would only weaken their position when they eventually realize their ambition and become *matai*. *Taulele'a* have almost as much interest as the *matai* in maintaining the *status quo*. Very few want to rock the boat.

Although the villagers respond to market incentives in a predictable way they rarely responded as fully as they could given their resource situation. They want a cash income because it allows them to have certain goods and services which otherwise would be denied them. It helps them up the social ladder, and to gain political influence and authority—the real objectives. Money is only one of many means to achieving them and, once achieved, money adds little to the enjoyment of the *fa'āSamoa*, the Samoan way of life.

Hence their interest in the outside world in general, and the market sector in particular, is limited.

There is little evidence to suggest that these attitudes towards economic development are changing. Yet population is rising very rapidly and by the end of this century most villages will start to experience a declining level of living as their resource affluence turns to scarcity. Major changes in attitudes towards future economic needs will be needed if this is to be averted, but it does not seem that this is likely. Perhaps future Samoans will regard shortages with the same fatalism with which present Samoans regard bunchy-top and the rhinoceros beetle.

# APPENDIX TABLES

Appendix Table 1   Four Villages: Population Data [a]
1950-65

| Year | Uafato | Taga | Poutasi | Utuali'i and Tufulele |
|------|--------|------|---------|----------------------|
| 1950 | 185 | 334 | 213 | 460 |
| 51 | 203 | 347 | n.a. | 486 |
|  | (178) | (393) | (287) | (425) |
| 52 | 170 | 353 | 272 | 513 |
| 53 | 204 | 372 | 293 | 525 |
| 54 | 215 | 415 | 324 | 555 |
| 55 | 223 | 403 | 314 | 606 |
| 56 | 242 | 382 | 352 | 603 |
|  | (186) | (386) | (367) | (243) [b] |
| 57 | 229 | 418 | 349 | 659 |
| 58 | 239 | n.a. | 365 | 718 |
| 59 | 228 | 474 | n.a. | 683 |
| 60 | 269 | 419 | n.a. | 719 |
| 61 | 271 | 475 | 394 | 769 |
|  | (247) | (481) | (468) | (296) [b] |
| 62 | 289 | 497 | 384 | 716 |
| 63 | 248 | 497 | 398 | 666 |
| 64 | 269 | 501 | 494 | 722 |
| 65 | 291 | n.a. | n.a. | 772 |
| Census of resident population taken during fieldwork | | | | |
| 1965 | 286 | 505 | 436 | 261 [b] |

SOURCES: Records of the Congregational Christian Church in Samoa, Apia.
Western Samoa Population Census, 1951, 1956 and 1961

NOTES:  [a] Census returns are shown in brackets. Other figures are the pastors' reports of resident population.
 [b] Utuali'i only

Appendix Table 2   Estimated Average Supply of Staple Foods by Months, December 1965-November 1966[a]

| Village | Staple | Dec. | Jan. | Feb. | Mar. | Apr. | May | June | July | Aug. | Sept. | Oct. | Nov. | Average for week | Total for village over 12 months |
|---|---|---|---|---|---|---|---|---|---|---|---|---|---|---|---|
| | | (lbs for consumption unit per week[b]) | | | | | | | | | | | | | ('000 lbs) |
| Uafato | taro | 10 | 10 | 5 | 16 | 10 | 10 | 8 | 10 | 12 | 16 | 18 | 22 | 12 | 128 |
| | ta'amū | 3 | 3 | 4 | 4 | 15 | 10 | 5 | | | | | 5 | 5 | 47 |
| | breadfruit | 8 | 8 | 12 | | | | | | | 1 | 4 | | 3 | 33 |
| | bananas | 10 | 10 | 10 | 10 | | | | | | | | | 3 | 26 |
| | | 31 | 31 | 31 | 30 | 25 | 20 | 13 | 10 | 12 | 17 | 22 | 27 | 23 | 233 |
| Taga | taro | 10 | 10 | 10 | 20 | 15 | 15 | 10 | 8 | 10 | 15 | 20 | 25 | 14 | 245 |
| | ta'amū | 8 | 8 | 5 | 7 | 10 | 8 | 8 | 4 | 2 | | | 5 | 5 | 95 |
| | breadfruit | 5 | 5 | 8 | | | | | | | 1 | 4 | | 2 | 44 |
| | bananas | 7 | 7 | 4 | | | | | | | | | | 2 | 28 |
| | | 30 | 30 | 27 | 27 | 25 | 23 | 18 | 12 | 12 | 16 | 24 | 30 | 23 | 412 |

| | 1 | 2 | 3 | 4 | 5 | 6 | 7 | 8 | 9 | 10 | 11 | 12 | 13 | Total |
|---|---|---|---|---|---|---|---|---|---|---|---|---|---|---|
| **Poutasi** | | | | | | | | | | | | | | |
| taro | 7 | 7 | 10 | 20 | 15 | 10 | 8 | 6 | 8 | 10 | 15 | 20 | 11 | 191 |
| ta'amū | 1 | 1 | 1 | 4 | 4 | 2 | 2 | 1 | | 1 | 4 | 5 | 2 | 24 |
| breadfruit | 8 | 8 | 9 | | | | | | | 1 | 4 | 5 | 3 | 49 |
| bananas | 15 | 15 | 10 | | | 1 | | | | 1 | | 5 | 3 | 54 |
| | 31 | 31 | 30 | 24 | 19 | 12 | 10 | 7 | 8 | 11 | 19 | 25 | 19 | 318 |
| | | | | | | | | | | | | | | |
| **Utuali'i** | | | | | | | | | | | | | | |
| taro | 8 | 8 | 8 | 4 | 2 | 1 | | | | 1 | 4 | 8 | 4 | 36 |
| ta'amū | 5 | 5 | 5 | 5 | 2 | | | | | | 4 | | 2 | 18 |
| breadfruit | 8 | 8 | 8 | | 1 | | | | | 1 | 4 | 5 | 3 | 29 |
| bananas | | | | | | | | | | | | | | |
| | 21 | 21 | 21 | 9 | 4 | 1 | | | 1 | | 8 | 13 | 9 | 83 |

NOTES:

(a) These are rough estimates of the supply of staple subsistence foodstuffs in the four villages, from December 1965 to November 1966. The quantities from December to June are based on data collected in the survey and more general observations in the villages. Those from July to November are what I expected to happen when limited quantities of breadfruit became available and the taro planted immediately after the hurricane began to be harvested. Both these changes had started before I left Samoa in August. The purpose of these estimates of subsistence food supplies is to allow some comparison between the villages of food supplies during the period, to provide a basis for a valuation of subsistence supplies (Tables 13, 23, 31 and 40), and to indicate the extent of subsistence food losses due to the hurricane. The quantities for Poutasi before the hurricane are supported by additional evidence published in Wilkins, Rosemary M. 1966.

(b) See p. 55 for definition of 'consumption unit'.

Appendix Table 3  Estimated Production from the Village Coconut Lands and Disposal of Output in 1966

| | Uafato | | Taga | | Poutasi | | Utuali'i | |
|---|---|---|---|---|---|---|---|---|
| | no. | % | no. | % | no. | % | no. | % |
| Coconut plantation land (acres) | 174 | | 325 | | 520 | | 85 | |
| Average number of palms to one acre (estimated)(a) | 50 | | 80 | | 40 | | 60 | |
| Condition of palms (estimated numbers)(b) | | | | | | | | |
| Under 7 years—not bearing | 500 | 6 | 2,000 | 8 | 6,000(a) | 29 | 300 | 5 |
| Aged and unproductive | 900 | 10 | 6,000 | 23 | 3,400 | 17 | 800 | 15 |
| Mature and unproductive | 7,200 | 84 | 18,000 | 69 | 11,200 | 54 | 4,100 | 80 |
| | 8,600 | 100 | 26,000 | 100 | 20,600 | 100 | 5,200 | 100 |
| Disposal of output (estimated number of coconuts)(c) | | | | | | | | |
| Subsistence food | 54,000 | 17 | 133,000 | 19 | 76,000 | 11 | 45,000 | 20 |
| Livestock | 20,000 | 6 | 79,000 | 11 | 22,000 | 3 | 4,000 | 2 |
| Copra | 125,000 | 39 | 433,000 | 60 | 515,000 | 77 | 126,000 | 56 |
| Nuts sold | — | — | — | — | — | — | 54,000 | 24 |
| Wastage | 124,000 | 38 | 72,000 | 10 | 57,000 | 9 | (−4,000)(d) | (−2) |
| | 323,000 | 100 | 717,000 | 100 | 670,000 | 100 | 229,000 | 100 |

NOTES:   (a) Areas of coconut lands include patches of open bush-fallow land. Much of the area planted in coconuts in Uafato and Taga contain well over 100 palms to an acre. These estimates are based on a count of palms and for Poutasi only, the results of a Coconut Survey carried out by the Department of Agriculture in 1965. The number of palms counted from the aerial photograph of Poutasi and the number counted in the Coconut Survey were similar enough, after allowing for recent plantings, to indicate that the numbers estimated for the other villages were reasonable.

(b) The data for Poutasi comes from the Department of Agriculture Coconut Survey of 1965. Those for the other villages are based on general observation.

(c) Based on my survey data of (a) nuts consumed as subsistence foods, (b) nuts fed to livestock, and (c) nuts used for copra and sold. The estimates of wastage and losses from the hurricane are balancing items only, but from observations they appear reasonable and at least indicate a real difference between the villages.

(d) Evidence from the survey and observation showed that some Utuali'i *taulele'a* were in the habit of taking coconuts from the Malua plantations both for subsistence foods (the Malua plantations were closer than the Utuali'i coconut lands to some of the families

Appendix Table 4    Copra Board of Western Samoa Price Order
February 1965

|  | Price per 100 pounds delivered to buyers' sheds | | | |
|---|---|---|---|---|
|  | HAD[c]<br>No. 1 | SD[d]<br>No. 1 | HAD[c]/SD[d]<br>No. 2 | Undried |
|  | s. d. | s. d. | s. d. | s. d. |
| All districts[a] | 38.6 | 36.6 | 33.6 | 19.3 |
| Independent traders and/or<br>  plantation copra[b] | 46.0 | 44.0 | 41.0 | — |
| Prices paid by the Board to<br>  holders of export licences | 50.0 | 51.0 | 47.0 | — |

SOURCE: Annual Report of the Copra Board of Western Samoa 1965
NOTES:    [a] Prices paid by village trade stores
               [b] Delivered to Apia, freight paid
               [c] Hot-air dried
               [d] Sun-dried

Appendix Table 5    Quantities and Value of Banana Sales[a]

| Year | Poutasi (II) | | Taga (III) | | Uafato (IV) | |
|---|---|---|---|---|---|---|
|  | Number<br>of cases | Cash<br>income | Number<br>of cases | Cash<br>income | Number<br>of cases | Cash<br>income |
|  |  | £ |  | £ |  | £ |
| 1959 | 12,526 | 6,263 |  |  | 2,712 | 1,356 |
| 1960 | 5,989 | 2,893 |  |  | 2,282 | 1,102 |
| 1961 | 10,699 | 5,349 | 79 | 40 | 2,471 | 1,235 |
| 1962 | 10,675 | 5,562 | 3,484 | 1,786 | 4,200 | 2,188 |
| 1963 | 4,829 | 2,516 | 4,159 | 2,112 | 1,798 | 936 |
| 1964 | 11,488 | 6,318 | 8,568 | 4,711 | 4,198 | 2,309 |
| 1965 | 4,762 | 2,619 | 3,821 | 2,102 | 3,209 | 1,765 |
| 1966[b] | 236 | 89 | 16 | 90 | 166 | 64 |

SOURCE: Records of the Banana Scheme, Department of Agriculture, Western
Samoa
NOTES:    [a] No bananas were sold from Utuali'i (I) during this period.
               [b] January only

Appendix Table 6 (a)    Household Daily Activities Questionnaire

household _____
date _____
day:      M  T  W  T  F  S  S

1. What things did this household purchase today from shops or from other persons?

| what was purchased? (name & quantity) | cost? £ | s. | d. | where was it purchased? | cash, account or goods? |
|---|---|---|---|---|---|
|  |  |  |  |  |  |
|  |  |  |  |  |  |

2. What other money has gone out from this household today for any other purpose?
(e.g. *tautua*, church, pastor, fares, billiards, gift, pay account etc.)

| who was the money given to? | how much? £ | s. | d. | who gave it? | why was it given, or on what was it spent? |
|---|---|---|---|---|---|
|  |  |  |  |  |  |

3. What did this household sell today to traders or to any other persons?
(e.g. copra, bananas, taro, fish, mats, thatches etc.)

| what was sold? (name and quantity) | where was it sold? | money received? £   s.   d. | account paid? £   s.   d. |
|---|---|---|---|
|  |  |  |  |

4. What other money came into this household today for any other reason?
(e.g. *tautua*, gift, wages, New Zealand etc.)

| who gave the money? | how much? £ | s. | d. | who was it given to? | why was it given? |
|---|---|---|---|---|---|
|  |  |  |  |  |  |

5. What goods (food, mats etc.) were given out from this household today?

| what was given? (name & quantity) | who was it given to? | why was it given? |
|---|---|---|
|  |  |  |

6. What goods were received into this household today?

| what was received?<br>(name & quantity) | who gave it? | why was it given? |
|---|---|---|
| | | |

7. Was any help received by this family in its work today by any visitor or member of another household?
   a. who helped?
   b. what work was done?
   c. where was the work done?
   d. how many hours were spent by this person?
   e. what food, money, other things were given to him/her?

8. Was any help given by members of this household in the work of another household today?
   a. who helped from this household?
   b. who was helped?
   c. where was the work done?
   d. what work was done?
   e. what food, money or other things were taken to the work?
   f. what food, money or other things were received during or for the work?

9. Was any member of this household out fishing during last night?
   a. who went fishing?
   b. time went out          , time came back          , total hours          .
   c. what was caught?

10. Did any member of this household leave the village on a visit or journey today?
    a. who went?
    b. where did he/she go?
    c. what was the reason for the journey?
    d. what money was taken for fares?
    e. what money was taken for other reasons?
    f. what food and other things were taken?
    g. when will he/she return?
    h. if he/she has already returned, what money, food and other things were brought back?

11. Were any guests or visitors received from another village today?
    a. who came?
    b. where did they come from?
    c. what was the purpose of the visit?
    d. how long did or will they stay?
    e. what food, money or other things did they bring for this family?
    f. what food, money or other things were given to them by this family?

12. Was there any village or church activity today in which a member of this household took part? (e.g. *fono*, Women's Committee, *'aumāga*, church, etc.)
    a. what was the activity?
    b. who took part from this household?

## Appendix Table 6 (a) cont.

    c. what was done?
    d. how long did it take?
    e. what food, money or other things were taken?
    f. what food, money or other things were brought back?

13. Was any member of this household too sick for normal work today?
    a. who was sick?
    b. what was the sickness?

## Appendix Table 6 (b)   Household Daily Production Questionnaire

days

BANANAS:
    bunches cut _____
        bunches packed for export _____
        bunches sold (not export) _____
    bunches used up in household _____

CACAO:
    pods harvested _____
    pods husked _____
        lbs beans sold _____
        lbs Sam. cocoa sold _____
    lbs Sam. cocoa used in household _____

COCONUTS:
    nuts gathered _____
    nuts husked _____
        lbs copra sold _____
        nuts sold _____
    nuts used up in household _____
                pigs _____
                chickens _____

TARO:
    taros harvested _____
    taros planted _____
        taros sold _____
    taros' used in household _____
    estimated weight of taros harvested _____

TA'AMU
    ta'amu harvested _____
    weight of harvest _____
    ta'amu planted _____
        ta'amu sold _____
    ta'amu used in household _____
    weight of ta'amu used _____

BREADFRUIT:
    number harvested _____
        number sold _____
    number used in household _____

YAMS:
    yams harvested _____
    weight _____
    yams planted _____
        yams sold _____
    yams used in household _____
    weight of yams used _____

PAPAYA:
    papaya harvested _____
        papaya sold _____
    papaya used in household _____

PINEAPPLE:
    pineapples harvested _____
        pineapples sold _____
    pineapples used in household _____

BEANS:
    lbs harvested _____
        bundles sold _____
        weight of bundle _____
    bundles used in household _____

TOMATOES:
    lbs harvested _____
        bags sold _____
        weight of one bag _____
    bags used in household _____

CUCUMBER:
    number harvested _____
        number sold _____
    number used in household _____

days

HANDICRAFTS COMPLETED:

papa _____
falalili'i _____
tapito _____
papa laufala _____
fala lau'ie _____
pola _____
'ietōga _____
ili _____
'ato laufala _____
ola _____
pola sisi _____
laulau _____
table mats _____
_____
_____
_____
siapo _____
'afa _____
na _____
ma'ata'ife'e _____
fana memei _____
paopao _____
_____
_____
_____
_____
_____

## Appendix Table 6 (c)   Household Particulars Schedule

village _____

household _____

### A.  MATAI:

a. title _____ ,

   other name _____

b. age _____ years

c. year elected to title _____

d. house name _____

e. cup name _____

f. rank in village _____

g. village office _____

h. other office—district, national

   _____

i. church denomination _____

j. church office _____

k. notes _____

### B.  POPULATION:

a. living in village or on village land (group in family units starting with that of the *matai*)

| number | names | male or female | relation-ship to *matai* | house number | occupation, special skills, school etc. | notes |
|---|---|---|---|---|---|---|
|  |  |  |  |  |  |  |

b. living away from village (other village, Apia, New Zealand etc.)

| names | male or female | relationship to *matai* | where living | occupation etc. | how *matai* is served (*tautua*) |
|---|---|---|---|---|---|
|  |  |  |  |  |  |

### C.  LAND HOLDINGS: (land under *pule* of *matai*)

| name of block | area | standing crops | who is working the block | notes |
|---|---|---|---|---|
|  |  |  |  |  |

Q

Appendix Table 6 (c) cont.

D.  HOUSEHOLD POSSESSIONS:

a.  Buildings:                                          Notes and hurricane
                                                               damage

Guest-*fale*

type_____      year built _____
floor _____    carpenter _____
roof_____      Samoan payment_____
ext. posts _____     _____
int. posts_____      _____
thatches _____       Cost of materials
blinds _____         _____
length _____         _____
width _____          _____

*Fale*

type_____      year built _____
floor _____    carpenter _____
roof_____      Samoan payment_____
ext. posts_____      _____
int. posts_____      _____
thatches _____       Cost of materials
blinds _____         _____
length _____         _____
width _____          _____

Small *fale*

number_____
years built _____
cost of materials_____
thatches _____
blinds _____
posts _____
floor _____
length _____
width _____

Cooking shelter

number_____
description _____
_____

Copra dryer

number_____
description _____
year built_____
cost of materials_____

Non-traditional dwelling or store

description _____
floor _____
roof_____
windows_____
length _____
width _____

Non-traditional dwelling or store (cont.)
year built_____
carpenter _____
Samoan payment _____
cost of materials_____
_____
_____
_____

Notes and hurricane
damage

b. Traditional handicrafts:
Mats: *pola vai* _____
*papa* _____
*tapito* _____
*papa laufala* _____
*tu'ulaufala* _____
*afiafi* _____
*fala pepe* _____
*fala laui'e* _____
_____

Other weaving:
*ili*_____
*'ato laufala* _____
*ola* _____
*laulau* _____
_____

Fine mats *'ietōga* _____
Tapa cloth *siapo* _____
Sinnet *'afa* _____
_____

Kava bowl _____
Food bowl _____
Cocoa-bean crusher_____
*Upeti* _____
*Fue* _____

*To'oto'o* _____
*Tuiga* _____

c. Fishing gear:
Canoes: *paopao* _____
*va'aniue* _____
*va'aalo* _____
Whaleboat _____
Other gear: _____
goggles _____
shanghai _____
,,     spears_____
throwing spear _____
rod *atu* _____
lure *atu* _____
lure other _____
line _____
hook _____
net: throwing _____
Japanese _____
*fa'amo'i* _____
lure octopus _____
_____
_____
_____

| | no. | age | how acquired | cost | G | F | P |
|---|---|---|---|---|---|---|---|
| d. Furniture: ___ | | | | | | | |
| foodsafe ___ | | | | | | | |
| table kitchen ___ | | | | | | | |
| ,,   side ___ | | | | | | | |
| chair wooden gdn ___ | | | | | | | |
| ,,   cane ___ | | | | | | | |
| ,,   other ___ | | | | | | | |
| bed ___ | | | | | | | |
| box ___ | | | | | | | |
| trunk___ | | | | | | | |
| case ___ | | | | | | | |
| other ___ | | | | | | | |

Appendix Table 6 (c) cont.

|  | no. | age | how acquired | cost | G | F | P |
|---|---|---|---|---|---|---|---|
| e. Household: | | | | | | | |
| sewing machine | | | | | | | |
| radio | | | | | | | |
| clock | | | | | | | |
| watch | | | | | | | |
| gun | | | | | | | |
| iron | | | | | | | |
| frames | | | | | | | |
| | | | | | | | |
| | | | | | | | |
| primus | | | | | | | |
| wick stove | | | | | | | |
| | | | | | | | |
| | | | | | | | |
| saucepan | | | | | | | |
| fryingpan | | | | | | | |
| cauldron | | | | | | | |
| kettle | | | | | | | |
| bowl large | | | | | | | |
| ,, small | | | | | | | |
| bucket | | | | | | | |
| 4 gall tin | | | | | | | |
| tub | | | | | | | |
| | | | | | | | |
| | | | | | | | |
| knife | | | | | | | |
| fork | | | | | | | |
| spoon des | | | | | | | |
| ,, tea | | | | | | | |
| | | | | | | | |
| mug large | | | | | | | |
| ,, small | | | | | | | |
| cup & saucer | | | | | | | |
| cup | | | | | | | |
| plate enamel | | | | | | | |
| ,, crock | | | | | | | |
| glass | | | | | | | |
| water jug | | | | | | | |
| teapot | | | | | | | |
| milk jug | | | | | | | |
| sugar bowl | | | | | | | |
| serving bowl | | | | | | | |
| | | | | | | | |
| | | | | | | | |
| | | | | | | | |
| | | | | | | | |
| | | | | | | | |
| | | | | | | | |

|  | no. | age | how acquired | cost | G | F | P |
|---|---|---|---|---|---|---|---|
| f.  Lighting: | | | | | | | |
| pressure lamp large | | | | | | | |
| ,,    ,,    small | | | | | | | |
| wick lamp | | | | | | | |
| hurricane lamp | | | | | | | |
| torch | | | | | | | |
| | | | | | | | |
| | | | | | | | |
| g.  Tools: | | | | | | | |
| hammer | | | | | | | |
| saw large | | | | | | | |
| ,,   medium | | | | | | | |
| ,,   small | | | | | | | |
| chisel | | | | | | | |
| screw driv. | | | | | | | |
| brace | | | | | | | |
| drill | | | | | | | |
| bits | | | | | | | |
| plane iron | | | | | | | |
| ,,   wood | | | | | | | |
| pliers | | | | | | | |
| spanner | | | | | | | |
| tin snips | | | | | | | |
| | | | | | | | |
| | | | | | | | |
| | | | | | | | |
| | | | | | | | |
| | | | | | | | |
| axe | | | | | | | |
| adze | | | | | | | |
| crow bar | | | | | | | |
| jemmy | | | | | | | |
| | | | | | | | |
| | | | | | | | |
| bush knife | | | | | | | |
| | | | | | | | |
| spade | | | | | | | |
| shovel | | | | | | | |
| pick | | | | | | | |
| *amo* | | | | | | | |
| *oso* wood | | | | | | | |
| *oso* metal | | | | | | | |
| | | | | | | | |

h.  Livestock:

horse _____

foal _____

cow _____

Appendix Table 6 (c) cont.

h. Livestock (cont.):
    bull _____
    calf _____
    pig  _____

    fowl _____


i.  Vehicles: _____


| j.  Accounts: | 1 | 2 | rounds 3 | 4 | 5 |
|---|---|---|---|---|---|
| village | | | | | |
| | | | | | |
| | | | | | |
| | | | | | |
| other villages | | | | | |
| | | | | | |
| | | | | | |
| Apia | | | | | |
| | | | | | |
| Bank | | | | | |
| | | | | | |
| | | | | | |
| Post Office | | | | | |
| | | | | | |
| | | | | | |

# BIBLIOGRAPHY

Administration of Western Samoa. *Handbook of Western Samoa*, Wellington, 1925.

Barrau, Jacques. 'Subsistence agriculture in Polynesia and Micronesia', *Bernice P. Bishop Museum Bulletin*, no. 223, Honolulu, 1961.

Barrett, W. J. Agriculture of Western Samoa, University of California, Berkeley, Ph.D. thesis, 1959 (unpublished).

Catt, A. J. L. *National Income of Western Samoa* (A preliminary estimate for 1952 and recommendations for regular compilation), South Pacific Commission, Noumea, 1955.

Churchward, William B. *My consulate in Samoa*, London, 1887.

Curry, Leslie. 'The physical geography of Western Samoa', *New Zealand Geographer*, vol. XI, no. 1, 1955, 28-52.

Davidson, J. W. 'The transition to independence: the example of Western Samoa', *The Australian Journal of Politics and History*, vol. VII, no. 1, 15-40, 1961a.
'The transition to independence in Western Samoa: the final stage', Australian National University, Canberra (mimeo), 1961b.
*Samoa mo Samoa: The emergence of the independent State of Western Samoa*, Melbourne, 1967.

Eden, D. R. A. 'The management of coconut plantations in Western Samoa', *South Pacific Commission Technical Paper* no. 48, Noumea, 1953.

Eden, D. R. A. and Edwards, W. L. 'Cocoa plantation management in Western Samoa', *South Pacific Commission Technical Paper* no. 31, Noumea, 1952.

Fairbairn, Ian. 'Samoan migration to New Zealand', *Journal of the Polynesian Society*, vol. 70, no. 1, 18-30, Wellington, 1961.
The National Income of Western Samoa, 1947-58, The Australian National University, Canberra, Ph.D. thesis, 1963 (unpublished).
'More on the Labor Potential—some evidence from Western Samoa', *Economic Development and Cultural Change*, vol. 16, no. 1, 97-104, Chicago, 1967.

Fisk, E. K. 'Planning in a primitive economy: special problems of Papua-New Guinea', *Economic Record*, vol. 38, no. 84, 462-78, Melbourne, 1962.
'Planning in a primitive economy: from pure subsistence to the production of a market surplus', *Economic Record*, vol. 40, no. 90, 156-74, Melbourne, 1964.

225

Fox, James W. and Cumberland, Kenneth B. (eds). *Western Samoa: Land Life and Agriculture in Tropical Polynesia*, Christchurch, 1962.

Goes, Jacobus, J. van der. 'Report to the Government of Western Samoa on processing and marketing of agricultural products', F.A.O., Rome, 1965.

Government of Western Samoa. *Population Census* 1951, Wellington, 1954.
*Report on the Population Census 1956* (Kathleen M. Jupp, Census Commissioner for Western Samoa), 1957.
*Western Samoa Population Census 1961*, Apia, 1962.
*Annual Report of the Department of Agriculture, Fisheries and Forests*, Apia, 1956—.
*Annual Report of the Banana Marketing Scheme*, Apia, 1956—.
*Report of the Copra Board of Western Samoa*, Apia, 1956—.
*Statistical Bulletin*, Apia, 1963-4.
*Trade, Commerce and Shipping of Western Samoa*, Apia, 1965.
*Western Samoa's Economic Plan for 1965*, Apia, 1965.
*Western Samoa's Economic Development Programme 1966-70*, (E.D.P. 1966-70), Apia, 1966.
Bonus Pay-sheets of the Banana Marketing Scheme 1956—(unpublished). These list the number of cases of bananas shipped by each grower for the whole year; details of the quota, receipts and rejects are also given.

Grattan, F. J. H. *An introduction to Samoan custom*, Apia, 1948.

Hiroa, Te Rangi. 'Samoan Material Culture', *Bernice P. Bishop Museum Bulletin*, no. 75, Honolulu, 1930.

Hirsh, Susan. 'The Social Organisation of an urban village in Samoa', *Journal of the Polynesian Society*, vol. 67, 266-303, Wellington, 1958.

Holmes, Susan. 'A quantitative study on family meals in Western Samoa with special reference to child nutrition', *British Journal of Nutrition*, vol. 8, no. 3, 223-39, 1954.

Jupp, Kathleen M. *Report on the Population Census, 1956, Territory of Western Samoa*, Wellington, 1958.
'Population expansion in Western Samoa', *Journal of the Polynesian Society*, vol. 70, no. 4, 401-9, Wellington, 1961.

Keesing, Felix M. *Modern Samoa: its government and changing life*, London, 1934.

Keesing, Felix M. and Marie M. *Elite communication in Samoa: a study of leadership*, Stanford, 1956.

La Perouse, J. F. G. de. *Voyage of La Perouse*, translated from the French (1798), in two volumes, 1926, London.

Lefort, E. J. E. 'Economic aspects of the coconut industry in the South Pacific', *South Pacific Commission Technical Paper* no. 92, Noumea, 1956.

Lockwood, B. A. 'Produce marketing in a Polynesian society, Apia, Western Samoa', in Brookfield, H. C. (ed.) *Pacific market place and market area*, (in press) Canberra.

Massal, Emile and Barrau, Jacques. 'Food plants of the South Sea Islands', *South Pacific Commission Technical Paper* no. 94, Noumea, 1956.

Mead, Margaret. *Coming of age in Samoa*, New York, 1928.

Mercer, J. H. and Scott, Peter. 'Changing village agriculture in Western Samoa', *Geographical Journal*, vol. 124, 347-60, 1958.

Nayacakalou, R. R. 'Land tenure and social organisation in Western Samoa', *Journal of the Polynesian Society*, vol. 69, no. 2, 104-22, Wellington, 1960.

New Zealand Department of Agriculture. *Food and agriculture in Western Samoa, 1950 survey*, 1950.

New Zealand Parliamentary Papers. 'Annual Report of the Government of New Zealand on the Administration of the Mandated Territory of Western Samoa', Department of Island Territories (annually), Wellington, 1924-9.

'Report by the New Zealand Government to the General Assembly of the United Nations on the Administration of Western Samoa' (annually), Wellington, 1947-60.

Oram, N. D. 'Household budgets in towns', New Guinea Research Unit, Australian National University, Canberra (mimeo), 1963.

Pieris, W. V. D. 'The manufacture of copra in the Pacific Islands', *South Pacific Commission Technical Paper* no. 82, Noumea, 1955.

*The coconut crisis in Western Samoa*, F.A.O. Regional Office for Asia and the Far East, Bangkok, 1965.

Pirie, Peter. The geography of population in Western Samoa, The Australian National University, Canberra, Ph.D. thesis, 1964 (unpublished).

Pirie, Peter and Barrett, Ward. 'Western Samoa: population, production and wealth', *Pacific Viewpoint*, vol. 3, no. 1, 63-96, Wellington, 1962.

Pitt, David. 'Some obstacles to economic development in Fiji and Island Polynesia', *Journal of the Polynesian Society*, vol. 71, 110-17, Wellington, 1962.

Rowe, N. A. *Samoa under the sailing gods*, London, 1930.

Stace, V. D. 'Economic survey of Western Samoa', *South Pacific Commission Technical Paper* no. 91, Noumea, 1965.

Stair, J. B. *Old Samoa*, London, 1897.

Stanner, W. E. H. *The South Seas in transition*, Sydney, 1953.

Schultz, E. 'The most important principles of Samoan family law, and the laws of inheritance', *Journal of the Polynesian Society*, vol. XX, 43-53, Wellington, 1911.

*Proverbial Expressions of the Samoans*, The Polynesian Society, Wellington, 1965.

Turner, George. *Samoa: a hundred years ago and long before*, London, 1884.

United Nations. *Economic survey and proposed development measures for Western Samoa*, prepared for the Government of Western Samoa by A. Lauterback and V. D. Stace, appointed under the United Nations Programme of Technical Assistance, 1963.

Urquhart, D. H. 'Cocoa growing in Western Samoa', *South Pacific Commission Technical Paper* no. 39, Noumea, 1953.

Watters, R. F. 'Cultivation in Old Samoa', *Economic Geography*, vol. 34, 338-51, 1958a.

'Settlement in Old Samoa', *New Zealand Geographer*, vol. XIV, 1-18, 1958b.

'Culture and environment in Old Samoa', *Western Pacific*, Department of Geography, Victoria University of Wellington, Wellington, 1958c.

'The nature of shifting cultivation: a review of research', *Pacific Viewpoint*, vol. 1, no. 1, 59-99, 1960.

Ward, R. Gerard. 'The banana industry in Western Samoa', *Economic Geography*, vol. 35, no. 2, 123-37, 1959.

Wilkins, Rosemary M. *Nutrition survey in urban and rural villages in Western Samoa: July-October 1965*, South Pacific Health Service, Suva, 1966.

# INDEX

Affluence, *see* Primitive Affluence

'*Āiga*, 16-17, 31, 193; *see also* Production; Social System

Apia, 6, 22, 25, 39, 62, 85, 87, 124, 139, 151, 155, 181, 198 (Table 49)

'*Aumāga*, 32-3; *see also* Effects of social and organizational institutions; Production; Social System

Bananas, *see* Foodcrops

Barrau, J., 28

Breadfruit, *see* Foodcrops

Buildings, 57-8, 102-3, 137, 167; *see also* Church; V. D. Stace

Bush Fallow Cultivation, 42-4 *passim*, 91-2 *passim*, 93 (Table 19), 127-9 *passim*, 131 (Table 28), 159-61 *passim*, 161 (Table 37), 165, 188-90 *passim*, 189 (Table 45)

Cacao beans, 107-10 *passim*; *see also* Production, Market sale

Capital works, '*āiga*, 71, 75 (Table 13), 113, 115 (Table 24), 144, 146 (Table 32), 173, 176 (Table 41); village, 71, 75, 113, 143-4, 173

Cash Crops, Copra and Coconuts, 55, 61-7, 107-11, 108 (Table 23), 138, 139-40, 140 (Table 31), 164, 167, 171; bananas, 56, 67-8, 111, 138, 140-1, 164-5, 170; cacao beans, 107-11, 108 (Table 23), 138, 141, 164-5 *passim*, 170; taro, 54, 56, 69, 111, 165, 172; fish, 57, 69, 101-2, 107, 139, 165, 166, 171; coconuts, 55, 140, 170-1; vegetables and fruit, 54-5, 56, 107, 165, 166, 171-2; handicrafts, 68-9, 105, 139, 143, 170; *see also* Costs, of earning money; Foodcrops; Income; Marketing, costs; Monetization factor; Production

Cash Income, *see* Income

Cash Outlay, 77, 117, 147, 152, 180; cash expenditure on goods and services, 78-9, 117-20, 147-50, 180-1; shopping facilities, 79-81, 120-1, 150-1, 181-2, 201-2; effects of social and organizational institutions, 81-4, 121-3, 146, 151-3, 182-3, 193-5 *passim*; food purchases, 78, 117-19, 147-9, 176 (Table 41), 180; church and pastor, 75 (Table 13), 82-3, 117 (Table 26), 122-3 *passim*, 146 (Table 32), 152, 182; fares, 79, 119-20, 149, 181, 196-7; schooling, 78-9, 119, 149-50, 181; schools, 72, 143-4, 173; *see also* Costs, of earning money; Education; Monetization factor

Chickens, *see* Livestock

Church, general, 33-4, 173; buildings, 73-5 *passim*, 97, 114-15 *passim*, 143n, 144-5, 174-6, 193; funds 82-3, 83 (Table 18), 109, 122-3, 122n, 174, 176, 178 (Table 43); pastor, 18, 33, 83, 97, 122, 123, 173; Congregational, 74, 82, 83 (Table 18), 87, 107, 143, 145, 156 (Fig. 10), 158, 173; London Missionary Society (LMS), 22, 25, 35, 82, 155, 156, 196, 207; Methodist, 158; Mormon, 82, 158, 180; Roman Catholic, 145, 158; *see also* Cash Outlay, church and pastor

Churchward, W. B., 84

Coconuts, *see* Foodcrops

Copra, 61-3; 107-11 *passim*, 138-40 *passim*, 170-1 *passim*; *see also* Costs

Communications, 13; *see also* Road communications

Consumption unit, 54-5

Costs, of earning money, 197-201; of marketing, 61-9 *passim*, 106-11 *passim*, 138-41 *passim*, 170-3 *passim*, 199-200;

Costs, of earning money—*contd.*
of subsistence production, 53-61, 99-106, 135-8, 164-70; of travel, 196-7; of labour, general, 56; of labour (subsistence), 62, 101, 135, 165-6; of labour (market), 62, 66-7, 108, 135, 140, 171; *see also* Cash crops; Cash outlay; Labour; Monetization factor; Wages
Curry, L., *see* Fox and Cumberland

Data collection, *see* Research method
Davidson, J. W., 22n, 23
Demand ceiling, 4-8 *passim*, 192-5 *passim*

Economic development, 206-10 *passim*
Education, 31-2, 48-9, 97, 133, 163, 181, 187; *see also* Cash outlay, schooling, schools
Effects of social and organizational institutions, 69-74, 111-15, 141-6,173-8; on production, 69-70, 112-13, 141-3, 173; on outlay, 71-2, 113-15, 115 (Table 24), 143-6, 146 (Table 32), 174-8; *see* Production
Exports, 28-9, 68

Fagaloa Bay, 39-40, 62, 66, 68, 69, 81, 121, 124, 200
Fagaloa District, 39
Fairbairn, I., 22, 26, 85, 96, 191 (Table 47)
Falealili District, 139
Fares, *see* Costs, Cash outlay
Fishing, 47, 55, 69, 95, 133, 136, 166, 170, 171, 191 (Table 46); *see also* Production; Subsistence
Fisk, E. K., 4-8, 9, 12, 21, 187-8, 192-3, 195
Foneti, J. B., 124
Fono, *see* Social system
Food, *see* Cash outlay; Production
Foodcrops, general, 28, 54-5, 100-2, 135-7, 165-7; bananas, 54-5, 100, 136, 165; breadfruit, 54-5, 100, 136, 165-7; cacao, 165-6; chickens, 54, 55, 136; coconuts, 54, 101, 136, 165, 167, 110-11 *passim*; European vegetables, 165-6, 199; fish, 54, 57, 101-2, 136, 165-6; pigs, 136; *taʼamū*, 54, 100, 135-6, 165-6; taro, 54-5, 100, 135-6, 165-6; production methods, 42-7

*passim*, 53-7 *passim*, 99-102 *passim*, 135-7 *passim*, 164-7 *passim*, *see also* Costs, of labour; Production; Subsistence food
Foreign Administrations, German, 23; New Zealand, 24
Fox, J. W., and Cumberland, K. B., 28 (Table 5), 42n (Wright, A. C. S. and Curry, L.)
Fragmentation of land holdings, 112
Funds, church and pastor, *see* Church

Handicrafts, 68-9, 70, 106, 139, 143, 173; *see also* Market sale
Hedstrom, M., 24
Household durables, 60-1, 105-6, 116 (Table 25), 138, 170; *see also* Production, subsistence use
Housing, 49; 57-60; 102-5; 137; 167-70; 168 (Table 39); *see also* Production, subsistence use
Hurricane, effects of, 15-16, 29-30, 54, 56, 67-8, 69, 70, 75-6, 78, 82, 84, 91, 93, 100, 112, 117, 136, 141, 142, 143, 163, 165, 166, 172-3, 178, 179, 180, 183, 205

Imports, 30-1, 31 (Table 7)
Incentive factor, 6-8, 195; *see also* Response factor
Income, 74-7, 76 (Table 14), 115-17, 116 (Table 25), 146-7, 148 (Table 33), 177 (Table 42), 178-80; cash, 74-7, 115-17, 146-7, 148 (Table 33), 178-80; subsistence, 74-5, 115, 146, 178
Indebtedness, 123, 153-4, 151 (Table 36)

Keesing, F. M., 51n
Keesing, F. M., and Keesing, M. M., 12, 22, 48, 113

Labour, village skills and specialization, 47-9, 95-8, 133, 161-3; *see also* Costs, of labour; Productive resources
Land Area, Western Samoa, 27-8; *see also* Poutasi village; Productive resources; Taga village; Uafato village; Utualiʼi village
Land, control of, 31, 43 (Table 8), 45 (Fig. 3), 46-7, 89, 93 (Table 20), 94

Land, control of—*contd.*
  (Fig. 6), 93-4, 112, 129, 130 (Fig. 9),
  131 (Table 28), 132, 141-2, 159, 161
  (Table 37), 162 (Fig. 12), 173; *see
  also* Productive resources
Land Use, general, 28 (Table 5), 42-7,
  43 (Table 8), 44 (Fig. 2), 45 (Fig. 3),
  89-95, 92 (Fig. 5), 93 (Table 19),
  112, 127-9, 131 (Table 28), 131-3,
  159, 160 (Fig. 11), 161, 162 (Table
  37), 188-90; *see also* Poutasi village;
  Productive resources; Taga village;
  Uafato village; Utuali'i village
Linkage, of market, 7-8, 195-6, 199-201
Livestock, pigs and chickens, 57, 107,
  136, 155
Local products market in Apia, 165,
  170-2 *passim; see also* Market

Malua, 14, 22, 155-7 *passim*, 173, 196;
  Malua College, 49, 167
Market, village trade stores, 52, 63-4,
  79, 107, 108, 139, 170; local products
  market in Apia, 165, 170-2 *passim;*
  participation, 203-6 *passim*, 209;
  substitution of market for village
  produced goods and services, 193,
  203-6 *passim; see also* Costs; Foodcrops; Linkage; Production
Marketing, 113; costs, 61-9 *passim*,
  106-11 *passim*, 138-41 *passim*, 170-3
  *passim*, 199-200
Market Sale, 61-9, 106-11, 138-41,
  165, 170-3; copra and coconuts, 55,
  61-7, 107-11, 108 (Table 23), 138,
  139-40, 140 (Table 31), 164, 167,
  171; bananas, 56, 67-8, 111, 138,
  140-1, 164-5, 170; cacao beans, 107-
  11, 108 (Table 23), 138, 141, 164-5
  *passim*, 170; taro, 54, 56, 69, 111,
  165, 172; fish, 57, 69, 101-2, 107,
  139, 165, 166, 171; vegetables and
  fruit, 54-5, 56, 107, 165, 166, 171-2;
  handicrafts, 68-9, 105, 139, 143, 170
*Matai, see* Social system
Mau movement, 24
Migration, 26, 48-9, 97-8, 133, 187
Monetization factor, 8, 75, 77, 115,
  146n, 176, 178, 203 (Table 51)

Nelson, O. F., 24, 85, 107, 120, 124,
  157, 170; *see also* Marketing

Oram, N. D., 15-16

La Perouse, J. F. G., 10-11, 12
Burns Philp, 24, 85, 107, 120, 121, 157,
  170; *see also* Marketing
Pieris, N. D., 207, 209
Pigs, *see* Livestock
Plantations, commercial, 28, 155, 170,
  178
Population, Western Samoa, 25;
  Poutasi, 127; Taga, 87; Uafato, 41;
  Utuali'i, 158
Poutasi village, description of, 124-7;
  land area, 125-6; land use, 127-9,
  131 (Table 28), 131-3; productive
  resources, 127-35; road communications, 124; population, 127; *see
  also* Land area; Land use; Productive
  resources; Road communications
Primitive affluence, 7-8, 187-8; *see also*
  Primitive economy
Primitive economy, 3-8; *see also*
  Primitive affluence
Production, 53-69, 99-111, 135-41,
  164-73, 188; subsistence use, 4, 53-61,
  100-6, 135-8, 165-70; market sale,
  61-9, 106-11, 138-41, 165, 170-3; *see
  also* Cash crops; Effects of social and
  organizational institutions; Subsistence food
Production methods, 42-3, 47-8, 49-52,
  91, 95, 163, 197-8, 207
Productive resources, Uafato, 42-53;
  Taga, 89-99; Poutasi, 127-35;
  Utuali'i, 158-64; land, 42-7, 89-95,
  127-33, 158-61, 188-90, 197-8;
  labour, 47-9, 95-8, 133, 161-3, 190-2,
  197-8; producers' capital, 49-53,
  98-9, 133-5, 163-4; *see also* Labour;
  Land use; Poutasi village; Taga
  village; Uafato village; Utuali'i
  village

Ranking of villages, 39, 85, 124, 155,
  195
Remittances, 26-7, 76 (Table 14), 77,
  115, 116 (Table 25), 117, 148
  (Table 33), 177 (Table 42), 179
Research method, 9-21 *passim*; selection
  of Western Samoa, 9-10; village
  selection, 13-14; data collection,
  14-15, 19-21, 41, 87, 127, 158; survey
  design, 15-16; household sampling,
  16-21

Response factor, 6-8, 193-4, 208; *see also* Incentive factor

Richardson, Administrator, 24

Road communications, general, 143, 196-7, 200; Poutasi village, 124-5; Taga village, 87; Uafato village, 39-40; Utuali'i village, 156-7

Road construction, 39, 53, 72, 96, 114, 134, 156, 176, 178, 193

Sala'ilua, 107, 121, 125, 196

Salelologa, 85, 108, 110, 120, 121, 124, 196, 198 (Table 49)

Savai'i Island, 13, 85, 87

Savings, 83-4, 123, 153-4, 183

School buildings, 48-9, 72, 73 (Table 12), 97, 114, 143-4

Social System, general, 16-17, 31-3, 83, 111-12, 135, 141, 173, 193, 208; *'āiga*, 16-21, 31, 72, 74, 112-13, 141, 173, 193, 194; *'aumāga*, 32-3, 70-1, 111, 141, 143, 173, 193, 194; *fono*, 32-3, 70-1, 74, 111, 129, 141-2, 173, 193, 194, 195; *matai*, 16-17, 31-2, 69-71, 112, 142, 173, 194; women's committee, 33, 70-1, 111, 113, 126, 141-3 *passim*, 173, 193, 194; *see also* Effects of social and organizational institutions

Stace, V. D., 73-4n, 209

Subsistence, 3-8 *passim*, 187-95 *passim*; production, 4, 53, 100, 135, 165; consumption, 4, 53, 100-1, 136, 165; *see also* Income; Production; Subsistence food

Subsistence food, 54-7, 100-2, 135-7, 165-7; housing, 57-60, 102-5, 137-8, 167-70; household durables, 60-1, 105-6, 137-8, 167-70; methods of imputing values, 49-50, 55, 76 (Table 14), 102, 116 (Table 25), 137, 148 (Table 33), 167, 177 (Table 42)

Substitution of market for village produced goods and services, 193, 203-6 *passim*; *see also* Linkage; Road communications

Taga village, 85-123; description of, 85-6; land area, 89; land use, 89-95; productive resources, 89-99; road communications, 87, 196-7; population, 87; *see also* Land Area; Land Use; Productive resources, Road communications; Villages

Travel, *see* Costs; Road communications

Uafato village, 39-84; description of, 39; land area, 42; land use, 45-6; productive resources, 42-9; road communications, 39-40, 62, 197; population, 41; *see also* Land Area; Land Use; Productive resources; Road communications; Villages

Utuali'i village, 155-83; description of, 157; land area, 158; land use, 159, 161; productive resources, 158-64; road communications, 156-7, 196; population, 158; *see also* Land Area; Land Use; Productive resources; Road communications; Villages

Villages, description of, Poutasi, 125-6, 125 (Fig. 7); Taga, 85-6, 86 (Fig. 4); Uafato, 39, 40-1, 40 (Fig. 1); Utuali'i, 156 (Fig. 10), 157

Wages, 25, 77, 96, 133, 147, 161, 163, 179; *see also* Costs, of labour

Watters, R. F., 11-12, 28

Women's Committee, *see* Social System

Wright, A. C. S., *see* Fox and Cumberland